Miami of Ohio . . .

The Cradle of Coaches

By Bob Kurz

Published by the Troy Daily News, Inc.
Troy, Ohio

©1983 Bob Kurz
Library of Congress Catalog Card Number 83-50645

Printed by Hammer Graphics
Piqua, Ohio, U.S.A.

I dedicate this book to all the Miami people everywhere, those special people who had the good fortune to attend an institution of which it has been said, "I've never met anybody from Miami who didn't love it."

To my wife Marian, my best friend and source of inspiration; and to my other Miami girl, Kelly, who has known the thrill of representing Miami in athletic competition. And to my two sons, Kyle and Chris, who at least would rather wear red than any other color.

B. K.

PROLOGUE

A generation ago, an associate, a young Miami University sports information director, groped for a better way to call attention to a phenomenon: that an institution known for academic excellence also was alma mater to an extraordinary number of successful athletic coaches.

The phenomenon, thought Bob Kurz, needed a label — a continuing instant-recognition factor which wouldn't need explaining all over again at each use. Miami already was recognized as Home of the McGuffey Readers because most of them had been compiled there by one of Old Miami's earliest professors. Miami also was known as Mother of Fraternities because six Greek-letter societies had been founded there.

"So why not Cradle of Coaches?" Bob Kurz one day asked his mentor, Bob Howard. And Howard, who said he had sought such a tag for a decade himself, responded, "Try it."

Kurz began using his coinage at every opportunity. It was picked up by others throughout the land, as Miami teams and coaching alumni achieved honor. There may have been a seed; yet I doubt that he dreamed then that some 23 years later he would be traveling, researching, interviewing, comparing responses, and agonizing, for a book about The Cradle.

Agonizing, most of all. Agonizing over how this book could be more than mere recitation of biographical details of men for whom a Miami diploma is linked with coaching success in high schools, colleges and professional sports.

So the agonizing part of his task was determining a theme. Just what was he trying to say? Gradually, he became assured in his direction.

It's much like building a team: pre-season meetings with staff, pre-season practice to blend the individual talents and personalities of players, the molding of offensive and defensive schemes, and then game day. With Bob Kurz, the painstaking harvest of fact and opinion, the extraction of some meaning from the mass, and tedious mechanical preparation for presstime.

I recall when playing for Woody and Ara at Miami, and then when coaching myself, the ultimate compliment could be just two words — "Nice Game" — and a pat on the back.

As this manuscript became ready for press, I spoke with Bob Howard, who all these years has stayed close to the legend, its source and its telling. Of Kurz' product, the mentor also had a two-word ultimate compliment:

"It's good."

Bob Kurz had found the theme.

John Pont, Miami '52
President, The Cradle of Coaches Association

PREFACE

Like a lot of others, I've had a long love affair with my alma mater, Miami University. It began in 1953, when Mom and Dad and I drove down in the fall of my senior year in high school to visit. It has continued unabated through four years of college, seven years as Miami's sports information director, a term on the Executive Council of the Miami University Alumni Association and the proud day in 1981 when our daughter decided Miami was her school, too.

And the flame hasn't burned any lower during the last 15 months as I have poured heart and soul into writing this story. Don't misunderstand. This isn't my story. This is their story . . . the story of the men who played and learned at Miami and in the process have written an intriguing chapter in American sports lore.

During 1959, when Miami was celebrating its 150th birthday, stories began to appear in the Ohio press as well as the national press, the **Christian Science Monitor** and the **New York News** in particular, calling attention to the name Miami graduates and former coaches were making as they plied their trade. Paul Dietzel's LSU Tigers, who were national champions the year before, and Ara Parseghian's Northwestern Wildcats, both undefeated, ranked first and second in the country midway through the season. There was Red Blaik at Army and Woody Hayes at Ohio State, Paul Brown with the Cleveland Browns, Weeb Ewbank with the Baltimore Colts and Sid Gillman with the Los Angeles Rams. Miami was becoming the Cradle of Coaches. Realization that the Cradle of Coaches meant something beyond the reaches of southwestern Ohio was evident when I moved to Dallas in 1965 and went to a sports gathering and found myself face to face with Mustang, Longhorn and Aggie followers. Somebody asked where I was from, and when I said Miami of Ohio, the quick response was, "Oh, the Cradle of Coaches."

I would not pretend to be an impartial chronicler of the story of the Cradle of Coaches. These men are my friends. I've worked with some of them; I've worked for others. Many I've known personally for a long time. But I'm enough of a journalist to be curious . . . to wonder what brought all of these people to Miami, and why their coaching careers have followed similar patterns of success.

As I wandered from South Bend to New Haven, from Greencastle to DeKalb, from Raleigh to Chapel Hill, to Ann Arbor, to Darrtown, even to Banner Elk, one thing was crystal clear. My love affair with Miami is surpassed only by the love and respect of these men for the institution which will always remain their home.

My son who got away from Miami went to the University of Alabama. There are many Alabama men in coaching, each of them disciples of one man, the legendary Bear Bryant. No one man is responsible for the hundreds of Miami men in the Cradle of Coaches. It's the institution . . bigger than any individual.

Obviously, writing this book has been a labor of love. Without the invaluable help of some very special Miami people, publication would never have been possible. My heartfelt thanks to Editor Bob Howard, who never realized when he hired me in 1958 that he'd still be correcting my mistakes 25 years later. His suggestions and checking of myriad details made my job much easier.

There's another special friend whose support has been my salvation. Joel Walker is the Publisher and Editor of the **Troy Daily News** in Troy, Ohio. TDN, Inc. is the publisher of this book, and mere words are inadequate when it comes to expressing my gratitude. Troy has been my home away from home on many occasions over the past several months, and always I feel welcome. To Nancy and Joel Walker, and Susan and Michael, a special thank you. And through them, many thanks to the people who make Troy a special place.

Thanks also to . . .

. . . the Miami Paper Corporation, for providing the paper.

. . . to the Cradle of Coaches Association and Mike Macechko, Director of Alumni Affairs, for the funds which enabled me to travel . . .

. . . to Miami's athletic department, and especially Sports Information Director Dave Young, Lori Brown and Carol Fink, for quick responses to every call for help,

. . . to Ed Meador and Miami's Audio-Visual Service for answering my call for pictures

. . . and to the coaches and others in the Miami family who took time to welcome me into their homes and offices in my never-ending quest for a new twist to this story.

Finally, thanks to the good Lord for guiding me through the ditch and back on the road when I slid off I-94 in a snowstorm after leaving Bo Schembechler's office in Ann Arbor. Were it not for His guiding hand, I was perilously close to having written only half a book.

Bob Kurz
Evanston, Illinois
August, 1983

ABOUT THE AUTHOR

It was a beautiful fall Saturday in Chicago in 1977. I was in the city on business and Northwestern was playing a home football game in nearby Evanston.

I remembered Bob Kurz was associate athletic director at Northwestern . . . the same Bob Kurz I'd worked for as a student assistant in the sports information office at Miami in 1960 and 1961.

It had been awhile since I'd seen Bob. We hadn't kept in touch, although our terms on the Miami University Alumni Council had overlapped a year and we'd seen each other a couple of times then.

Bob left Miami in the mid-1960s to work in the promotion department of the **Dallas Times-Herald.** After five years there he bought two weekly papers in Hallsville and Waskom, but sold them two years later and joined an advertising agency in Dallas where he worked for two years before returning to his hometown to take the Northwestern job in 1974.

The weather was perfect for a football game on this particular fall day. I decided I'd go out to the game. I'd call Bob in the pressbox when I got there and he'd get me a ticket. No problem.

But when I made that call I reached John Pont instead. He was athletic director at the time, and he said he wanted to talk with me about Bob before I saw him at the game.

"You know Bob's been sick," Pont said. I responded that I didn't.

In June of 1977 Bob had surgery to remove a benign tumor on the upper part of his spinal column. The operation was difficult because the tumor was wrapped around the spinal column. When it was removed it caused a stroke and Bob was in the beginning of rehabilitation therapy when I saw him on that October Saturday.

He could barely speak and his body movements appeared laborious at best. He was sitting in the stands and he recognized me. His wife, Marian, was at his side and she was as cheerful and happy as ever.

She explained to me what had happened, but Bob Kurz was a different Bob Kurz. I felt uncomfortable, for myself, for him. I excused myself, watched part of the game from another part of the stands and then took a train back downtown.

I felt sorry for Bob, for Marian, for their children. Bob was down and appeared to be just about out. I figured he'd never really be able to walk again, maybe not ever talk. I felt an extreme emptiness.

But Bob Kurz wasn't giving up.

"I was in the hospital 13 weeks," he says in relating the story today. "At the time I figured there are two kinds of strokes . . . one you die, one you live. And I was still alive so I decided to make the most of it.

"I went through a long period of paralysis on my left side. I couldn't write my name. I had no control of my mental processes. Part of the therapy was learning how to read and write. Those things you learn in grades two through six I was having a tough time with. It was about a year after the surgery before I felt I could make a contribution to society. I became more independent."

Our relationship was renewed. And it has blossomed to the point that our company, the Troy Daily News, Inc., is the publisher of this book.

Bob has not only written this book, he's been active with his wife in the Nancy Williams public relations firm in Chicago and he's playing golf on a regular basis again.

He's played in a tournament with me in Troy the past three years and he'll probably keep coming back as long as he can be around people like Kees Scarff, a Troy native, who went to Indiana and played football for John Pont.

"Kees is a breath of fresh air," said Bob.

But really Bob Kurz is a breath of fresh air . . . to his family, his friends, to Miami.

You'll enjoy this book.

Joel H. Walker
Miami '61

Author Bob Kurz (center) with two of the stars of this story: Weeb Ewbank, (left) and Trainer Emeritus Jay Colville, examining Jay's collection of Miami sports memorabilia.

Football is a multi-faceted game. The relationship with your people, because it's a people game, is very important. The relationship with your players . . . your ability to maintain communication with them: your ability to motivate them . . . to make them understand the purpose of what they're doing . . . to extract hopefully the best from them . . . it starts with that.

It starts with loyalty. It starts with staff, and everybody working together. You can't work together if everybody doesn't believe in what you're doing. That's a job of selling by the head football coach, I think. Unite the staff, unite the players, and have everybody together. There's no one individual greater than the whole, under any circumstances . . .

Ara Parseghian, 25 years a head football coach, at Miami, Northwestern and Notre Dame, with a little of his coaching philosophy.

I
ARA

WHEN YOU'RE a sports junkie like me, it's strange how your recall on certain events is forever.

On a game day, he always wore a brown suit, this man with the uncommon name who was head football coach at Miami University.

It was 1954, my freshman year on the Miami campus at Oxford, Ohio, and I hardly could wait to see my first football game coached by Ara Parseghian. So I was at Miami Field on that October afternoon when the Miami Redskins took the field for their home opener against Xavier University. The contest was part of what then was a unique four-way neighborhood rivalry in southwestern Ohio, a geographical thing outside of any conference commitments: Xavier and the University of Cincinnati as cross-town participants. The University of Dayton only an hour away. And 1954 was a long, long time before Xavier abandoned football and Dayton retreated to Division III in favor of emphasis on basketball.

Sitting in the end zone at Miami Field, I saw holes opened wide by guys with names like Dick Mattern, Stan Jones and Tom Jones, Roger Siesel, Dick Chorovich and Teddy Bear Smith. And I saw runners like Ed Merchant, or Bobby Wallace, or Tom Troxell or Tirrel Burton glide or power off those blocks to chew up huge chunks of that beautiful green real estate. The quarterbacks, Dick Hunter and on occasion Denny Studrawa or Tom Dimitroff, executed flawlessly. There was nothing the team from Cincinnati could do to stop the onslaught. And defensively, the team wearing the red and white was overpowering. When Miami's confusing scoreboard clock finally signaled the end of the game, there was no mistaking the other numbers: Miami 42, Xavier 7.

The Redskins continued dominant through the first half of the season. Looming ahead, however, was a Big Ten team from Indiana, coming off a most impressive victory over Michigan. It boasted Olympic Decathlon Champion Milt Campbell at running back and Florian Helinski, at that time holder of the NCAA record for passes without interception, at quarterback. It had been some years since Miami had faced a Big Ten foe; and though the next 15 years would see Miami more than hold its own against Big Ten and other major opponents from all over the country, nobody really expected what took place on a later October day in 1954 at the old IU stadium in Bloomington.

Campbell was held almost totally in check (his longest gain was seven yards), and his fumble at the Miami 30 with less than two minutes to go snuffed out Indiana's final glimmer of hope. Helinski threw three interceptions, his second, third and fourth of the season. He was so frustrated by the swarming Miami defense that on Indiana's last two possessions he never attempted a pass, completely disdaining what had been his favorite weapon. Miami, on the other hand, used its first possession of the second half to score the game's only touchdown. That came when Helinski fumbled on the option, and Moody Baker recovered on Indiana's 30. On fourth and four, Hunter's pass to Bobby Wallace was gathered in at the 16, and the chunky Miami halfback tore himself from the grasp of one defender and outsprinted four others into the end zone. As the final seconds ticked off the clock, many of the 3,000 Miamians among a crowd of 23,000 swarmed the field to salute their heroes and the 6-0 victory.

However, the story everybody likes to tell about that game had been played out Friday afternoon, during the brief workout time allotted in the stadium. It had rained a lot in Oxford that week, and the Redskins' practice gear showed it. Bloomington weather hadn't been much better; footing remained damp, with more rain possible. Rather than risk dirtying the game uniforms, Parseghian suggested to his equipment manager that the squad take Friday's workout in already-dingy practice gear. In the press box above the stadium, Ben Garlikov of the **Dayton Daily News** was watching as Miami appeared on the field to limber up in mud-caked pants and miscellaneous jerseys, many of which could be described most charitably as faded. As Garlikov watched, so did many of the Indiana players, by this time arriving from class.

Garlikov thought he had a story. What a stroke of genius by the young coach, sending this team of unsuspected talents out in full view of the

A scene I got used to during my freshman year. Tirrel Burton has the ball, and the other Miami players are Russ Giganti (52) and Tom Troxell (43). Check out the scoreboard clock. It's not quarter 'til one. The game is in the first minute of the third quarter. Miami was leading Marshall, 33-0 at the time, and won, 46-0. This was only the second game I watched at historic Miami Field.

opposition, looking like "ragamuffins", as Bill Mallory, who was on the team, would refer to them years later.

"I got credit for a psychological ploy," said Parseghian as he recalled how Garlikov had written the story. "And even now, I have to admit it made a great story, even with the telling and retelling. But believe me: all I was trying to do was keep the game uniforms clean."

*****

That Parseghian ever got to Miami University and thus was in position to be its head football coach in 1954 is a story that bears telling.

Graduate of Akron South High School, Ara had started his collegiate football-playing career at the University of Akron. But there was a war going on, and he preferred not to be drafted. Enlisting in the Navy through its V-12 program, he wound up as a company commander training boots at the Great Lakes Naval Training Station north of Chicago. Great Lakes had a heckuva football team in those days. Students of football will recall that the coach of those Great Lakes teams was the legendary Paul Brown, Miami '30.

One of Parseghian's service responsibilities involved escorting freshly-trained boots to their next duty station. He was on his way back from Norfolk on such a mission when the train stopped at Cincinnati. He had 24 hours or so to kill. Recalling that a cousin was attending Miami 35 miles up the road, he decided to hitch-hike to Oxford for a visit.

"That was my first introduction to Miami," he remembers. "I had played football at Great Lakes, and I was getting some opportunities — Ohio State was one of them — to play after I got out of service. I saw Miami — the location and the general setting. It was just absolutely what I wanted, and I said that if the Good Lord is willing, that if I get out of service and all goes well, then I'm going to Miami."

In December 1945, Parseghian was discharged from his military obligation, and he applied for admission to Miami. He was admitted and enrolled for the second semester in February 1946. His first taste of athletic competition as a Redskin came on the basketball team coached by W.J. (Blue) Foster. Come spring Parseghian, an all-around athlete, wanted to give baseball a try. After a couple of spring football drills, he headed for the diamond, to the undisguised chagrin of Football Coach Sid Gillman. Certainly such a bold move would be challenged by coaches today, undoubtedly with good reason. Parseghian, however, had come to Miami as a true walk-on, as the expression is used today, and he was enrolled under the GI Bill. His scholarship was with Uncle Sam, not Miami. Parseghian himself has even more to say on the subject:

"You have to understand now that I wasn't a 17- or 18-year-old kid. I was 21 years old, and I'd been in the service for three years. I think the coaching staff was not very happy about my going to baseball and somewhat, I would imagine, discounted me for the fall even though I was hopeful of being back . . . which I was. I came back in the fall and made the football team."

(And 37 years later, he remains the most recent winner of Miami's varsity M in three separate sports.)

Having been exposed to the exceptional organizational genius of Paul Brown while at Great Lakes, Parseghian found Miami's practices

Ara Parseghian in football gear, as a left-handed basketball player, and strolling to class. He also played baseball and golf in his spare time.

somewhat disorganized. Even so, the future Miami coach had a "profound respect for Sid Gillman's technical approach to the game, which was excellent."

"Maybe I wasn't the easiest guy to handle in those days," adds Ara, "and maybe that, coupled with my previous exposure to Paul Brown, set the tone for a situation which I guess you could call not necessarily agreeable between the head coach and myself. The guy who poured the oil on the water, which kept it amiable in a sense, was George Blackburn, the backfield coach."

*****

In a two-year Miami football-playing career, during which the Redskins won 16 of 20 games (a 6-6 tie with Xavier was the only blemish on the 1947 record), wins might be expected to dominate Parseghian's reminiscences. Not so. The game he remembers most was the 1946 season windup against arch-rival Cincinnati. In his South Bend office, rummaging through stacks of media guides for the Miami press book which could confirm his total recall of that game, he was engaged in a mild form of self-criticism:

"I remember it so well because I figured I was responsible for the defeat. I hadn't been at Miami very long, but I was very much aware of the intense rivalry between the two schools, particularly among the people who lived in Cincinnati and who had gone to either Miami or UC. Anyway, after all that buildup, in the waning moments of that game, we were either ahead or tied; and I was playing defensive right halfback, and they completed a pass in my general area for a touchdown which made the score 13-7 against us. I felt very much responsible for that loss."

After his research had confirmed his memory of that game's final score, he checked the next season and proclaimed in a way that you could appreciate fully only if you were sitting in the room, "the following year, we got revenge. Thirty-eight to seven . . . ," the words clipped off his tongue, "we beat 'em down there." The man who had been so quick to understand the Miami-UC thing obviously had forgotten that for as long as he was at Miami, either as player or as coach, the game always was played in Cincinnati.

*****

As a freshman, my initial contact with Parseghian turned out to be no contact at all. I had joined **The Miami Student** as a sports writer. Late in the 1954 season . . . I think it might have been just after the victory over Indiana . . . I was asked to look in on football practice. But it happened to be one of those days when things weren't going particularly well, and the coach decided to send a manager over to ask all of us who were along the sidelines, including aspiring sportswriters, to leave. My formal introduction to Parseghian would have to wait for another day.

The next season, which turned out to be Parseghian's last at Miami, saw the coach at his fiery best in a game situation.

In the season opener for both teams, Miami's opponent was Northwestern. On the first play from scrimmage, Miami's Tirrel Burton went 77 yards to the end zone — but the score was nullified by a Miami offside call. Later, Burton did race 59 for a touchdown that counted; yet Miami did trail 7-6 as the second half began. Northwestern received the third-quarter kickoff, but two plays later, Miami regained the ball. And that's when the fireworks really started. From Northwestern's 40, Tom Troxell on the belly swept left end to the Wildcats' 13. Parseghian's teams "repeat successful plays," and Northwestern wasn't stopping that play. A rhubarb followed, and all of a sudden Miami was being penalized 15 yards for a personal foul and Miami Center Butch Mattern was being escorted from the game. Parseghian's brown coat flew off in rage, and that resulted in another 15 yards, this time for unsportsmanlike conduct. It still was first down; but instead of being in scoring position, the Redskins had half the field to go. Let Parseghian pick up the story from there:

"When I look back on it, I can't evaluate my explosiveness of those days with what I'd like to think is a maturity at 58; but anyway, I don't remember what I said or did on the sidelines . . . I don't remember whether it was a justified penalty or not. In any event, I know we came back and threw a tight end screen. The ball was on our hash mark, and I remember faking action; and it was a beautifully set-up screen, absolutely beautiful, I remember that, and I felt . . . I said to myself . . . poetic justice. I thought, I would have guessed, that we went for a touchdown. We ran right down to the one-yard line and punched it in. That's the way I recall it."

Twenty-seven years later, Parseghian's recollection of the situation was pretty accurate. Two plays left Miami still 34 yards away from the end zone and even 31 from the first-down marker. No big deal, as today's young people would say. Quarterback Tom Dimitroff's screen pass went to Pres Bliss, and he went in untouched. And the avalanche was on. Miami scored twice more before the third quarter had ended. Burton's 46-yard punt return led to one score, and a four-play, 41-yard drive, with Burton going the final nine, made it 25-7 Miami with just under five minutes remaining in the third quarter. The final score was Miami 25, Northwestern 14, as Miami cleared the bench.

Northwestern, under Lou Saban, never won a game that year. Miami, under Parseghian, won 'em all. Northwestern, to no one's surprise, began the search for a new coach. Also to no one's surprise, that new coach turned out to be Ara Parseghian.

*****

John Brickels had been Miami's basketball coach and backfield aide to Woody Hayes when Ara forsook professional football to return to Miami early in 1950. This same Brickels who had been the Cleveland Browns talent scout and backfield coach when Parseghian signed with the Browns as a halfback was to have important influence on Parseghian the coach. But a handful of decisions by Brickels at Miami may have determined the course of Parseghian's career.

Let's look back a bit farther: Having been one of the stars of an undefeated 1947 Miami team, Parseghian was Miami captain-elect for 1948. Then he signed with the Cleveland Browns with a season of eligibility remaining. Already 23, seeing most of his GI teammates moving on, he needed only six hours for graduation; the move made sense. He played well with the Browns in 1948. He completed Miami degree requirements in the off-season. He went into the 1949 season looking great — until a serious hip injury squelched his prospects.

Returning to Miami for spring-semester graduate work, he also took "temporary" spare-time work as a line assistant to Hayes in Miami's 1950 spring football practice. Then on June 15, 1950, he accepted appointment as freshman coach for football and basketball, varsity coach for golf. Brickels' promotion to athletic director was announced just a week later, although Brickels was to continue as both basketball coach and backfield lieutenant to Hayes.

Parseghian's freshman football squad was undefeated and his freshman basketball team off to a sharp, aggressive start by the time Hayes' varsity had capped an 8-1 regular season with a Mid-American crown and a post-season Salad Bowl victory over Arizona State at Tampa. The timing was so right: Ohio State said goodby to Wes Fesler, and Woody Hayes was in the limelight at just the right time to succeed Fesler as head coach at Ohio State after only two seasons at Miami.

And at age 27, after one year of coaching experience and serious consideration of at least one other candidate, Ara Parseghian became the first Miami graduate to coach at a school gaining recognition for its alumni in coaching — and the first in what was to become a long line of Miami graduates to ascend to the head football coaching position at alma mater.

Timing: Brickels could have left the basketball job open in February 1950, or in June 1950. Brickels could have made a bid for the head football job in February 1951, with or without the directorship, most certainly without the basketball job. Given a different decision at any of those points, there's no telling where Parseghian's career might have led.

"When I went to Miami as coach, I always had a great interest in basketball as well as football," Ara has said. "When I went into those two positions, I think that if either one of those jobs had broken — football or basketball — I would have become a candidate because of my interest in either one of the sports. Hypothetically, let's say that the basketball job had opened: I think I would have made a legitimate appeal for that job. You never know which way the paths along the road are going to go. Let's say John Brickels decided to take the athletic directorship and relinquish the basketball job, then I'd become a serious candidate. I could very well have become the basketball coach and not the football coach.

"That's how the little things in life, things you have alsolutely no control over . . . the fact that I was interested in coaching, the fact that I did go to Miami of Ohio, the fact they hired me to those two positions, and the very fact that I had equal interest in those two sports . . . and if one job had opened before the other, who knows? I may have become a basketball coach and lasted a season and a half.

"There was a period of time before they made the decision that John Brickels came to me and said that Vivian Anderson, president of the Board of Trustees at that time, had suggested the possibility that John Brickels take the job for a year or so, essentially in name only, and let me do the coaching. Then see how things go, and then be elevated. Well, I was not going to have any part of that. I figured I was either going to be the head coach, or not be the head coach, and I took a very strong

Parseghian's first Miami staff, and his last. The 1951 team had a 7-3 record, and was coached by, left to right, Bruce Beatty, Doc Urich, Warren Schmakel, Bill Hoover, Parseghian, John Brickels and Woody Wills. The 1955 team went undefeated and Parseghian had added John Pont, to the left of Parseghian, to the staff. Shoults is to the right of Ara, and Wills, Urich and Beatty are to the rear.

stand."

What other influences came to bear on the ultimate decision remain unclear, but the fact remains that Parseghian got the job.

And it was only four weeks after Parseghian committed himself to the football challenge that Brickels did relinquish the basketball job. It went to Bill Rohr, intense and successful coach at Portsmouth High School, an Ohio Wesleyan graduate but a protege of Miamian Paul Brown.

*****

The move from Miami to Northwestern was made without much hesitation, albeit there would be times throughout Parseghian's years at Northwestern when he questioned the wisdom of the change.

The Northwestern bid came from Athletic Director Stu Holcomb, himself a former Miami coach. Holcomb, assisted by Gillman, had created a turnaround at Oxford launching a string in which Miami was to go from 1943 and into the Seventies without a losing season. Holcomb made the first contact with Parseghian when the coach was on a recruiting and speaking trip. Checking with Brickels convinced Parseghian that any Miami salary increase would be modest, so he felt free to consider the Northwestern position. It was a step up in the profession, it was the Big Ten, and the salary was an improvement over the $7,800 level he had attained at Miami. He accepted Holcomb's offer, and then began a soul-searching which would continue until the Notre Dame years.

"I was so naive that I didn't realize Northwestern was a privately-endowed school in a state conference," he confesses. "It was going to be a very difficult job. Little did I know, and I'm very grateful; my career could have ended there. But I didn't know that in those days. I was just stupid, I guess, and not knowledgeable enough."

The first year was alright, pretty good by Northwestern standards today. The Wildcats won four games, lost four and tied one.

But the coach was realistic enough to assess the season in terms of what really had happened. And he didn't like what he saw. Three of the four victories had come at the end of the season, when the opponents were out of contention in the Big Ten race. Trouble was just around the corner.

"The problem was, beyond those we're well aware of today, an old-time philosophy . . . they had the coaches, and they had a recruiter. The recruiter did the recruiting, and the coaches did the coaching. If things didn't go well, the coaches blamed the recruiter and the recruiter blamed the coaches. Well, you can't work that way; and as a result, this whole Northwestern situation was in a terrible turmoil. I could see that there was a tremendous rebuilding job to do. Attitude-wise, talent-wise, recruiting-wise. What we had to do was pay the price for this philosophy that had been in vogue at Northwestern for a number of years. It doesn't work that way. The coaches are responsible for the recruiting. They're the ones that know what they have to do. That old philosophy had to go by the wayside."

The whole process of change was painful, to say the least. The next year, for the only time in 25 years of coaching, a Parseghian-coached team lost an opening game. That's not all. Northwestern lost **every** game during that 1957 season.

But Parseghian had known well before that disastrous season that the only salvation for the Northwestern football program was the reshaping process which he already had begun. Recruiting was a priority, to be sure; but even before that, there were some attitude problems which needed to be corrected, and it quickly became clear to the new coach that there was only one way to correct the problem.

"There were some attitudes that needed to be corrected, and the only way to correct them was to dismiss them from the team. And we did so. I figured I was not going to put up with this. There are certain sacrifices you have to make to play, and certain guys were unwilling to do so. So there was somewhat of an upheaval."

If the 1957 season was a "traumatic experience to go through," Parseghian realized from the opening game of the 1958 season that "my career was on the line." The recruiting, even during the disastrous 1957 season, had gone well. Players were coming to the Evanston campus who Parseghian felt could produce. But since freshmen were ineligible to play in those days, the wait seemed interminably long. Among those recruited for that class were names like Dick Thornton, a quarterback who was to rank among Northwestern's best, and halfback Ron Burton, who became legendary in Northwestern's annals, and Mike Stock, another outstanding offensive performer who stirs fond memories among the Northwestern loyalists.

Twenty-four years later, Parseghian had no trouble remembering some of the details of that pivotal 1958 season. The opening game was against Washington State, a team which featured a fine passing attack centered around Gail Cogdill, who went on to enjoy great success in professional football. Northwestern beat Washington State, and then Stanford, and "we're off to a start." Then came the Big Ten season, and the turn-around in the program that Parseghian wanted so desperately. When Michigan fell behind the Wildcats, 40-0, by halftime, and Ohio State, which had embarrassed Northwestern in Columbus the year before, lost 21-0, people around the country who had expected nothing from Northwestern reacted with surprise. Injuries and a decided lack of depth, eventually took a toll, but the Wildcats finished second in the Big Ten. Maybe things were going to be OK at Northwestern after all.

"Well, when you say OK, we had a chance, we were competitive. There was one of the years in there, fifty-nine or sixty, somewhere in there, where we took the Wildcats to the top of the polls, and we held it for a few weeks."

It was 1959, and Parseghian's Northwestern team was battling for the top ranking with LSU's Chinese Bandits, coached by Paul Dietzel. Miami Teammates Parseghian and Dietzel, ranked one-two in college football for a brief period of time.

"We were competitive. We were starting to win some games. Nobody was going to take us apart. We started to win some games we weren't supposed to. We started to take on Oklahoma and Notre Dame, and we never lost to either one of those teams. We beat Notre Dame four years. We beat Oklahoma in their hey-day."

But some of the problems inherent at Northwestern, problems which

Parseghian recognized when he realized his team was the only private school among the Big Ten's giant public universities, remained and seemed insurmountable. Admission requirements were higher, costs were substantially higher and because of the costs, Northwestern was limited when it came to the number of scholarships available. There was no national limit then, yet Northwestern had a limit, usually 25; the most was 30. It wasn't enough, and depth was a constant problem as each season wore on. In fact, it was that lack of depth which seemingly would lead to Northwestern's lack of staying power late in the Big Ten season, and to a "can't win in November" tag which obviously still rankles Parseghian.

"First of all, I was upset with myself because we had not won the Big Ten championship, and you feel certain inadequacies. You get 'em going, and they can't survive. But I came to recognize that we did have some shortcomings. Yet it wasn't until I left there and could look back on what happened through those years, that I became truly aware how difficult the job is."

In 1963, Northwestern was favored to win the Big Ten championship and earn that elusive trip to the Rose Bowl. But the injuries came earlier than usual that year; the Wildcats lost a couple of games and appeared incapable of living up to the pre-season promise. All of a sudden there was pressure from certain factions, Chicago media included, indicating that Parseghian might need to look for other work at the end of the year. Wishing to clarify his situation with Holcomb, Parseghian went directly to the athletic director and said, "What's this I read?" He was stunned when the response was, "You can't coach forever."

The season ended on a high note as the Wildcats beat Ohio State in Columbus, but Parseghian, even though he had a year remaining on his contract, was not particularly anxious to stay where he was not wanted. Notre Dame had just named Hugh Devore as interim coach, so Parseghian picked up the phone and called Father Edmund Joyce, faculty representative in control of intercollegiate athletics at Notre Dame.

"I told Father Joyce I was aware Hugh Devore had been named interim coach. 'If you're contemplating making a change,' I said, 'I'd like to be considered as a candidate.' Apparently he did have an interest, because approximately a week or so later, he called and said, 'I'd like to meet and talk with you.'"

That first meeting took place in Chicago, and there was a subsequent meeting in New York. Eventually, all the details were worked out, and Parseghian was offered the spot at Notre Dame. Meanwhile, Harold Anderson, a most influential Northwestern supporter, was working behind the scenes to keep Parseghian in Evanston. A new five-year contract was offered, but Parseghian refused to sign it, feeling even though Anderson obviously wanted him to stay, Holcomb wasn't sure, and working in an environment like that could lead to nothing but trouble.

The contrast between Northwestern and Notre Dame was like night and day. Parseghian had found that being physically separated from the lakefront campus at Northwestern (Dyche Stadium and the athletic department offices were about a mile away in a residential-business area) contributed to the overall lack of interest on the part of the students and the rest of the university community. Winning had changed much of that, but the enthusiasm had to be manufactured.

"The relationship that existed between the athletic department and its station in the university was nothing at all like it is at the University of Notre Dame. You're respected, you're admired. There's a genuine interest in your program just like there is a genuine interest in the chemistry program, in the math department, and the president is just as much involved in what happens Saturday afternoon . . . I remember Father Hesburgh saying, 'we don't have to have winning seasons . . . being representative and once in a while having a good season, but if you cheat to win, you're gone.'

"The administration at Notre Dame is very loyal. You hear a lot about these external pressures at Notre Dame. The external pressures are being voiced by those who have absolutely no authority."

*****

Twenty-five years as a collegiate head coach, from the age of 27 to the age of 52, took its toll. After one of the most memorable football bowl games of all time, when Parseghian again defeated the legendary Bear Bryant in the Orange Bowl, the man who started out in a brown suit at Miami but is remembered by most wearing his Notre Dame coaching sweater, was ready to retire. He is in business now in South Bend, the president of Ara Parseghian Enterprises, primarily a specialty insurance company dealing in accident, health and credit life insurance. Although the idea for using the Parseghian name on the business originated through a South Bend business acquaintance, Parseghian says Miami gets at least some of the credit. He had considered a business career before coaching interfered; so when the business opportunity came, his background at Miami gave him at least a partial head start.

When Ara's doctors suggested to him that it might be wise to step aside, even they probably didn't realize that 25 years as a head coach is a never-ending job. Parseghian himself thinks he might have lasted longer in coaching had he had more years as an assistant. The responsibility of the head coach is impossible to escape.

Yet men drift into this business, not by accident, but by design. Many from Miami have risen to the top rung of their profession. Why? Is there a good reason?

"Miami provides an excellent background, not only in my field, but others. But they can only teach you so much. From there, you grow. You grow from the experiences you have in the field. I personally feel Miami provides you with an excellent fundamental background; that the type of guy they have apparently attracted there goes on and amplifies as he goes through that profession. Obviously, there's no way you can turn out a guy from that school that would be a polished football, basketball, baseball coach. I think it was Paul Brown who made the statement when I became the head coach, speaking about my youth and experience, and it stuck with me in a sense: 'Ara really doesn't know what he doesn't know.' There's some truth to that. I was energetic. I had some knowledge of the game. But I really didn't know what I didn't know, and I came to know those things by experience."

*****

The Notre Dame experience obviously was one that Coach Parseghian cherishes. The enthusiasm of the student body, the memorable games with Southern Cal, the first meeting ever with Bear Bryant, the Bowl games with Texas and Alabama, the chance to win national championships — those are Parseghian memories of Notre Dame that probably never will fade. Two games particularly stand out in his mind: the Cotton Bowl game against Texas, when the Longhorns were working on a 30-game winning streak, and the Sugar Bowl game that ended Alabama's bid for a national championship.

"The Cotton Bowl game when we broke the wishbone and had to come up with a mirror defense . . . necessity is the motherhood of invention . . . we had to come up with something, and we never lost to another wishbone team . . . that game was very memorable. The other memorable one was certainly the Sugar Bowl game when we played Alabama. Again, Alabama was on a big winning streak, Bryant had said this was the best team he'd ever had, offense and defense, Alabama and Notre Dame had never played, Bryant and I had never coached against one another, it was the North against the South, it was the Catholics and the Baptists . . . it was a whole gamut of things . . . they were ranked number one, we were ranked number two, both undefeated, so that game became memorable because all the marbles were right there. The winner was going to become national champion, and undefeated. So everything was riding on that game."

And it truly was a memorable college football game, as a fourth quarter field goal put Notre Dame ahead, 24-23. But it was Parseghian's courageous call for a pass on third down, with Notre Dame in the shadow of its own goal posts that turned out to be the key play in a game filled with dramatic moments. The successful gamble enabled Notre Dame to run out the clock, and Ara had another national championship.

Dramatic as that game was, still another Notre Dame game with Alabama, the very next year in the Orange Bowl, was more so. Ara had announced this would be his final game as Notre Dame's coach. As his friend and long-time aide, Tom Pagna, said in his book, it was the end of Notre Dame's "Era of Ara." And it ended with a 13-11 Notre Dame victory. But this is a Miami story.

In the beginning, the trainer did not make athletic trips, due to hotel, food and travel expenses. Often the coach would like to take an extra player rather than a trainer. However, it was not long before the trainer was considered very important and made all the trips the same as the team doctor.

Jay Colville, who has seen Miami as few have, recalling the years.

II
GUARDIAN OF THE CRADLE

HE HOLDS COURT now in a setting that befits his status as Miami's Trainer Emeritus. Its first, its only.

For nearly fifty years, E.J. (Jay) Colville practiced his art, becoming in the process able "to recognize hundreds and hundreds of athletes by the bottoms of their feet." Until his retirement in 1970, when the intercollegiate athletic history of a 161-year-old university spanned 82 years, Jay was the only person Miami ever had called varsity trainer.

Today, he picks up his mail regularly in a below-decks office of spacious Millett Assembly Hall, a grotto adorned with memorabilia which he calls "my archtives." On recruiting season weekends, he regales visitors with yarns of Miami athletes and coaches from Red Blaik and George Rider to Rob Carpenter and Tom Reed.

There is no greater authority on Miami athletics than this warm, hearty and plainspoken man who was born June 30, 1903, on the 80-acre family farm outside Greenville in Darke County, Ohio. At 18, he was a railroad section hand spending his spare time learning to box in a neighbor's barn. He enjoyed both pursuits. He would have been perfectly content to continue that combination. But an older sister, Mabel, was determined that he go to college. She kept dropping casual comments about college. He'd come home from work and find new clothes on his bed. One day, there was a trunk in his room. And almost before he knew it, the budding welterweight and his trunk and his sister were loaded into the family Model T, college-bound. The 49-mile journey from Greenville down Route 127 to Miami University took nine hours in 1921. But it began a 60-year odyssey around the world . . . focal point, Oxford, Ohio.

In any attempt to dissect the Cradle of Coaches phenomenon, Jay Colville sees it most clearly. Not only does he know why it had a chance to happen, he knows that it did happen because of the people who have been a part of it. He never would say so, but the role he has played over the years in interfacing with those people has had more than a little to do with their success, and thus with Miami's recognition as the Cradle of Coaches.

*****

The Roaring Twenties provided more than relief for a nation which had endured World War I and a horrible flu epidemic. They provided the country with its first honest-to-goodness sports heroes.

"The people were entitled to a decent living," Colville recalls, "and they really had it for ten years. Sports were at an all-time high. There was Big Bill Tilden in tennis, Dempsey and Tunney were having their great bouts. Newspapers kept you alive on that. We lived in the country, and I think it took me two days to find out how Dempsey and Firpo came out. There was Bobby Jones, the Four Horsemen, there was Rockne,

This sketch by Ted Patterson, Miami '68, speaks volumes about the man lovingly referred to as "The Guardian of the Cradle".

there was Red Grange. There was Hagen. There was just a tremendous amount of sports . . . I think maybe Weeb (Ewbank) and me, and Paul (Brown) got caught up in it. That and Lindbergh flying the ocean, bathtub gin, and Al Capone."

It was into that type of sports fervor that a pretty good boxer from Greenville was thrust when he first arrived on the Miami campus the same day as another small-towner named Tuffy Potter. Tuffy's little sandwich shop with the delicious toasted rolls became a campus landmark, just as Jay's training room was to become a mecca in its own right.

Miami athletics in that era were the domain of a single individual . . . one individual who had the coaching and administrative responsibilities for everything. George Little was that man for a while. Then George Rider pinch-hit through two remarkable years while Little was overseas as an artillery captain in the AEF. Little returned in 1919, and in Colville's first college semester Little's 1921 Miami football team went 8-0. Little was off to Michigan, boosted into the big time; a pattern which was to be repeated often at Miami some years laters.

Colville calls Little "perhaps the greatest of the Miami coaches," adding that "his addresses to the student body at Friday chapel before the team would depart for a road game were something to hear." And Colville believes that before he left Miami, Little the all-sports wonder was talking up the need for diversification. However, after Little there was one more round of the one-man regime. Little's successor at Miami was Harry E. Ewing, a Nebraska graduate with some success at Ohio Wesleyan; but this time the magic wasn't there. With the 1924-25 school year Miami brought back George Rider as director of physical education and athletics, to coach track and cross country; Chester M. Pittser, for football and baseball, and Roy E. Tillotson for basketball. New ideas accompanied the new format.

After his two Miami years as a relief man wearing four hats, Rider had spent a year at the University of Maine, as director of physical education and athletics, coach of track and cross country. He had been brought back to Miami from Washington University, St. Louis, where he coached football and track besides being director of physical education and intercollegiate athletics. And he brought to Miami with him a deep respect for a new "coaching school" concept which had emerged at the University of Illinois. The new football coach, Pittser, was a product of that program, having started his playing career at Colorado School of Mines, 1915-19. Pittser had become Montana School of Mines' first paid coach in 1920 without a college degree. He had moved on to Illinois to receive the bachelor's degree there in 1924; so he technically was a recent college graduate as he came to Miami, although he had maturity and experience. Tillotson, an Oberlin graduate who had coached successfully in a Pittsburgh high school and engineered a turnaround at Hiram College in four years as physical education director and coach, had attended summer coaching schools at both Illinois and Notre Dame.

"When Pittser, Rider and Tillotson came to take up the coaching duties and expand the department . . . as I mentioned before, it had been in the hands of one man too much . . . these people came in and they had views they'd picked up from pretty good experiences, and they wanted a trainer," Colville reveals.

"Nobody knew very much about what a trainer was . . . whether it was to train horses or what have you . . . but there I was with some knowledge of rubdowns and taping, from my boxing . . . and as a student I was asked if I could be a trainer, part time.

"So there I was. And I started in the basement of old Herron Gym, or what is now called Van Voorhis Hall. I had a little room that's still there . . . and some coach or somebody along the line had the idea of putting a cement bathtub in that very small area. I didn't know who the coach was. It wasn't too bad an idea . . . hydrotherapy is great treatment . . . but I really needed the space more than I needed that tub. So I boarded it over and used the top of it for space. In there also were two little tables. They were alright for length and width, but they were only about two feet off the floor. Now if you ever tried to give a massage bent over to meet the demands of a table only two feet off the ground . . . you can use your body weight good, but it sure is bad on the back. So the first thing I had to do was extend the legs on those tables. I only had two in there and I had to take care of two patients at a time. There was no ventilation, and it was hot . . . it wasn't the best, by any means.

"It was right off the dressing room, and the football players, they didn't

Coach Pittser at the blackboard during a baseball class. "There were a lot of eyebrows raised," remembers Colville.

get a complete change of equipment like we do now, they didn't get a clean athletic supporter every practice . . . T-shirts, or short-sleeve jerseys to wear under the pads was far out of the picture at that time. I've seen these boys . . . I remember one in particular, Gordon Wilson . . . he wound up as an English professor . . . I can still see him beating his pants around an iron support in the dressing room there . . . Needless to say, it didn't take long to fill the place up with dust . . . just trying to get the mud out of the pants. Then in the drying room that Pittser thought up . . . and made it out of chicken wire . . . we did have some steam pipes in there and did have the benefit of startin' out each day with dry clothes . . . but it was unheard-of to get a clean towel. Mr. Roudebush, who ran the University for years . . . I remember him saying you don't need a clean towel every day. Economy was quite a thing in those days. So you'd see a boy lay his towel on the floor and jump up and down, tramp on it, try to get the rough places out of it . . . but if you'd ask a boy today to go out without a clean T-shirt and a clean athletic supporter, he'd stand at the window all day until he got it. Practice twice a day, two T-shirts."

Thus did Jay Colville, who had come to Miami only at the insistence of his sister, who hung around the gym a lot because he had some experience as a boxer, through a series of circumstances which he feels were really a result of the enormous interest in athletics during the Twenties, find himself while still a student, beginning the training career which would span five decades.

*****

As he looks back from the perspective of those five decades, Colville realizes that as a young student trainer he was beginning to see the emergence of the organization which would lead Miami men into coaching. Pittser had come to Miami from the school "which at that time was enjoying the greatest collegiate sports program of any college in the United States . . . the University of Illinois — they had everything."

It was the Zuppke era in football, and Red Grange was the greatest college football player in America. The track coach, Harry Gill, was widely-acclaimed. Illinois' track team was the best. People like Jay Colville, at the urging of Pittser, went to learn at the feet of the masters; and when they left, they had to sign affidavits saying they only had participated in a six-week summer course, lest there be any misrepresentation about where an individual's degree was from. Jay himself won the friendship of Illinois' famous trainer of those days, Matt Bullock, and "became very close to Matt — learned lots."

So, obviously, did Pittser. What Pittser, Rider, Tillotson and eventually Colville brought to Miami was the Illinois concept of physical education, with a few embellishments which became uniquely Miami.

"They brought a whole program, almost lock, stock and barrel, as it was presented and founded at the University of Illinois," Jay reports. "Pittser was familiar with it. He was there as a baseball coach and assistant football coach, under the famous athletic director, George Huff."

Was there ever any question raised about how such a course or series of courses fit in with the general courses of study required?

"Let me say this," responds Colville. "There were a lot of eyebrows raised by the faculty and the Senate about what was going to happen with a basketball team in the classroom."

Apparently it took some doing to get that concept past the faculty. Leave it to Colville to see the humorous side. He tells a story of a football coach who walked into class the first day, held up a ball, and announced, "Boys, this is a football." A big tackle in the front row piped up, "Now, Coach, let's not go too fast." Colville also liked to jest, "You get A in football and F in math, it averages out — helps eligibility."

But through all the spoof and the skepticism, one would have to say the coaching school was an unqualified success. It almost immediately led to an even better understanding by players of the game they were playing, contributing to realization that a Miami team "played smarter."

"It also opened the door for graduates to use their training to be considered for better jobs," Colville suggests, "and it was the Miami faculty which kept the program under tight rein and headed in the right direction."

*****

Attempting to measure the contributions which Jay Colville has made to Miami athletics — the many roles he's played — it's hard to know where to begin. He's the "Will Rogers of the Miami athletic department;" by longevity alone, he reigns as unofficial historian-archivist; he has been Miami's good will ambassador around the world, serving as trainer for the United States Olympic boxing team in Melbourne in 1956.

When Jay Colville went to Melbourne in 1956 to train the Olympic boxers, he returned with memorabilia of all kinds.

What he did best, though, was heal and counsel the thousands — "acres and acres," — he says of athletes who came under his care beginning in 1924.

How does Colville remember his days as trainer, once he graduated in 1926? (He spent so much time on training chores as a student that he was in school longer than anticipated.)

It was early summer when he was still contemplating returning to work on the section gang, or helping with the farming, when George Rider pulled up in front of the Colville home one morning. It was customary for the Riders to spend the summer months in Michigan, so Colville presumed this was simply a social visit en route. It wasn't. Pittser and Rider apparently had agreed that there still was a need for a trainer, and that the recent graduate filled the bill quite nicely. Rider was stopping at Greenville to ask Colville to return in the fall to help with the football team. This wouldn't turn into a full-time appointment for several months, but it was a start. And considering Rider's reputation, it represented a victory.

Colville tells this story about this man who was his boss and who went on to become one of America's great track coaches:

Several of the players, Colville noticed, were beginning to show the effect of the constant rubbing of the pads on their bare chests. One player in particular was in considerable pain and was a regular visitor for treatment. Colville thought it might make some sense to have the players wear T-shirts under the pads for better protection, a common practice today. So he approached Rider with such a request.

"George would have been a great banker, because he had the bluntest no of anybody, and that's all a banker ever said in those days. The gist of his answer was that he couldn't afford me and the T-shirts both. So that set the T-shirts back."

Much of what Colville learned in his early days as Miami's trainer, other than what he learned from his friend Bullock at Illinois, was learned by trial and error and from association with coaches he had learned to respect as Miami traveled Ohio. Besides Miami's Pittser, Tillotson and Rider, Jay learned from George Gauthier of Ohio Wesleyan, Walter J. (Livvy) Livingston at Denison, C.W. Savage at Oberlin, and others.

Colville remembers learning about the use of ice from Gauthier: "When he'd come to our place to play football, he'd call me and ask me to get him a cake of ice and have it in the dressing room. A cake of ice meant going to the ice house down by the depot and chipping off your 300-pound cake of ice, which is what you needed; and then you bellied that out and put it in the dressing room down there. I mean you did it yourself. The iceman didn't bring it. You did everything for yourself. Then I'd go in the dressing room after the game, and that ice wasn't hardly touched. The next time I had a chance to talk to George — maybe it would have been a track meet in the spring — I said, 'George, you get that ice, and I never see you do anything with it.' And then Gauthier said, 'When I get a boy injured, I'll chip that ice off . . . some of it, and I'll make a pack with a towel, and if it's a boy's knee or ankle, I'll tie it on his leg; and by the time we get home, it'll keep the swelling down.' That's where I learned to use ice."

That Colville was somewhat of a pioneer in the training profession is a tribute to the Illinois experience and the foresight of Pittser and Rider. Many of the coaches at the other Ohio schools were still doing their own taping. Colville tells the story involving John Brickels, who was to become Miami's athletic director in 1950, and Ernie Godfrey, a coach Brickels had played for at Wittenberg.

"I've heard Brickels say Godfrey would take that strip of tape up the side of his ankle, and would be saying 'Now if that team does this, you do this,' and he'd jerk that tape and tighten and go the other way, and John said he couldn't wait to get away and cut the tape off. His feet and toes were turnin' blue. A coach didn't necessarily make a very good trainer."

Eventually, new equipment for use of trainers began to be developed, even beyond some of the early discoveries of people like George Gauthier. There was the electric pad and the infra-red lamp, and "I thought at one time that might be as good as we were gonna get." The use of such innovations would be explained by a salesman. Specific techniques remained a matter of trial and error.

Today it's different, and Colville isn't sure all the changes are for the good. In no way would he be, or was he, one to stand in the way of progress. But he sees another problem which has surfaced in this age of "modern new equipment."

"Trainers today, they've got all these whirlpool baths, they've got ultra-sound, they've got the paraffin bath, they've got the Nautilus training, weight machines, they've got special devices to exercise the knee . . . They've just got so many things to work with that the last thing they wanna do is **touch** a boy."

Here was the Will Rogers . . . the healer and the counselor . . . beginning to surface. He already had retired when he began working on the injured leg of Rob Carpenter, an all-time great running back of the Seventies who has gone on to play for the New York Giants after several years as the other back with Earl Campbell, on the Houston Oilers. Massage and talk, talk and massage . . . lots of talking . . . Jay spent countless hours working on Carpenter's leg — and on Carpenter's confidence in that leg. And the result was a fabulous final collegiate game — 28 carries for 117 yards, playing hurt — for an athlete most coaches and trainers might have given up on.

*****

Anybody who's been around as long as Jay Colville, and who professes to have learned his craft by trial and error, is bound to have come up with an innovation or two. Born of necessity, these inventions may or may not become universally adopted. George Rider had a magnificent track athlete who went on to become a great coach at Bowling Green, Miami's Mid-American Conference rival. Bob Whittaker, it seems, had a huge problem with a blister which, though it never became infected, was so sore that Whittaker simply couldn't run. Nothing Jay tried worked, including the normal procedure of making a donut. Colville finally went up to the cobbler in town and had the shoe rebuilt by taking from here and replacing there, enough so that it relieved the pressure and enabled Whittaker to run — right into Miami's Athletic Hall of Fame.

The neck yoke, used commonly now by football players, is a Colville invention for which he never got a dime. "That came about in about 1962, when Miami had a pretty good football team, and Lowell Caylor, a quarterback turned linebacker, suffered a cervical spine injury. He was laid up in the hospital for a time, and when he was released and back in school, Colville was sure he had to do something to protect that neck before letting Caylor practice or play again. He tried several possible solutions without much success before experimenting with a type of material which he and Dr. Richard Mackey from Miami's physical education staff had used with success to make and market a practice golf ball. With that and a little bit of a design idea, Colville went to the Capitol-Varsity Athletic Reconditioning Co. in Oxford to see if they could help. Jay's idea of what he wanted combined beautifully with Capitol's capability and experience. Jay watched while a fellow named Russ Hawkins produced a neck yoke, held it up and said "Is this what you want?" And thus was born the forerunner of what has become almost a staple piece of equipment for every football team in the country. Did Jay ever think about getting a patent on his invention? "Well, you didn't think about it. You invented those things just for your own use."

*****

We already have noted that in his younger days, in and around Greenville, Jay Colville learned to box. At Miami, his German professor, Dr. Charles H. Handschin, was also the boxing instructor. Jay continued to polish his boxing skills under Doc Handschin. In fact, it was the boxing which led to a contact with the football team. He was out doing his road work when George Little spotted him and invited him to try out for the team.

"Since I only weighed about 148 pounds, there wasn't a place for me to play," he relates. "So they stuck me at guard."

Colville didn't play much football, but between the boxing and the football, he was around the gym a lot. Boxing was a popular intramural sport at Miami in those days, and Jay competed for his fraternity, Sigma Alpha Epsilon. Even after he wound up as Miami's trainer, he continued his boxing career. He boxed on a card down at Ft. Thomas, Ky., and over in Dayton. What about the purses? Colville was asked.

"Lunch money, maybe. Cold cuts."

His boxing reputation grew, and Si Burick, who remains the Sports Editor of the **Dayton Daily News**, wanted to start a newspaper-sponsored boxing tournament in the Dayton area, the winners to go on to Chicago to compete in the **Chicago Tribune's** annual Golden Gloves event. Burick, along with the ever-present Ben Garlikov, solicited Colville's aid in staging the Dayton event. And it was Colville who took the Dayton-area champions to Chicago.

*****

Over the years, as he has watched this phenomenon develop, Colville obviously has seen some changes.

"When I first came here, and George Little was the coach, one man would coach two or three sports. They might get somebody off the faculty to coach baseball in the spring. If you could imagine one man in 1921 compared to this year, 1979, past season, where we have probably seven

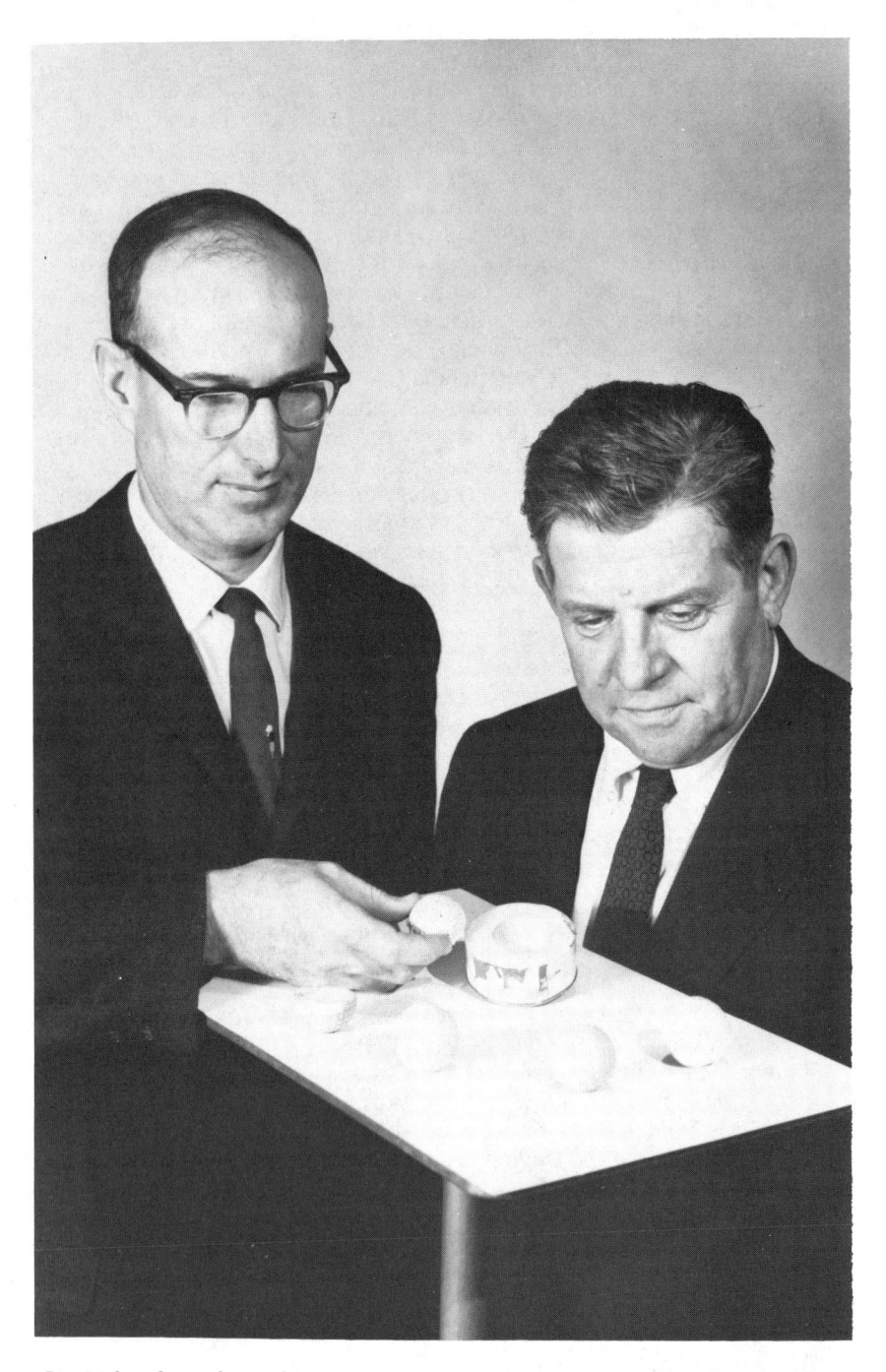

Dr. Richard Mackey of Miami's physical education staff and Jay Colville developed a practice golf ball. It had some of the same properties that were evident when Colville needed to protect Lowell Caylor's neck with the "yoke."

permanent coaches . . . football . . . didn't do anything else . . . coach football . . . plus three or four graduate assistants . . . that might give you a better idea that there've been some changes."

Little had precious little help. Colville recalls that after he had graduated, Red Blaik and a couple of his friends from Dayton, Red Steele and Eddie Sauer, would drive over to Oxford to lend what help with practice as they could. Little did his own taping, and treated injuries, what few there were, as best he could. The players took pretty good care of themselves, because the equipment in those days didn't afford the protection it does today. "Today, with the equipment, they might figure there's no way they can get hurt, so they don't protect themselves and one another."

The modernization of Miami football started with Chet Pittser. Pittser had known success at Illinois, and he had a system.

"Chet . . . he was an organized guy," Colville continues. "I've heard him before a game . . . say his quarterback was Weeb Ewbank or Eddie Wohlwender . . . 'If we receive the ball, we'll run this play, and that'll take us about here, then this play . . . and I've seen that go all the way to the goal. He had a game plan, and I've seen Pittser do that."

A few years ago, late in a game involving the Oakland Raiders, a trick play decided the game. The quarterback took the snap from center and laid the ball on the ground next to a guard. The lineman then scooped up the ball, picked up blocking, and swept into the end zone. Phil Samp, the Cincinnati broadcaster, asked Paul Brown on his radio show the next day, if he'd ever seen such a play before.

"Well, I did," said Brown. "When Mr. Pittser was the coach at Miami, and I was the quarterback at Miami we used that play."

Besides well-organized game plans and innovative plays, Pittser brought other ideas to Miami which proved particularly advantageous. He believed in scouting an opponent; and the phys ed man, Tom Van Voorhis, who likewise was to become a Miami institution, was his scout. With freshmen ineligible to play, Pittser still deemed it wise for them to get good early training, develop good habits, and have someone they could have daily contact with. To say nothing of running the next opponent's plays against the varsity. So a freshman coach was hired.

What wasn't necessary until much later, and thus kept the staffing requirements somewhat under control, was recruiting and the need for coaches to make weekly appearances at booster clubs. In fact, it was considered quite inappropriate, even at places like Illinois and Michigan, to stoop so low as to recruit a football player. And as far as booster groups were concerned, the need for that didn't surface until the advent of game film. The coach who succeeded Pittser was Frank Wilton, and it was he who persuaded the "banker with the bluntest no," George Rider, to permit filming the games.

"Wilton was a progressive guy, but he was steadily going downhill in the late Thirties," Colville proceeds. "He was gonna take one last shot at it. He got a couple of renegades to come in — rejects from other schools . . . and he was gonna have a great year. He was gonna play Illinois . . . I think the opening game . . . And he was gonna outfox the Old Fox, Zuppke. He got some people interested in town, and he approached

Tom VanVoorhis was one of the additions to the Miami staff when George Rider returned as athletic director. Coach Pittser believed in scouting an opponent, and VanVoorhis was his scout. VanVoorhis directed the intramural sports program at Miami for many, many years.

Rider on the feasibility of takin' pictures of the game. Would you believe that took a lot of doin'? Took a lot of doin' to get Rider to say he was gonna fund that kind of thing. Now, they film every practice. Then Wilton was gonna take those films uptown after the game and show 'em. Try to build up interest in the boosters, but it was so sad he had to do that all through that season. I think he had one game we won. But that was good thinkin'."

While Colville never could understand the circumstances of Pittser's leaving ("I think he was forced to leave") he had no doubt about Wilton. He just didn't, or wouldn't change his basic coaching philosophy as the game changed elsewhere. And it was during the Wilton era that Miami suffered its only prolonged slump: four wins and two ties in the 27 games of 1939, 1940, and 1941. Even then, technically Wilton wasn't fired; official discussion of his status still was current when he went to the colors early in 1942.

*****

Colville's years at Miami have embraced virtually all there is to tell about Miami athletics. He wasn't around when Red Blaik came to the Oxford campus. But he was around when Blaik came back afternoons to lend a hand as a volunteer. When Miami started an Athletic Hall of Fame in 1969, Jay Colville was among the eight charter inductees. And the athletes and coaches who have joined him on the Hall of Fame roster in subsequent years all have felt the touch of the sage from Darke County.

And sage he has been. As the Miami coaching legend has unfolded, his sideline vantage point was as visionary and inspirational as it was therapeutic. After more than 50 years on the Miami campus, Colville thought he'd seen it all. And then came a period, from 1973 through 1975, when Miami won 31 of 33 games, losing one and tying one. It gave Colville pause.

"I wonder if we're going to be able to keep up," reflects Colville as he considers some of the talented athletes on those teams. "Because those guys just more or less walked in here.Can we be lucky enough to catch guys who'll be good enough to keep us great? I don't know."

Time will tell, but history and tradition are solidly in Miami's corner.

I don't know any particular reason for that. I really don't. I think it's just something that evolved by nature. Like I said, I didn't even realize it was a fact. It shows you how much thought I had given it . . . I should commend the people at Miami for doing this.

Paul Brown, upon realizing that beginning with Ara Parseghian in 1951, five graduates of the Cradle of Coaches had become head coaches at their alma mater.

III

THE CRADLE'S PIONEERS

JAY COLVILLE CALLED the Roarin' Twenties the golden age of sport in this country. There are those who would argue the point with Jay; but in Miami lore, there is no argument that the Twenties brought to Miami the first wave of the student-athletes who were to make a significant impact on the sports world as their coaching genius became recognized.

Weeb Ewbank was to recall many years later that when he returned to Oxford in the early Thirties to coach at McGuffey School and to help coordinate the student teaching activities of the Miamians in the "coaching school," by his own rough count there were more than 180 Miami graduates in high school coaching positions around Ohio.

One decade followed another, and by the Fifties and Sixties two men from Colville's Roarin' Twenties emerged to pre-eminence in the world of sport. Wilbur C. Ewbank, Miami '28, was one of those, and his friend Paul E. Brown, Miami '30, was the other. As the history of professional football is written, these two Miami contemporaries have provided much of that saga.

They had followed different paths to get to Miami, and they followed different routes to the pinnacles each attained; yet both stand as testimonials to the Miami connection that clearly exists in the coaching profession. Ewbank explains:

"A Miami man would get a good job, and he'd hire a coupla Miami assistants. They'd have good success, and then one of the assistants would get a job, and he'd hire more Miami people. Then these coaches who were out there would send players back. That's where we had good teams, because a lotta those people out coaching were former Miami people and so they would naturally be interested in Miami and they'd funnel 'em back to Miami.

"I think that's where the coaching school really mushroomed. The other thing is, I think they always had, starting with Pittser, good fundamentalists as head coaches, who stressed fundamentals, which is the name of the game, and stressed teaching, which is coaching."

Paul Brown, who transferred to Miami from Ohio State as a sophomore when Weeb Ewbank was a senior, learned how the system worked. After more than a decade of separate coaching experiences, heaven only knows how much the Miami chemistry was augmented as they coached together at Great Lakes in World War II. Brown already was organizing the Cleveland Browns by the time he left the service. Ewbank went on to an assistant's job at Brown University, then got his first head-coaching spot at Washington University in St. Louis. Within a couple of years, Paul Brown was in need of an aide who shared his philosophy, and the "Miami funnel" as Ewbank had called it, was working. Brown knew where Ewbank was, and that's the man he wanted. Ewbank had said that's the way it worked, and now he had personal testimony.

Weeb Ewbank emerged on the Miami scene in 1925, a product of the playing fields and gymnasiums of nearby Richmond, an eastern Indiana city with a perpetually outstanding sports program. His father had introduced him to sports, and he recalls throwing the ball against the side of the house to create difficult fielding plays for himself, or shooting at the basketball goal erected in the back yard.

"There's a fella by the name of Bob Evans, who's a Phi Delt, and I was on championship teams (at Richmond)," explains Ewbank, "And he was interested in Miami and tryin' to get athletes and fellas for the fraternity . . . . that type of thing. I sorta sifted myself through. I think a lotta players do this. I'd been to Indiana, they'd taken me out to the state basketball tournament, they'd taken me out to the University of Illinois, and I remember old G. Huff out there. If I'd gone to a Big Ten school, I think I'd have made a baseball letter, and that would have been all. They wouldn't even look at me in basketball and football . . . . I was still only five-seven, so they wouldn't even give me a suit. They'd just say grow up. So I sorta thought this (Miami) would be a place where I could play a little."

And play he did. Football, basketball and baseball, although he didn't play football as a freshman. The Miami baseball teams were perennial conference champions during the Ewbank years; and though the basketball teams were only average, Weeb just marveled at the talents of one of his teammates, Paul Taylor. Taylor subsequently shifted his personal emphasis from filling baskets to filling teeth, as he became one of Oxford's finest dentists.

"When I'd get the ball, I always figured I'd get it to Paul Taylor, because he can do something with it," chuckled Weeb in recalling the man he thought was as good a basketball player as Miami ever had. "He was fabulous."

Ewbank was a business major when he started at Miami. But by the beginning of Ewbank's sophomore year, plans were being made by the Miami coaching staff to launch the "coaching school." Ewbank was tempted, yet he was concerned about being able to pursue business studies as well. Given that assurance, he was in the first class of Miami students to be enrolled in a four-year course in Athletic Coaching and Physical Education.

Here is how Miami's President Raymond M. Hughes described the new curriculum:

"During the year 1925-26 Miami offered a four-year course in Physical Education and Athletic Coaching for the first time, and its reception was so enthusiastic that we are continuing it with great interest. It is designed to combine a liberal education with preparation for directing the work in physical education in the high schools.

"We believe this is an important course, which will appeal to young men who love athletics and who are fond of boys. It should develop teachers of a type that is now much sought for in Ohio.

Miami University

Four Year Course in
ATHLETIC COACHING and PHYSICAL EDUCATION

"Men of high character, scholarly tastes, fine sportsmanship, should find it interesting and profitable, and through it should reach a fine field of public service."

This, of course, was the new program already referred to briefly by Colville in explaining the new philosophy whose needs included providing a full-time varsity trainer.

President Hughes noted that the new curriculum was being presented by an impressive four-man staff — not, by modern standards, a large complement; yet a coaching-teaching team nearly four times larger than Miami ever had known before. In addition to Coaches Rider, Pittser and Tillotson already identified, Hughes listed in this quartet Thomas P. VanVoorhis, a blustery martinet whose justification for any duress was the predictable assurance: "It'll make a man of you!"

George L. Rider headed this staff as professor of Physical Education, director of athletics and track coach. Chester M. Pittser, coach of football and baseball, and Roy E. Tillotson, coach of basketball and assistant coach in football, held associate professorship in Physical Education. VanVoorhis, director of intramural athletics, held assistant professorship in Physical Education.

The University of Illinois influence already described was an overlay on solid all-round preparation, mostly in small yet high-quality colleges. Rider, who had been one of Michigan's finest athletes as a 1914 graduate of Olivet College, had coached just about everything at Hanover, Miami, Maine and Washington before returning to Miami. Pittser's four seasons at Colorado Mines included starring on its undefeated, untied 1918 team; he topped off the experience of being Montana Mines' first paid football coach by working as an assistant under the great Zuppke at Illinois while completing a bachelor's degree in the Illinois coaching school. He had come to Miami directly from that experience. Tillotson, we have noted, already had taken work at Illinois and Notre Dame as a 1916 graduate of Oberlin (they'd tied Ohio State and beaten Cornell, Western Reserve, Case, Miami, Ohio Wesleyan and Wittenberg while he was there). He had done successive four-year coaching stints in high school and college.

VanVoorhis deserves special mention. Although his role in team coaching was incidental, he had unique impact on future coaches through his supervision of service classes, through implementing one of the nation's earliest and most extensive intramural sports programs, and through staying around long enough to become a legend in his own right. And he remains the only one of these four to have a Miami building named for him: VanVoorhis Hall, formerly Herron Gymnasium. Van had gone to Hiram College before and after overseas Army service; had finished up at Miami in 1921, spent a year in Mexico as a YMCA physical education instructor, and returned to Miami as a physical education teacher in 1922. He had earned a Harvard physical education diploma in summer sessions, 1921-24.

So those who chose this course of study were apprised of the opportunities in Physical Education and then, in the University literature describing the curriculum, they read these words:

"The athletic director, the coach, or the physical educator finds himself today in a position of no less responsibility than the college president, superintendent of schools, or the minister of the gospel. Probably no person has greater influence in building the character and the ideals of the boys with whom he comes in contact."

Then came the challenge . . . . and the admonition:

"Some may have the idea that this is a 'SNAP' course. On the contrary, it is not intended to be easy, but is planned to give a person a thorough, general and scientific education. It will require a great deal of study and outside work, as well as diligent application to the practice work on the field. If you expect to slide thru college, having a good time and doing little work, 'Don't Come to Miami,' expecting to take this course because such people will never complete the work. We want men in this course that we will feel free to recommend for a responsible position on the completion of the work."

In the first year, students enrolled in the four-year course took a three-hour introductory course in Teaching and Psychology, English Composition, Physical Education 110, Football and Basketball (both one-hour courses), Public Speaking and selected courses from the major field of study. The second semester, Track and Baseball were substituted. Zoology (Hygiene and Sanitation) and Physiology, along with a choice of Economics, Sociology, Government or History and Social Sciences, were additions to the sophomore year requirements.

The junior year was the year for observation and participation in practice teaching, in addition to a continuation of Physical Education courses and selections from the teaching major. Training and First Aid was a senior requirement, as was a one-hour course in History and Philosophy of Physical Education. A School Administration course, Organization in Secondary Schools, was an important part of senior year study. And so it went, a complete program leading to the Bachelor of Science degree, preparing the young man for a career as a teacher-coach. And Weeb Ewbank was one of those who learned his lessons well.

*****

The Miami baseball team in 1926 won 15 of 16 games played and earned the right to be declared Ohio and Buckeye Conference champions. By Ewbank's senior year, Coach Pittser's football squad was beginning to get its act together. The 1929 Tribe won eight of nine games, losing only to Wittenberg. Miami finished out that year with three games on the road and defeated Ohio Northern, Dayton and Cincinnati in succession. Weeb was the backup for an outstanding quarterback of his day, Eddie Wohlwender.

What was a football game at Miami Field like in those days? Ewbank remembers:

"There were two wooden stands, one on either side; and in those days the girls sat over where the faculty and the other people sat . . . . and if a fella came with a girl, he'd go right over to the other side and yell for the team."

Ewbank doesn't recall there ever being more than 10 or 12 rows in those stands, and this probably was true so long as any of the sideline units of wood bleachers existed. However, a photo taken at the 1926 Homecoming

Coach Weeb Ewbank's first job after graduating from Miami in 1928 was at Van Wert, Ohio, High School. That's Weeb at the right underneath the goal post.

game shows the first section of the steel stands which were still in place when the 1982 Redskins played the last of 334 games stretched over 87 seasons on the historic field.

"At the halftime," continues Ewbank, "the big thing was the snake dance. About three or four guys would get arm in arm and others would fall in behind, and they'd just snake-dance all over the field. And we didn't have girl cheerleaders then . . . . They were all boys."

Ewbank's first job as a high school coach was at Van Wert, Ohio; but it wasn't long before he "got the big break" and came back to Oxford as a teacher and coach in the William McGuffey Schools, laboratory system for Miami's School of Education. In those days McGuffey included a high school, separate from the Oxford public high school, and Ewbank was to coach all sports for the high school.

One year, 1939, when Miami's basketball coach left for another job near the opening of the season, Ewbank agreed to take on Miami's team as acting coach, while also coaching McGuffey High School.

"Boy, I really had to work pretty hard that time, runnin' back and forth between McGuffey Gym and Miami's Withrow Court," Ewbank recalls.

Knowing what we know now, in fact there were testimonies to its success almost from the day it started, it is not surprising to find graduates of Miami's four-year course in Athletic Coaching and Physical Education moving into responsible coaching positions in Ohio high schools and elsewhere. But what about the Miami players, and more importantly, the Redskin teams? Were they better because of the "coaching school?"

"Oh, I don't think there's any question about that," answers Ewbank. "When they first started, they did it all in the college classes. When I came back in 1930, they used the McGuffey School, and they also used the Oxford high school, Stewart. My job . . . . I taught Methods in Physical Education after I came back, and I also was in charge of the critic teaching of all those students." The cycle, Ewbank says, was sending good young men out into the coaching field, bright young student athletes were being funneled Miami's way, and Miami was better because of it.

******

The war came along, and that took care of the next chapter of Ewbank's life in Oxford. But his entry into the service also reunited him with Paul Brown, and there were new challenges ahead.

"I went into the Navy, and I ended up at Great Lakes, and Paul Brown was the football coach, and so I coached with Paul up there," explains Ewbank. "And when I was shipped out of there, later on they brought me back, and I coached basketball. They then wanted me to stay in the Navy and wanted me to coach baseball; but I had enough points to get out, so I thought I better go to work."

Even though he spent the next three years in the collegiate ranks, Ewbank was destined to follow Brown into professional football. Having shared in Brown's successes with the Cleveland Browns, before too long he was making his own mark — as head coach first with the Baltimore Colts in the National Football League, then with the New York Jets in the old American Football League. With those two franchises, Ewbank etched his name forever into the pro football record books. Just four years after he signed on with Baltimore, his Colts became world champions in that epic 1958 overtime struggle with the New York Giants. Ten years later, he had another world champion — this time the Jets, after four years at their helm. Nobody ever had won each league. He remains the only coach to have done so. And since the merger of the American and National Leagues, it's not likely to happen again.

It was Ewbank's characteristic hard work and dedication which eventually led to the opportunity with Baltimore. But earlier, Weeb hadn't been so sure there was any sense to what Brown was asking him to do at Cleveland: coaching the offensive and defensive tackles.

"I thought he was out of his mind," Ewbank admits, "but as things turned out, it probably was the best thing that ever happened to me, because I had to really study. I got hold of those movies and looked and studied the players and studied pro football and all that went with it."

Later, as a head coach, Ewbank was able to put to work that knowledge gained under Brown studying the play in football's trenches.

"We had owners at the Cleveland Browns who were friends with Art Rooney (of the Pittsburgh Steelers)," Ewbank comments. "The story that I heard was that when Carroll Rosenbloom was looking for a coach, Art Rooney said (to Rosenbloom), 'I've got some friends who are owners up in Cleveland that say that Ewbank is doing one helluva job. I'd recommend you look into that.' That's the way Carroll Rosenbloom and Don Kellett got interested in me."

In his Cleveland days, in addition to his line coaching responsibilities, Ewbank also was assigned by Brown to prepare for the draft of college talent. There weren't any scouting combines in those days, or even the sophisticated, computer-oriented methods of talent search like those used by the Dallas Cowboys. Out of necessity, Ewbank developed his own. One was to contact various college coaches who were friends of his, asking them to write a letter recommending some of the best players in the college ranks. Ewbank would pay those coaches $40 or $50 for their recommendations.

Another Ewbank innovation was the post card which he would send to some of those who had been recommended asking that they pass along the names of people they had played against who were particularly talented. "When I found somebody's name that kept coming up that people thought was tough that they'd played against, to me I was getting an evaluation from a player who had to play against somebody," and that carried significant weight.

The situations Ewbank walked into in Baltimore, and later with New York, were desperate situations. He wasn't being asked to breathe new life into a proven organization which had, for one reason or another, fallen on hard times. He was building from scratch, which would seem to make finding the talent more important than the tactical, strategic part of the game.

"The people who win, anyplace, whether it's college or high school, right away when they haven't been winning, you can figure that the material was there.

"When we went there," recalls Ewbank of his Baltimore days, "we thought we had about ten players. In looking at film and grading players, we thought we had about ten players. At the end of the first year, we thought we had 14; but in the meantime, we're gettin' the devil kicked out of us."

It was even worse with the Jets. They hadn't even signed a draft choice in two years. "We always laughed about the first year at the Jets. We said we had yesterday's team, today's team and a team comin' in tomorrow. We looked at about one hundred twenty, one hundred thirty ballplayers that year. Just bring 'em in, look at 'em, keep the ones that were better than . . . ."

Ewbank brings his own brand of coaching philosophy to any discussion about sideline strategy during the course of a game:

"For example, you get down near the goal line to score, the first thing I always said, 'How'd you get here?' Then number two is, 'What did we work on all week to get in that end zone?' and you always went to your plan. I always liked to have a good plan for everything, and if something would come up, you'd go with your experience."

There were times, he would acknowledge, when game plans and experience went out the window, and the human qualities, or frailties, of the men who played this physical, yet mentally demanding, game were decisive. In that memorable world championship game in 1958 between Ewbank's Colts and the New York Giants, the Colts were down on the goal line, looking for a touchdown. The game plan in this situation called for a toss play to the big fullback, Alan Ameche, with Ameche faking the run, then passing to Jim Mutscheller in the end zone for the touchdown.

"A toss-out play for us was twenty-eight," remembers Ewbank, "and a four twenty eight meant the back was gonna throw it. In this case it was the fullback. Down there on the goal line, Ameche didn't hear the four. He just heard the twenty-eight. There was Mutscheller in the end zone, jumpin' up and down, and Ameche never looked at him. And we didn't get in there."

Inevitably, the former Miami quarterback would get around to talking about his two pro quarterbacks. Joe Namath was "a great quarterback," says Ewbank.

"He was a winner. He had a quick release . . . . and a lot of people can throw the ball long . . . . we used the long pass, when it was there, we hoped to complete it . . . . but early in the game we would generally throw one with the idea of makin' the short pass good. We'd figure, hell, if it should happen to be intercepted, it was as good as a punt. And Joe was a good leader. He just didn't have the mobility. But what he did do was amazing, when he had two braces on, and he looked graceful. I remember a woman saying one time, the value of her ticket was just watching him take that ball from center and set up. He did it so gracefully. He did it about a half a second quicker than John (Unitas). And when John did it he looked like a plodder. Joe just did it gracefully. But John was equally as good a quarterback. I wouldn't take one over the other."

During his long tenure as a successful head coach, Ewbank hired many

The Namaths, father and son, congratulate Weeb after the Super Bowl victory.

assistants. No doubt he thought frequently about the time in Oxford when a campaign was mounted in his behalf as Miami was looking for a head coach in 1942. Stu Holcomb was hired. Even though Weeb wanted the Miami job at the time and was disappointed when he didn't get it, he realized later that he lacked the experience, particularly as a defensive coach. That, perhaps, is why he worked so hard, studied so much football, and went to so many clinics. It is this work ethic which undoubtedly led him to search out and hire the type of people he surrounded himself with as a head coach.

"I always prided myself in the type of people I put around me," he explains.

Continuing to paint a word picture of that type of individual, Weeb says, "First, I figure if he has intelligence and is interested in the sport, I could always teach him. Then I'd want to look at his background to see if he was a good teacher, because that's coaching. I also wanted to find out what kind of person that man was, and his wife, because he has to be happy in that situation. Those were the main things I would look for. Plus, the guy had to be a worker. Of course, I always believed that if I worked hard, they would work hard."

Ewbank retired from coaching in 1973 and moved into a front office position with the Jets. Two years later, he retired from his active life in football, to a little slower pace in Oxford, where he can watch his favorite team play every Saturday the Redskins are home.

******

Paul Brown doesn't enjoy the same luxury.

First, as part-owner and general manager of the Cincinnati Bengals, he remains active in professional football. He tries to see Miami play at least once a year and in 1982, when Miami closed Miami Field with a fitting ceremony, Paul Brown was among those who participated in the festivities. He and Weeb, along with John Pont and Paul Dietzel, representing the "Cradle of Coaches," were there as the game ball from Miami's 23-0 victory over Central Michigan was passed along to members of the 1983 Redskins, to be used in the inauguration of the new Yager Stadium.

Weeb Ewbank was raised in a rural setting outside Richmond, Indiana. Brown was a product of urban northwestern Ohio. Massillon was his home town; and like Richmond, Massillon enjoyed, and has continued to enjoy, a reputation for good high school sports. Brown was a multi-sport athlete at Massillon, captain of the basketball team, quarterback of the football team. But because of his size, football was out of the question for him at Ohio State.

"I just wasn't big enough," Brown says now.

In the spring, "which is a beautiful time in Oxford," Brown went down to visit some boyhood friends who were in school at Miami: "I became enamored of the place; I really thought this looked like a school should be."

He finished the year at Ohio State and finally persuaded his father that Miami was where he wanted to be, and his credits would transfer without question.

His book, **PB: The Paul Brown Story,** written in collaboration with Jack Clary, talks about his arrival at Miami University the next fall, and he says he never will forget it. He was beginning his sophomore year, but his first year on the Miami campus. After a train ride from Massillon to Hamilton, he was aboard a bus crammed with Miami students — among them, it turned out, a lad who was a varsity cheerleader. As the bus topped a final hill and the campus buildings loomed into view, the cheerleader shouted, "Crimson Towers, everybody up!" And with that, the busload of Miami students began singing the Miami fight song, to the utter amazement of a young man from Massillon who didn't know the words but nonetheless was caught up in the spirit of the moment.

Looking back on his Miami experience, Brown obviously has no regrets: "I had a very happy time. I played football, I was the quarterback, I was the punter, I was the passer, I held for the placekicker . . . . I was in it thick."

A transfer, Brown had to sit out a year, playing only with the freshman team. But he thinks the experience matured him, inasmuch as he had been only 16 when he graduated from high school. At the very least, he was bigger.

Not only was Brown enamored of Miami, he respected the coach, Chet Pittser, Like Ewbank, who sang Pittser's praises as a strong fundamentalist, Brown apparently learned a lot of football from the man he still referred to as Mister Pittser at the time of Pittser's death in 1976 at age 86.

"Mr. Pittser was a very gentle man," intones Brown. "He had some modern ideas about football at the time. He had been a disciple of Bob Zuppke at Illinois (how many times have we heard that reference?) . . . he was the fellow who really had the system that we were brought into by Mr. Pittser."

Brown was a member of Delta Kappa Epsilon fraternity at Miami, and in addition to football, he was the leadoff hitter and centerfielder on the Redskin baseball team. But football was Brown's game, and he had some glorious moments in his two-year career as the Redskins' signal-caller.

Despite his admiration for Mr. Pittser, the two occasionally had differing philosophies about how the game should be played. The teacher was conservative; the player was not. A good example of those differences came during Miami's 1928 game against Wittenberg. It was a big game for Brown, because he had so many friends from Massillon on the Wittenberg team. Let Brown pick up the story:

"The plan was to attack their defense cautiously and try not to make any mistakes that would give them cheap touchdowns. One of our receivers was Jim Gordon, who later would be a 400-meter finalist in the 1932 Olympic Games. I figured no one on either team could touch Jim for pure speed; so the first two times we had the ball, I sent him straight down the sideline and threw the ball as hard as I could so he could run under it, make the catch and go for touchdowns. We won the game 18-0, and I had the satisfaction of outpunting Jim Price (a friend from Massillon and Wittenberg's quarterback) as well. I never felt I went against Coach Pittser's orders because I wasn't taking any chances — I

In 1971, Weeb was in San Diego with the Jets, and his college coach, Chet Pittser, was there to see the game.

simply knew the defensive back on that side could not stay with Gordon."

Miami finished that season with six victories in eight games, and the next year won seven of nine. Brown closed out his collegiate playing career on Thanksgiving Day in 1929 as the Redskins upset arch-rival Cincinnati, 14-6, despite Quarterback Brown playing with a sprained ankle.

******

The career course Brown had charted for himself, with considerable guidance from his father, was law. Physical Education and Athletic Coaching was not his major: he majored in English and History with an eye toward law school. The master plan was sidetracked, however, by a series of unpredictable events. First, he and his high school sweetheart, Katy Kester, were married. That was predictable. But since both Miami and the Western Reserve School of Nursing forbade it, they had to keep their marriage in 1929 a secret, from all except their parents, until Paul's graduation. Because of his academic prowess, Brown was eligible to apply for a Rhodes Scholarship. But the country was in the middle of a depression, and for a newly married couple, a job, if one were available, seemed best. When Severn Prep in Maryland contacted him and said he had been recommended for a coaching and teaching job at the preparatory school for the Naval Academy, his prayers were answered. So were Katy's, because as a registered nurse, she was placed in charge of the infirmary.

In Brown's growing-up in Massillon, the man who had the greatest influence on him was his coach, Dave Stewart. Stewart had left Massillon, and when he did a lot of what he had built was left to die. Massillon needed to rebuild, and Brown learned that his old school was in the market for a football coach. The guy who tipped him off was Dave Stewart. And when Dr. H.W. Bell, president of the school board, asked Stewart for his recommendation, Stewart unhesitatingly threw his support behind the 22-year-old who had used his two years at Severn Prep to pick up the necessary courses to qualify for a teaching certificate in Ohio.

Where did this leave the dream of a law career? Brown did complete two years of law school. And though his father doubted the course his son's career was following ever would lead to anything, he eventually became resigned to the reality of the situation.

"He took a dim view of what I was doing, for a while," Brown recalls. "Well, he got into the spirit a little when I was coaching Massillon, but then when I got to be the coach at Ohio State, why then at that time he said, 'Well, this might be alright, at that.'"

Brown still was working toward the law degree in night school classes, however, when he got another assignment at Massillon.

"What happened was," he says, "the basketball coach at Massillon falsified a score, believe it or not, of his team, and they fired him. And so this man who was head of the board, Dr. Bell, called me in the morning and said 'Paul, you've gotta coach basketball, too.' And so I did."

With an assist from stalwarts Billy Rohr and Carroll Widdoes, who did much of the coaching, although Brown remained in charge of the basketball as well as the football program. Ironically, Widdoes perhaps gained his greatest acclaim as the football coach at one of Miami's hated in-state rivals, Ohio University, and Rohr made his mark as a highly successful basketball coach at Miami, and then Northwestern, and ultimately director of athletics at Ohio University. Now a highly successful insurance salesman in Cincinnati, Rohr makes his home in . . . you guessed it . . . Oxford.

Brown pauses to explain his special relationship with Rohr, and how it has an impact on Rohr's career, and even on the careers of other Massillon products who, at one time or another, came under the Miami influence.

"When Billy was a senior, I loaded up a whole group of guys . . . . I had a good team at Massillon, many of them good players . . . . and I'm going to get some of the key ones down at my alma mater, where I hoped they'd go. Howard Brinker, Ray Hoyman, Billy Rohr . . . . I can remember those . . . . Bob Elias, the Snavely boys. Unfortunately when we got there, Frank Wilton, the coach . . . . I kept those guys at the Deke house . . . . he wouldn't even come over to see us. Wilton was, at that time, doing very well at Miami and he just wasn't interested in some high school coach bringing these people down.

"And I was tryin' to do the right thing. In fact, I took Howard Brinker and Fritz Heisler out in the country, and they got a job milking cows, morning and night, for a stock farmer named Ray Brown, a Miami alumnus. They'd go to school during the day.

"Brinker was inducted into the Miami Athletic Hall of Fame in 1982; Heisler died the same year. But these two guys are there, and they came back to Massillon, and I put them on as assistants in our system of football, and teaching.

"And now you can see how this thing grows from just that kind of a thing. Billy Rohr became a basketball coach, and his interest . . . . he saw Miami as I did, and eventually he coached at Miami, and then at Northwestern, and then Director at Ohio University, now on the board at Ohio University.

"This is how this thing develops from a small kernel, from one person in my case here."

Brown was at Massillon for nine years, and by the time he left there certainly wasn't anybody in the state of Ohio . . . . indeed in many parts of the country . . . . who knew anything about high school football who didn't know about the Massillon Tigers, their outstanding marching band, and their powerful football team.

When Paul Brown left Massillon, it was only to have a shot at another coaching job he coveted, the position as head coach of the Ohio State Buckeyes. Dave Stewart, his old friend from Massillon, didn't figure in this appointment. It was the Ohio Coaches Association which put pressure on the Ohio State Athletic Director, L.W. St. John, and urged him to consider Brown as the primary candidate. He was interviewed several times; the fact that he had a master's degree from Ohio State didn't hurt his case, and he was acquainted with a number of people on the campus from his student days . . . . all of these factors weighed heavily in the young coach's favor. That plus the pressure group of high school coaches and, of course, his remarkable record at Massillon.

"You know," Brown says, "I was fortunate. I coached places, Massillon and Ohio State, for example, where they wanted it to be good. That's an advantage to coach someplace where they really want you to be a winner. Where the public's in favor of the program."

Like Miami?

"Oh, yes," he responds. "Miami's very proud. The Cradle of Coaches has added to it. It just enhances it all the more. I mean coaches to be coaching there, players to play there, is something special."

Ohio State lost a game the first year under Brown, but the second year the Buckeyes were national champions. And then came the war. "And we were only allowed to play with 17-year-olds. They called us the Baby Bucks." Then it was off to service for Brown as well . . . . as the athletic officer and coach at the Great Lakes Naval Training Station north of Chicago.

******

Carroll Widdoes. Arch Ward. John Brickels. Each in his own way contributed to the direction Paul Brown's career took after the service commitment.

Widdoes had been a Brown assistant from the early days at Massillon, and it was Widdoes who had succeeded Brown at Ohio State. For Brown to return to Columbus, which he certainly could have done, didn't seem right, because it would have been "disruptive" to Widdoes and the others at Ohio State who were Brown's friends. Besides, Arch Ward had an intriguing idea.

Ward was the sports editor at the **Chicago Tribune,** the man who conceived and nurtured the All-Star baseball game, the College All-Star football game and the Golden Gloves, among other promotions for his newspaper. His latest brainstorm was the All-America Football Conference, which Ward hoped would bring another football team to Chicago and provide some excitement and competition for the National Football League. Great Lakes and Notre Dame had some classic struggles during Brown's tenure at the Training Center, and Ward became an admitted Brown admirer. One of the cities Ward had in mind for a franchise in his upstart league was Cleveland, because the Rams were moving to Los Angeles. Brown while still in the service signed his contract as coach and part owner of the new team in the Tribune Tower.

He had a team, but he didn't have any players, and the team didn't have a name. And Brown was still at Great Lakes, and would be for a little while longer. Enter John L. Brickels, coaching basketball at West Virginia University.

"John Brickels was the coach at New Philadelphia High School and I was the coach at Massillon High School," Brown begins as he describes how Brickels became his confidante and liaison when the new team was being formed. "John's assistant and line coach was Woody Hayes. John's team developed a string of wins. I think it was around 26, if I remember correctly, so I . . . . used to look around the state and find somebody who had a pretty good winning streak and offer them a game with us . . . . The big payoff would be to play in Massillon, where we had the stadium and twenty-thousand people. So John elected to play the game, and the check would be bigger than they realized from probably half the season put together."

"The game was not a contest in terms of being close, and it was embarrassing to me because John was coming out to my house afterward .... At the half, we were ahead, I think about forty-five to nothing, and I said to John walking off the field, 'John, I don't get any kick out of this, what do you suggest we do? I don't want to embarrass you by just kicking the ball every time.' He said, 'Kill 'em, run it up on 'em, kill 'em,' which is typical John Brickels if you knew him like we did."

Brickels and Brown became close friends and were together in Columbus when both were working on their advanced degrees, and that friendship developed through the years. To the point that John Brickels was the man Brown turned to when he needed somebody in Cleveland to go out and sign the players Brown designated for the nucleus of that first team . . . .

Brickels also was designated to run a contest, with the help of the Cleveland media, to name the team. Brown wanted something animated, like the Tigers of Massillon. And the name selected was Panthers. Unfortunately, there had been a semi-pro team in Cleveland named the Panthers, and the guy who owned that team was still around. He wanted money for use of the name.

Brown recalls "It irritated the people I was associated with in Cleveland," and they decided trying another contest. What did Brown suggest?

"Whatever name comes up the most, make it the name of the team. What the heck, let's not fight these people. Remember I had been coaching at Massillon and Ohio State, and it fit right in. It was always 'Brown's this or Paul's that' or some such thing, so that's how it got named. That's what came up the most."

And the other owners agreed to stick with it and not try any more for some type of logo that would lend itself to animation.

Brickels, after he signed the players, stayed on to become the offensive backfield coach. And, of course, the Browns became one of professional football's legendary teams. They so dominated the All-America Conference that Brown found the toughest challenge was keeping some of the other franchises afloat. The only other alternative was not to win, and "I'm not about to stop doing that because of somebody else's inadequacies."

The merger with the National Football League in 1950 proved, to Brown's way of thinking, the soundness of Ward's idea. The cities that emerged as the strong franchises were cities that fit with Ward's original concept, as he envisioned a setup similar to baseball, with the American and National Leagues. And today, the American and National Conferences of the NFL would appear to be extensions of that type of vision.

Statistics, they say, are for losers. And Paul Brown has been anything but a loser. An examination of his record can serve only to point out how he . . . . his teams . . . . dominated the game of football at every level.

Miami teammates and close associates through the years were on opposite sides of the field when Ewbank's Colts came to Cleveland to play Brown's Browns in 1960.

In the 18 games played by Severn Prep under the young coach, Paul Brown, there were 16 Severn victories and a tie. At Massillon, the Tigers won 89 per cent of the time. As college coach at Ohio State, it was no different. In three years, a loss and tie the first year, only one loss and a national championship the second year, and three victories in nine games in 1943 with the Baby Bucks, so called because it was mainly 17-year-olds who played. At 18, they became subject to call for military service, and most went.

In two years at Great Lakes, there were only five losses in 24 games, and there was the memorable 39-7 victory over Notre Dame in the final game ever played at the oval stadium which served as the Training Station's home field. It was a victory which avenged a loss the year before.

Brown's record in Cleveland stamped him forever as a coach whose record would be looked upon as the standard by which others would be measured. Seven championships in seventeen seasons and 11 trips to the championship game of the league.... either the All-America Conference or the NFL. His record was 167-53-9, hardly the kind of mark that would cause a firing, yet that's exactly what happened in 1963, two years after Art Modell had purchased control of the club.

******

"This is like being an older man and having a new family," is the way Brown describes his association with the Cincinnati Bengals. He really wasn't ready to leave pro football when he left Cleveland under a cloud and took up residence at LaJolla, California. Paul's son Robin had a couple of radio stations, and the family was looking carefully at that industry with the hope of some day owning a TV station in the San Diego area. In fact, it wasn't an idle dream; and when Pete Rozelle assured Brown that the Cincinnati franchise would be available, it was time for a family conference. The family was gathered at the Brown home, and it was determined that the following morning, the pros and cons of tackling the television opportunity, or returning to football would be weighed. The meeting never got off the ground. After breakfast, Brown was ready to start the discussion, but Katy intervened:

"We've already decided. We'll go back into football."

So it was back to Ohio, and on to the road that led the Bengals (it isn't the Massillon Tigers, but it is adaptable to animation, and there is a family resemblance) to the 1982 Super Bowl.

Along the way, Brown lost his wife Katy, after a long struggle with a diabetic condition, and son Robin succumbed to cancer when his body rejected chemotherapy. However, sons Mike and Pete have joined Paul in the Bengals' front office, and he has remarried. The entire Brown family lives within a few miles of one another in the Indian Hill section of Cincinnati.

Paul Brown made the decision not to coach anymore. Although he misses it, he remains philosophical about that change in his life.

"I did it myself," he says. "I can have my cake and eat it. I control the thing. I have the vote. I control most of the stock. So all's well that ends well."

I don't know that he was any more innovative. He was obviously a very hard worker — industrious — night and day he dedicated himself to coaching, and I really think that's the reason he succeeded. Now over the years he has really become a great student of the game, but at that time, I don't think that he was, any more than anybody else.

I think Sid had a great feeling for the ability of his players, and to use the type of a system that would complement the talents of the players. I think that's really . . . basically in my 30 years of coaching . . . I really think that's what football is all about. Whether you're an offensive coach or a defensive coach or a head coach, it really doesn't matter, because you have to take the players that you have, whether it's the college level, the pro level, and put it into a system whereby you can utilize their talents, and exploit it into a team aspect, and I really think Sid, way back in those days, was ahead of his time with that ability.

**Richard (Doc) Urich,
captain of Miami's 1951
Salad Bowl team, describing Sid Gillman,
the man who recruited
him and whose career in collegiate
and professional football has spanned half a century.**

IV
ROCKING THE CRADLE

TO IMPLY THAT everything has been consistently glorious for Miami would be to forget the University has faced repeated crises in its history. Created as a frontier institution by legislative action in 1809, it was thwarted by fifteen years of war, depression, isolation and poverty before its doors finally could open for collegiate instruction in 1824. Struggling more often than not, it barely managed to survive the Civil War — or maybe it didn't. Dwindling enrollment and a financial panic which swept the country forced Miami to shut down in 1873. It didn't reopen until twelve years later — the beginning of its football history in 1888 was a product of a new, young faculty — and it was nearly two more decades before any really steady growth began.

As recently as 1982, whole programs were slashed, including sports programs, so the University could withstand an economic crisis brought on by recession and the high unemployment rate Ohio shared with the rest of the nation. And while it wouldn't do to suggest that football fortunes overshadowed the health of the entire institution, it's only honest to concede that there have been low spots in a football legend which, over all, has been formidable.

Miami football dates from an 1888 scoreless tie with the University of Cincinnati, played on the lawn just outside the Old Main Building. Since then, through the 1982 season, Miami had won more than two-thirds of the 774 games played. In 93 years (no games were played in 1890), Miami teams had experienced just 21 losing seasons. Twelve of those losing seasons came before 1912.

You will recall Jay Colville talking about his arrival on the campus in 1921, about George Little as the coach, and about the subsequent arrival of Chet Pittser and the return of George Rider in a new role as athletic director.

Pittser was relieving Harry Ewing, who had bowed out with only three victories and a tie for the eight games of 1923. And for his own first year, Pittser had a 2-6 record. From 1925 to the present, however, a span of 58 years, Miami has had only seven losing seasons, and four of those came in succession, 1939 through 1942.

Or look at it another way: From the inception of the four-year program in Physical Education and Athletic Coaching, excluding the four-year drought just mentioned, Miami football teams have won 368 games, lost but 137 and tied 16. That's better than 70 per cent.

Included in the record are three Buckeye Conference championships, 12 Mid-American Conference championships, and victories in five of six post-season bowl games. The undefeated though once-tied 1947 Redskins beat Texas Tech, 13-12, in the Sun Bowl at El Paso on New Year's Day 1948. The 1950 team, only seven points away from a perfect season, overwhelmed Arizona State in the post-season Salad Bowl game at Tempe, 34-21. Then from 1973 through 1975, the period referred to earlier by Jay Colville, Miami beat Florida, 16-7; Georgia, 21-10, and South Carolina, 20-7, in consecutive Tangerine Bowl appearances.

But we're getting ahead of the story. As both Weeb Ewbank and Paul Brown had observed, they had profound respect for the teaching of Chet Pittser, the football gospel according to Bob Zuppke at Illinois. Yet Brown, it will be recalled, had called Pittser "conservative."

"It's something I'll never know," says Colville, referring to the fact that following the 1931 season Pittser moved on to coach at Montclair State Teachers College (now Montclair State College at Upper Montclair, N.J.), and Frank Wilton, 26, was brought in to be the new Miami coach.

"I'll never know," puzzles Colville. "Pittser was let out. I don't know if you could say he was fired, or things would be better if he left, or what it was; but it was a sad thing. And I'm so happy that they've seen fit to bring him back here and give him his just desserts."

(In 1970, Pittser was among the second class of inductees into Miami's Athletic Hall of Fame.)

"If he'd stayed here . . . he had this great team comin' up, 1932 and 1933, great team, couldn't have missed with it . . . it was his team all the way."

Wilton, a Stanford disciple of Pop Warner, immediately installed Warner's double wingback offensive system. With Pittser's players, Miami did in fact win a Buckeye Conference crown in 1932, losing only a season opener at Illinois. And the next year, there was a Buckeye co-championship for Wilton.

Pittser's fall from favor may have been because, in his tenure, no conference crown could be celebrated. Yet here in the first two years under Wilton, there were celebrations both years. And to his credit, Wilton continued to have success, as Paul Brown found when he attempted to deliver some of his Massillon standouts to Miami. There was even another Buckeye Conference championship in 1936.

Colville recalls how things started to slide after that: "He didn't change anything. The smart coaches like Don Peden (at Ohio University) . . . the word got around and they didn't bother to scout him anymore . . . they just took out the files from the year before, and they knew we were gonna run this double wing stuff. Morale got down . . . things get bad enough there's no way nobody can do anything with it."

Testimony from those days comes from Dr. Charles Heimsch, internationally-known Miami botanist. As professor emeritus, he still teaches a course or two, continues research on campus, and remains chairman of Miami's Athletic Advisory Board, faculty representative to the Mid-American Conference and the NCAA, and member of the Miami Athletic Hall of Fame selection committee. He played on Wilton's football teams and remembers him as "arrogant."

There seems to be no doubt that Wilton brought some progressive thinking with him from Stanford; yet the fact he remained a loner and put himself above those who had an interest in Miami's success cost him a measure of respect.

Ewbank, who was in Oxford through most of the Wilton era, says: "He was hard to get to know. He didn't let people get too close to him."

Such a thought also must have occurred to Paul Brown when he brought the Massillon players to Oxford and found the Miami coach not very interested in seeing Brown or the players.

Others who were close to the situation seemed to see it the same way, although until his last couple of years Wilton's record was quite good.

John Carsten, a retired IBM executive who once served a term as president of the Miami Alumni Association, was a student manager for the Wilton teams.

"He was hard to get to know . . . standoffish . . . stoic," recalls Carsten, who also remembers that Wilton seldom had a word of praise for the players and was without humor. From where he stood, Carsten had the feeling Wilton was a finesse-type coach and didn't have the material to pull it off.

Which goes back to recruiting, which Carsten feels may have been Wilton's Achilles' heel, a perception obviously shared by Brown. Carsten even recalls one of those people Brown brought to the campus who stayed, Fritz Heisler.

"One of my jobs as manager was to hold the blocking dummies during practice," remembers Carsten. "I'll tell you, for a little guy that Heisler could hit it harder than any of 'em."

Ewbank, you will recall, had described the enthusiasm the students brought to the games during his playing days. What was the student reaction as Miami was going down the tubes to defeat in the late Thirties?

"Apathy," says Carsten.

And Bill Moeller agrees. In fact, he can paint a word picture. Moeller, who became sports editor of the **Hamilton Journal-News** in 1942 and holds that same post today, used to drive to the games with George Hutchison, a Miami alumnus who was sports editor then.

"We'd be driving into town, and the students would be hitch-hiking out of town," says Moeller, "and George would say, 'We've gotta do something about that.'"

Moeller further describes Wilton as others have portrayed him: cold.

"And I've heard it said he didn't use a system fitted to his players," Moeller adds.

But that seems to be begging the question. There were more immediate concerns. Low player morale was turning into open grumbling. Early in January 1941, following a meeting of varsity athletes, not only football players, a petition for change was presented to the executive committee of Miami's Board of Trustees by an elected committee of three lettermen.

According to **Miami Student** accounts, the athletes' petition implied a demand for Wilton's removal by asking for "a change in the school's coaching policy." It charged that Wilton failed to inspire the players, that his football system was outmoded, that his personal attitude toward the team was one of indifference, and that his conditioning program was too severe.

The trustees' public response was announcement a month later of its approval of President Upham's recommendation for some realignment of authority: George Rider, who had been director of physical education and athletics as well as coach of track and cross country, would be redesignated "director of physical education and head of the athletic department" while continuing his coaching duties. Freshman Coach Merlin A. Ditmer would become "assistant director in charge of intercollegiate athletics and freshman coach." And Tom Van Voorhis would become "assistant director in charge of intramural athletics."

Nothing was said publicly about Wilton. When he finally submitted his resignation after a 2-7 1941 season, **The Student** said his reappointment for 1941-42 had been "conditional."

Maybe Pearl Harbor provided the real answer. Ten days after declaration of war, Wilton submitted a resignation, effective in June. He served out the year as baseball coach, leaving a day after the final baseball game for a Navy indoctrination school at Annapolis. He received a full lieutenant's commission and in July 1942 was assigned as physical education director at a naval flight training base at Memphis.

He wouldn't be back. At war's end, he grasped a business opportunity, and never returned to football coaching at any level.

The man who succeeded Wilton as football coach was Stu Holcomb, an Ohio State graduate who came to Miami from Washington & Jefferson College. He had been athletic director and coach at Findlay College 1932-36 and at Muskingum College 1936-41. Perhaps it's safe to assume that Holcomb was brought in as much for his ability to restructure and rebuild as for his technical approach to the game. Maybe Miami needed to rekindle some of the enthusiasm for football, and the spirit of those high school coaches who had become disenchanted during the Wilton years. Whatever it was, Holcomb came on. The rebuilding he accomplished, with a completely new staff and almost a new squad, launched a new era in Miami football.

*****

Up in Louisville, Ohio, near Canton, in the summer of '42, a high school football player was finding out about Miami from one of Holcomb's assistant coaches, a fellow named Sid Gillman. Holcomb had dispatched Gillman to Louisville to get a red-hot quarterback prospect, Don Skelley, and bring him to Miami. Gillman suggested to Skelley that he bring a few of his football-playing buddies along. Bill Hoover was one of those buddies.

Hoover played the '42 season at Miami as a freshman, and so did Skelley. But the war beckoned, and that was it for the time being. Skelley never did resume schooling at Miami, although he remains in Ohio as an engineer for Timken Company. Hoover, on the other hand, returned to Miami even before he completed service, in an officer-candidate program. Already into football again before phasing-out of the Navy program made him a civilian again, he stayed on to play three full seasons, under the coaching of Gillman; for Holcomb had moved on to

Bill Hoover, 1947 team captain, student entrepreneur, assistant coach and Oxford businessman.

West Point via army enlistment after the 1943 season.

Miami wasn't simply a stopping-off place for Hoover. He and another returning Navy veteran, Art Goldner, and their wives as post-war Miami seniors opened a High Street eatery and watering hole, the College Inn. And the roster of collegians who worked in the CI through those years is almost as impressive as the roster of the Cradle of Coaches; because varsity athletes were foremost among those who helped out — some paid, some fed, some volunteer. Many have become successful coaches. But that's another story. A part of the story about how Hoover as a senior was businessman, husband, football captain, and a Business Administration student carrying an academic overload of 18 hours, all at once.

On graduation in 1948, while continuing the CI, Hoover was a part-time end coach with three consecutive Miami head coaches: George Blackburn, who had been Gillman's backfield coach in Hoover's last two playing seasons; Woody Hayes, and then his former teammate, Ara Parseghian.

Thirty-five years later, with Frank Dodd, another Navy veteran who played varsity tennis for Miami, Hoover is co-owner of Capitol Varsity Athletic Equipment, Inc., the same enterprise referred to earlier under a slightly different name, in the story about Jay Colville's inventing the neck yoke for Lowell Caylor. This partnership includes a sporting goods store just a block from the old College Inn location.

Hoover explains that Miami football was a far cry from its current level when he first arrived on campus in 1942. Recalling the low morale of those remaining from three consecutive losing seasons, he adds:

"Holcomb had dismissed all of the seniors, and we only had two juniors. Sophomores and freshmen made up the whole team. And by the time the Cincinnati game rolled around, seven freshmen were starting."

It was an initial season of only three wins in nine starts, with those underclassmen, but it was a start. And it was as many wins as Miami had accomplished in the three previous seasons.

As Holcomb had begun his reclamation project with the hiring of a new staff, the first was Gillman, a former Ohio State teammate who had been assisting Tommy Rogers at Denison University. Next was Walter C. (Pinky) Wilson, Muskingum '28, whom he had known as a Findlay high school coach. They'd been fellow graduate students in Ohio State summer sessions, along with such as Paul Brown and John Brickels. The new basketball coach, W.J. (Blue) Foster, was a Texan with postgraduate work in the Illinois coaching school. Since he'd coached football successfully in high schools at Harrisburg, Illinois, and Newport, Kentucky, he doubled as an aide to Holcomb. Ditmer took over the freshmen who weren't actually varsity regulars.

Of these Gillman clearly was foremost. Indeed, he was so assertive an assistant that many thought he had taken over. Yet Hoover is sure, after all these years, that enlisting Gillman was Holcomb's best move and perhaps his greatest legacy.

"Holcomb was personable," Hoover adds, "and he and Sid got along well."

Which may have been an accomplishment; because as Hoover's

teammate Doc Urich would point out, "Sid would rub a lot of people the wrong way because he was so intense."

At least one other conspicuous figure in the legend of the Cradle who got his Miami start among Holcomb's juveniles was Paul Shoults, a speedster from Washington Court House who managed a freshman season under Holcomb in 1943 before the army picked him up to send him into European combat as an infantry sergeant. We'll pick up his story later.

Holcomb's turn at military service was coming, too. He volunteered for the U.S. Army after that 1943 season, his second at Miami, and lo, Private Holcomb's assignment to duty became the United States Military Academy at West Point; and lo some more, he there became an aide to Col. Earl H. Blaik, the 1918 Miami graduate and 1920 West Point graduate who had come back to West Point as head football coach after high success at Dartmouth.

Although Blaik hadn't been around when Miami's "coaching school" was launched, he nevertheless was a positive influence on hundreds of Miami coaches during his great years at Dartmouth and West Point. And as we shall see later, Blaik's staff at West Point was a stepping stone for bright young Miami graduates on their way up in coaching.

Holcomb's career as a football coach led from West Point to Purdue; and from there he went on to become Director of Athletics at Northwestern. Holcomb left the college game not long after Parseghian left Northwestern for Notre Dame; yet he remained involved in Chicago-area sports as he joined the front office staff of the White Sox, then launched a Chicago professional soccer franchise. Holcomb retired to Florida, where he died in 1976.

Before he left Miami for West Point via enlistment, Holcomb had produced a winning team in his second season, 1943, registering 7-2-1. It would be 1976 before Miami suffered another losing season. And in 1944, Miami had Holcomb's former lieutenant, Sid Gillman, to pick up where Holcomb had left off.

When Bill Hoover returned from the Pacific, Gillman was still around; so from 1945 through 1947 Hoover was playing for the coach who had met him in Louisville in 1942. That wasn't all that Hoover found different. For maybe a year, Gillman had continued to utilize the short punt as his basic offensive formation. But an 18-year-old 1946 freshman named Mel Olix changed all that.

There was an evolution taking place in football. The T formation was becoming the vogue. And Gillman recognized that Olix had the quarterback skills suited to effective utilization of the T formation.

Edwin E. (Red) Morgan has been an Oxford resident since the dean of the School of Business Administration, Raymond E. Glos, called him back to teach a course in Business Law on an emergency basis in 1944. Graduated from Miami in 1938, Morgan had been hearing tales of the renaissance in Miami football. Although he had gone to the games as a student, he had been infected with the apathy of that era. Back now, he caught the new fever, and Sid Gillman became a close friend. Morgan remembers when Gillman switched to the T formation in 1946.

"I suppose that it was prevailing in football at the time was part of it. I think maybe the other part was that Mel Olix came on the scene," says Red.

"Mel Olix developed into as good a quarterback as there was in the country. I know Sid had great faith . . . he saw great things in Olix before he even played. He knew he had a star."

The 18-year-old started at quarterback in the 1946 opening game against Purdue and alternated throughout the season with Veterans Bob Wieche and Jack Robinson. He even played quite a bit on defense. Yet he was emerging as the major quarterback, an offensive specialist, by season's end.

Gillman's teams lost but six times in his four years at the helm. During the war, Miami had been the home of a Navy V-12 program, and the number of mature football players in that program enhanced Miami's chances of success. The culmination of the lengthy rebuilding of Miami football came at the end of the 1947 season, with the Sun Bowl victory. You'll recognize the names of some of the other stars of that team — names like Ara Parseghian, Paul Dietzel, Wayne Gibson, Doc Urich, Paul Shoults, Ernie Plank, Jack Faulkner, and yes . . . Bill Hoover.

Recognizable as those names are . . . particularly to the fan of Miami football . . . Morgan feels, and no doubt there are many who would concur, that the Redskins of that day, like their brethren today, were overmatched against the stronger teams on their schedules.

Says Morgan: "I always thought that Sid felt that we had to do things a little bit better than most of the teams we played. In many cases, he was outmanned physically, and it was almost impossible, when you look back at the size of some of the people who played on those football teams . . . so I think Sid felt that the fundamentals had to be completely sound, because probably when we played teams like Purdue and Miami of Florida and Cincinnati, you were definitely going to be outmanned."

Gillman countered, according to Morgan, with devotion to fundamentals and perhaps a more open style of play. The T-formation, with some derring-do, permitted that, if you had speed, conditioning and technique.

"Sid liked to throw the ball and use a little more deception, although Sid basically was a fundamentalist. Sid believed in fundamentals as much as any football coach ever did. Some of the coaches who . . . went out and made successes of themselves say the main thing they learned from Sid Gillman was basic fundamentals."

So, perhaps after the lapse of nearly a decade, Miami had reestablished an emphasis on fundamentals as one of the measuring sticks for success in coaching. At least so thought Miami practitioners of the art.

******

Morgan's friendship with Gillman is one of those things that can happen in a small town like Oxford, and it's not an isolated occurrence. A business law prof becomes a confidante of the football coach, his lodgings become a regular after-hours hangout for the coaches, a place where football is the primary topic of talk, even a place where new strategies may be formed.

"Soon after coming back (to Oxford)," recalls Morgan, "I met Sid and got to know him rather well. I certainly was struck by his hard-working and enthusiastic devotion to the game. I really then became quite interested in football from that point on."

Gillman and Morgan spent a lot of time together, over coffee almost daily at the Purity, and even in the evenings at Morgan's apartment, especially after Joe Madro, like Morgan then a bachelor, came aboard as a Gillman assistant. It was in one of those evening sessions that Morgan came up with something that went into the Gillman playbook and later would come back to haunt the fan-professor.

"I felt at times like I was a little bit a part of the coaching staff. I used to come up with some crazy play once in a while, and they'd look at it and laugh. But you know, I gotta tell you one story.

"I did come up with one, and after Sid went to Cincinnati, darned if they didn't run that play against Miami, and it went for a touchdown. Sid came around afterward and said, 'That was your play.'"

The play was a jazzed-up version of what in those days was known as a "Sally Rand" — a naked reverse. The "Sally Rand" was a part of the Miami offensive repertoire, and the coaches were discussing it one evening when Morgan wondered out loud why a forward pass couldn't be thrown after the reverse handoff. Today, that's the flea-flicker; but Red Morgan remembers it as the play Sid Gillman used to turn the tables on Miami after he had moved on to its arch-rival, Cincinnati.

******

Miami's successes under Gillman probably could be attributed to a number of factors, not the least of which was the maturity of most of the players. Many of the squad members were older than the average college student because of their service experience, and with each successive game, the young Quarterback Olix was mastering the intracacies of the precise ball-handling required by Gillman's system, which Phrasemaker Madro labeled "the Calibrated Slide-rule T."

Even though Olix became one of the nation's most effective passers as a 1947 sophomore, he is remembered equally well for pure sleight-of-hand as the ball-dealer in an offense which depended so much on timing and deception. Madro used to explain that the handoffs and fakes all took place within an area no larger than a card table. The sure, deft hands of Olix, the future surgeon, made it work.

Gillman himself enhanced the Miami football fortunes with his attention to detail, including the grading of player performance through regular review of game films. He was in the forefront in this dimension of the game, and has remained so throughout his career, which has embraced virtually every level of football known to man.

After achieving considerable acclaim in professional football as the head coach of the Los Angeles Rams in the National Football League and then as the offensive-minded genius in charge of the high-flying San Diego Chargers in the fledgling American Football League, Gillman at 71 still defied any "senior citizen" label when he accepted an assignment to help coach the Tulsa entry in the new United States Football League.

Let's get back. Miami's 1946 Gillman-coached team lost just three games: 13-7 to Purdue, 20-17 to Miami of Florida, and then 13-7 to Cincinnati in that game for which Parseghian assumed the blame for permitting a Cincinnati receiver to sneak behind him in the waning minutes for the winning touchdown.

Miami was leading that game against Cincinnati when the Bearcats began their final drive; and in Florida, the Redskins shunned a shot at a tie and went for a touchdown instead of a chip-shot field goal — even though Tom Cole was a consistent kicker. When Miami was stopped inches short on a fourth-down try, Backfield Coach George Blackburn was in tears as he descended from the press box and put an arm around Gillman.

"That was the only way to play it," Blackie assured his boss. "You gotta go for the win."

So it wasn't surprising when Miami went undefeated the following year.

It was Mayor Morgan, student-entrepreneur-football star Hoover and Coach Gillman congregating in the Mayor's office.

The die may have been cast in the narrow loss to Cincinnati after one-touchdown deficits at Purdue and the other Miami. Gillman's charges entered the 1947 season determined to prove their greatness. And the post-season Sun Bowl victory made it Miami's best season since 1921.

There were two flaws to an otherwise perfect 1947 season: The 6-6 tie with Xavier, attributed to a questionable interference call at the goal line, required the tag "unbeaten, though once-tied;" and a 3-0 conference record for Miami's first year in the Mid-American Conference still didn't win the crown because four games were minimum for title eligibility.

However, a close call at Bradley could have ruined it. Going into Peoria Stadium, Miami was coming off a rewarding yet costly 21-0 victory over

Miami's Sun Bowl trophy, awarded after the 13-12 victory over Texas Tech to Coach Sid Gillman and Placekicker Robert (Jake) Speelman.

Ohio University. Both regular halfbacks, Ara Parseghian and Paul Shoults, injured, were standing around on the sidelines in street clothes and windbreakers as the teams warmed up.

Miami still had Mel Olix to orchestrate its offense, but Bradley's Quarterback Gib Carl also had a formidable season record: 32 completions in 55 passes, seven for touchdowns.

And the way the game started, it looked as if Carl was determined to make his total more impressive. Bradley got on the scoreboard first when he completed a 46-yard touchdown pass to put Bradley in front, 7-0. The touchdown had been set up by a Miami fumble. Bradley returned the favor shortly afterward, fumbling a punt which Miami recovered on the Bradley 38. An Olix pass to Jack Bickel carried to the five. From there, Sam Wippel exploded into the end zone. Placekicker Cole had a rare miss, and Miami trailed 7-6 with four minutes gone in the first quarter.

Carl and Olix traded touchdown passes in the second quarter, and the game became a 13-13 tie. Miami finally took its first lead by resorting to a ground game, moving 82 yards with Wippel again scoring.

Everybody had a good time when members of Miami's victorious Sun Bowl team were reunited in Oxford. That's Ara Parseghian with his arm around Teammate Robert Raymond. In the middle is George Blackburn, who succeeded Sid Gillman as head coach. Next to Blackie is the team's center, Paul Dietzel, and then the "Guardian of the Cradle", Trainer-Emeritus Jay Colville.

Frank Wilton returned to the Miami campus in 1951 for a visit, along with his son, Warner.

Miami's 19-13 halftime lead grew to 26-13 as the Redskins took the second-half kickoff and marched 95 yards, mainly on the running of Bickel and Bill Stoner. And Stoner scored from the three.

Bradley wasn't done, though. An Olix pass was intercepted, and the Braves drove 45 yards to pull within six points. Then a Miami shovel pass went awry, and the Redskins fell behind 27-26, late in the fourth.

With less than two minutes remaining, Miami was backed up deep in its own territory, third and 12. Olix heaved a desperation pass to Stoner, who caught it on the Bradley 35 and was hauled down on the 16. The play covered 69 yards. Another Olix-Stoner pass carried to the four; and on fourth down with 25 seconds to go, no time-out left, without a huddle, Olix frantically ordered his line down, whispered to Center Paul Dietzel, and sneaked Miami a 32-27 victory. Dietzel's block on that play helped him to win Little All-America selection that year.

After that 1947 season, Gillman went to work for Miamian Red Blaik at West Point "because there's so much to be learned from him." The Miami reins were turned over to Blackburn, the aide whom Gillman regarded as one of the finest backfield coaches in the country. Madro and Ben Ankney stayed with Blackburn, who also brought in his boyhood buddy Woody Wills, a successful high school coach.

Then an odd thing happened: Blackburn in his first year as a college head football coach had one of the most successful seasons in Miami history, and then left to become an assistant again. His team won the Mid-American crown in its first season of title eligibility, outscored nine opponents 249-90, and needed regret only a 7-0 loss to Dayton and a 14-14 tie with Virginia. But Cincinnati backers wanted the brains behind three solid Miami wins over Cincinnati out of the four most recent meetings. They wooed Gillman away from West Point to take charge of the Bearcats. The pay, the opportunity to work together again, and various other apparent advantages understandably were irresistible to both Blackburn and Madro. They rejoined Sid at Cincinnati. Blackburn eventually succeeded Gillman as Cincinnati's head coach and still later became head coach at the University of Virginia. More recently, he has been conducting a scouting service.

Morgan, friend of both Gillman and Blackburn offers an appraisal:

"George was a very diplomatic individual. And George was a very well-liked, nice person. In fact, if he had any shortcoming as a head coach, or if there was any reason he wasn't quite comfortable in that role, I think that was it — he was just too nice a guy."

Apathy toward Miami football had been erased by high success, and the level of interest in Miami on the part of young high schoolers had been increased. Now, in less than ten years, Miami had had four head coaches, and another was on the way.

Enter Wayne Woodrow Hayes.

******

Like the others after Wilton, he was Ohioan by birth or adoption. Holcomb and Gillman, born in Nebraska and Minnesota, respectively, had become great athletes at Ohio State; Holcomb had coached at two Ohio colleges, Gillman at one. Blackburn was native of Columbus, Ohio, starred at Findlay College, and earned his coaching credentials at Pomeroy, Gallipolis and Western Hills High Schools. Woody Hayes, born at Clifton, Ohio, a Denison University graduate, was head football coach at his alma mater when he was offered the opportunity to succeed Blackburn as football coach at Miami. An assistant at Mingo Junction for a year after graduation, he had begun learning under John Brickels at New Philadelphia, inherited the top job there when Brickels moved to Huntington, and became Denison's head coach when he returned from the Navy in 1946.

So Woody Hayes was picking up where Holcomb, Gillman and Blackburn left off — except that he had the not-uncommon experience of first-season problems. After an opening romp over Wichita, Miami suffered consecutive losses to Virginia, Xavier and Pittsburgh.

That, however, was simply an uncertain prelude to great things. The record books show that Miami lost only one game in 1949 and only one in all of 1950. Plus a post-season victory in the Salad Bowl. It looked good on paper, and it was. But there was more to Miami football at that juncture than simple arithmetic. Looking back, those Hayes teams at Miami were dotted with names which were to become legend . . . not only among Miami people, but almost everywhere in the world of football.

Study of a photograph of the 1950 Salad Bowl football team reveals this astounding portfolio of accomplishments. Right there in the front row, wearing number 74, is Glenn Edward (Bo) Schembechler, erstwhile left-handed pitcher from Barberton, Ohio. Even the most casual of football observers will recall the memorable season-ending battles between Schembechler's Michigan teams and Hayes' Ohio State Buckeyes.

In the middle of that row, holding the football symbolic of the team captaincy, is Richard (Doc) Urich, long-time assistant under Ara Parseghian, head coach at Buffalo and Northern Illinois, then assistant in the pro ranks, most recently with the Green Bay Packers.

Next to Coach Hayes in the second row is Clive Rush, who coached the Toledo Rockets before he went to the Jets as Weeb Ewbank's assistant and later was head coach of the Boston Patriots. Rush was 49 when he died in London, Ohio, in 1980. In the same row, next to Rush, is Jim Root, one of two outstanding quarterbacks on that team. Root was 1967 College Division Coach of the Year at New Hampshire, and went on to coach at William and Mary.

John McVay, next to Root, became head coach at the University of Dayton and now is general manager of the San Francisco 49ers.

Yale's head football coaches from 1963 to the present are also in that row. John Pont and Carmen Cozza were roommates at Miami; when Pont left Yale in 1965 to become head coach at Indiana, Cozza succeeded him. Ernie Plank is there, the only representative at the Cradle entitled to wear both the Rose Bowl ring (from Indiana University) and the Super Bowl ring (from the San Francisco 49ers).

Rounding out the lineup in the second row are Joe Codiano, whose long string of successes as head coach at Brookville (Ind.) High School has placed him in the Indiana Athletic Hall of Fame. John Brickels, who had been Hayes' boss at New Philadelphia High School, is there, this time as

Miami 1950 Football squad

First row (left to right)--Bruce Beatty, Ed Schembechler, Norbert Wirkowski, Sam Estell, Tom Pequignot, Jerry Beckrest, Art Jastrzebski, Richard Urich, Bob Marquardt, Al Macciolli, George Acus, Verl Mangen, George Galat, Bob Ellison
Second row--Woody Hayes, Clive Rush, Jim Root, John McVay, Milton Niergarth, Roger Brown, Jack Rogers, Paul Cary, Vern Orth, John Pont, Don Green, Dale Doland, Bob Podsiadlo, Carmen Cozza, Joe Codiano, John Brickels
Third row--Jim Williams, Jay Colville, Andy Arvay, Charles Williams, Dick Huebner, August Holubeck, Bob Hengartner, Charles Lucas, Charles Lucas, Charles Harrison, Bob Saltmarsh, Larry Hawkins, James Bailey, Al Ward, Al Habinak, John Zachary, William Wehr
Fourth row--James Mullen, William Arnsparger, Woodrow Wills, Bob Boylan, James Powers, David Pershing, Earl Jones, William Combs, Kenneth Zelina, Kenneth Lazarus, Paul Sautter, Howard Schuster, Jay Fry, William Hoover, Bob Howard.

both Hayes' assistant and as Hayes' boss, although he also had become head coach in another sport, basketball.

Also in the 1950 picture, in the back row, wearing coaching garb, is a 1950 Miami graduate, Bill Arnsparger. He played on Miami's 1948 and 1949 teams, had extensive college coaching experience, was head coach of the New York Giants for a time, and has gone on to be recognized for a significant role in professional football as Don Shula's defensive coordinator with the Miami Dolphins.

Bill Hoover was an assistant coach for Hayes with that 1950 team and is pictured next to Jay C. Fry — longtime assistant with John Pont, a coach in both collegiate and professional ball in Canada for several years, now back in Oxford as president of Camp America, a summer sports center — and father of Miami's current defensive backfield coach, Jay T. Fry. Having followed the late John O. Fry, who played basketball during World War I, these Jays are second and third generation Miami lettermen.

The 1950 picture includes Norbert (Nobby) Wirkowski, whose name has become a Canadian byword — as quarterback and then coach of the professional Toronto Argonauts, as a television football announcer, as a businessman and as coach and athletic director at York College, Toronto.

Under Hayes in 1950, and indeed for most of the year before, Miami was an offensive juggernaut. In 19 games, only twice did Miami score fewer than three touchdowns.

Mel Olix had completed his playing career with the 1949 season and headed for medical school, eventually to become a distinguished orthopedic surgeon. So Wirkowski had picked up where Mel left off, and Root in 1950 already was coming into his own as a rangy sophomore alternate.

The T formation which Gillman had established was in high gear. And so was Hayes' voltage meter.

When Woody's temper got the better of him and he punched the Clemson player in the closing minutes of the Gator Bowl game and it cost him his job, Red Morgan was reminded of a more comic Hayes outburst. It was in Oxford, on the day Miami had accepted invitation to play in the Salad Bowl, after a 28-0 Snow Bowl victory over Cincinnati had concluded a highly successful 1950 season.

Morgan still was mayor of Oxford as well as a business law prof. By virtue of his office and also because he continued close to Miami football, Hayes called to share the good news and to invite Morgan to stop by the football office in Withrow Court.

Permit a digression: Until Bill Mallory's return to succeed Bo Schembechler as Miami's head coach, an event which more or less coincided with the Athletic Department's move into the new Millett Assembly Hall in 1969-70, the Miami football office consisted of two rooms next to the men's washroom in the building called Withrow Court. The head coach shared one of those rooms with a couple of other coaches. The remaining assistants were squeezed into the other room, only slightly larger.

New to the staff that year was Ara Parseghian, fresh from the

Cleveland Browns, assigned to coach not only the freshman football team but also the basketball yearlings. In the midst of the mini-celebration, as coaches and friends gathered in the small office, Hayes suddenly suspected something might be amiss. Would Parseghian be permitted to make the trip to Arizona with the rest of the staff which had shaped the triumph?

"Not possible!" countered Basketball Coach-Athletic Director-Backfield Assistant Brickels. Parseghian's responsibility during the winter months was to the freshman basketball players, Brickels insisted.

This on the eve of Miami's annual football banquet, already scheduled to celebrate the successful season regardless of the pending bowl game. Trophies to be presented at the banquet were there on the office floor, in a cardboard box.

Frustrated by the adamance of an assistant who also was his boss and mentor, Hayes turned for a temper target. He aimed a helluva kick at the nearest inanimate object: that cardboard box — and stormed out of the room.

The assemblage hardly needed to be told that the kick had shattered the Most Valuable Player trophy, scheduled for presentation at the banquet to Team Captain Doc Urich.

"We just sat there," recalls Morgan, "not knowing what to do."

After a cooling-off period, Hayes returned and made his apology to Brickels. But at the banquet the next evening, Urich's Most Valuable Player trophy "just hadn't arrived yet."

Urich did get a replacement later on, he acknowledged when members of the Salad Bowl team gathered for a reunion 30 years later as part of Miami's 1981 annual Alumni Weekend.

Those from that team who came, and there were many who did, including Woody, were able to rejoice over some amazing facts about that team.

Yes, they won nine of ten games. But consider that they did it with fantastic offensive balance — a daring, deadly passing attack complementing a fast, hard-blocking ground game — and consider that this was the coaching of the Woody Hayes who for nearly thirty years at Ohio State was committed to the "three yards and a cloud of dust" offense.

Miami easily won the Mid-American Conference title that year as the second of 12 MAC football championships the Redskins either have won outright or shared since Miami became eligible for the title in 1948. The 1950 Redskins scored 19 of their 48 touchdowns — that's nearly five a game — on passes. Wirkowski and Root threw 20 times a game, netting more than 1,800 yards in the air as an explosive ground game accounted for nearly 2,400 yards.

We have looked at a picture of that team and identified the easily-recognizable. Let's look at the team another way. Nine members of the squad have filled a total of 19 head football coaching jobs in colleges and four with pro teams. Six have played pro football. Three have become college head coaches in sports other than football. Four have become college athletic directors.

No less than six — Pont, Cozza, Root, McVay, Schembechler and Urich

— have been enshrined in Miami's Athletic Hall of Fame. At least eight have been head coaches at Ohio high schools, and at least two dozen assistant spots in college or pro football have been filled from the 1950 roster. In this case, statistics aren't for losers.

Lest you think, however, that this is simply a recitation of the accomplishments of a particularly gifted group of Miami athletes, Bill Hoover has an entirely different perspective.

Having been the end coach under Hayes, Hoover was at the reunion in 1981 and compared the Salad Bowl team to Gillman's Sun Bowl team:

"This Salad Bowl team is one of the unusual teams in that these kids have stayed closer, probably, than the team that I played on and was captain of in 1947. This group of kids, for some reason, are probably the closest group that I've ever been associated with. Many of them did stay in coaching . . . but for some reason, and I don't know what their great attraction was for each other . . . but they've remained friends all their lives and I think this is a real tribute to the boys and to Miami University."

One of the contributors to the success of that team was a young man

Woody Hayes' Miami coaching staff included, in the front row, left to right, Warren Schmakel, Hayes and Ben Ankney. Standing, John Brickels, Woody Wills and Bill Hoover.

from nearby Hamilton named Jim Bailey. Hoover recalls Bailey, who was nicknamed Boxcar, as one of Miami's most natural athletes. Bailey returned to the campus for the reunion, the first time he had been back in 30 years, and Hoover remembered this story about his athletic skills.

"Jim played fullback, but his last year, when Ara was coaching, a couple of the ends got hurt. Ara said, 'Take Jim Bailey and make him into defensive end this week.' So Monday night at practice, Boxcar Bailey went with me, and we talked about playing defensive end, and we worked with him for a night or two. Saturday afternoon, he played defensive end for us, first string, and he had a great day. That's a tribute to his truly great athletic ability."

Some of the lesser-known among the celebrities on that team, when they were gathered together once again, offered additional insights on Coach Hayes and what made that group tick.

Bob Saltmarsh, a tackle on the 1950 team, now is a professor in the Department of Educational Psychology and Guidance at Eastern Illinois University. He started as a football coach at Lemon-Monroe High School, near Oxford (his first job was as a high school head coach); but at the urging of Woody Hayes, he decided to pursue his doctorate, which has led him to his present position.

Dr. Saltmarsh remembers Coach Hayes drawing a play on the blackboard one day during a skull session, and one of the Miami players who had been around for a few years remembered it as one of Sid Gillman's plays.

"Damn right it's one of Sid's plays," said Hayes, as Saltmarsh remembers. "And I'll tell you something else, whenever I find something that somebody is doing that's better than what I'm doing, then I'm a goddam fool if I don't change."

"I've used that as a guide in my professional life," says Saltmarsh, who also was one of the many returnees who recalled with nostalgia the jobs they had had to perform in the dining halls as a condition of their scholarships.

"I think I got an excellent education here," Saltmarsh commented during the Alumni Weekend festivities. "My football career . . . I was never very good . . . I was a fourth or fifth string tackle, and there was a lot of pain involved in that for me, but I've come back here and found good friends among the famous and among the ones who are not, and I think I've drawn a great deal of strength from my days as an athlete."

Bill Gunlock is a former football assistant and head baseball coach at Heidelberg, as well as assistant football coach at Bowling Green, Ohio State and West Point. Today, he is president of Sabre Systems & Service, Inc., in Dayton.

"I would only say that in my business career," says Gunlock, "I relate all the things that I learned as a football coach, and I guess I went to college to become a football coach and that was my ambition from a youngster in high school, I never thought I'd leave coaching, and I apply all the principles that I learned as a football coach to my business environment."

Perhaps there is no greater testimonial to the closeness of the 1950 team, the closeness which Bill Hoover noted, and to their feeling for Miami, than to realize that the sons of four of them, Gunlock, Fry, McVay and Tom Pequignot, all have pulled on the Miami football uniform.

****

Doc Urich didn't even know it at the time, but he was the original "Chinese Bandit." Paul Dietzel, when he was riding the crest of Bayou popularity at Louisiana State University, called his aggressive defensive unit the Chinese Bandits. That was 1959. Joe Madro, as one of Gillman's assistants, gave Urich that monicker in 1947, when he was a freshman.

Bob Howard, who was Miami's sports publicist at the time, recalls that Madro described Urich as a Chinese Bandit for the press guide because of his "aggressive and stubborn, and almost reckless style of play."

Urich had been recruited by Ohio State as well as Gillman at Miami, but had decided to enroll at the Columbus school and was actually there for pre-season training . . . until the day before registration.

"It was post-war time," Urich recalls, "and they had a lot of lettermen back, and a lot of former All-Americans, and I just wasn't real happy with the situation. So I called Sid, and Sid said, 'Well, gee whiz, lay out and come down here at mid-term.' and I was very happy to."

So Urich came to Miami as an 18-year-old freshman, following a pattern not unlike that of Paul Brown, although Brown had stayed through his freshman year. Urich had immediate success on the football field, grabbing a starting role, and wound up playing in two bowl games.

But that was really only the beginning of Urich's football experience. On graduation, he was named to Parseghian's first staff. He stayed with Ara in moves to Northwestern and then on to Notre Dame.

After a couple of years under the Golden Dome, Urich had a head coaching job at the University of Buffalo, and then came the head post at Northern Illinois, during the period when the Huskies aspired to join the Mid-American Conference. The Green Bay post he now holds is his fourth spot in the NFL, the others being Buffalo, Denver and Washington.

Looking back on nearly four decades of association with football at the collegiate and professional levels, Urich can smile and say, with firm conviction:

"I'll tell you, my years here (Miami) and the associations with the people, and the education and the training is just . . . you can't add it up . . . you really can't. At the time I came here, at that time, I don't think you could get that anywhere else."

Urich, as captain and Most Valuable Player on Woody Hayes' last Miami team, an innocent victim of Hayes' temper in the trophy incident, is in a unique position to share some thoughts on the man whose entire coaching career was spent in Ohio:

"He was one of those very rare people. He certainly is a great gentleman . . . I have a great deal of respect for him, and a lot of admiration for his coaching ability. His record will attest to how good he has been over the years. But, along the way he obviously has had many, many cases where his temper got the best of him, and he couldn't handle it, and afterwards he was the first one to admit that he did wrong."

****

There were plenty of memories that late spring night in Oxford in 1981. These men were celebrating their on-field exploits of thirty years ago. Many were celebrities, in or out of coaching; but for this evening, these were memories of past glories.

But the real guest of honor, and the man they would salute as the evening wore on, was the man who held them all together, their coach, Woody Hayes. Maybe he was the glue that produced the "closeness" which Bill Hoover describes. Regardless, you knew that at a time like this, the coach would rise to the occasion.

After saluting the doctor who was attending him and had permitted him to be in attendance despite recent surgery, Hayes turned to those he considered the honored guests, those who had wrapped up that glorious season with "two great games," which he maintains "put me in at Ohio State."

"As you get older," Woody told the crowd, "you come to realize that there are so many, many people you owe. So many. And I got to thinking over there in the hospital, I don't know of any group I owe more to than this group right here."

Then came a tip of the hat to a couple of guys on that team who had followed him as Miami's head coach, first John Pont and then his old coaching rival from Michigan, Bo Schembechler.

"There was a little guy . . . I forget his name (grinning at Pont,) but he's sittin' right here . . . down there at Cincinnati in the snow, played like a madman.

"And then you know why we're down there? I thought we only scored four touchdowns. Well, we scored five. Do you remember that? Bo, do you remember that?"

"Unfortunately, Woody, yeah, yeah. And I want you to know that after all these years, I apologize," came Bo's reply.

"But the thing that was so unbelievable, it was a draw play, and tackles on draw plays drop back. You know what he did? He started charging . . ."

And laughter reverberated throughout the room.

But after he had needled Bo, Woody paused to deliver this tribute: "After Bear Bryant, Bo is the greatest college coach around."

And then Woody revealed that when he woke up after his second operation, "Who did I see sitting there at the foot of the bed but Millie and Bo Schembechler?"

By now, the convalescent coach was growing tired, and it was time to say good night. He concluded:

"I want to say again, I'll always be beholden to you, for the great help you've been in my career, because I never saw a better team to coach. I'm not sure there ever was a better team here at Miami . . .

"Yet I find you don't pay back to people. It can't be done. They don't need it. But you always are in a position to pay forward, to help somebody else out. And that's what you and I have got to do, is to keep paying **forward** as long as we live.

"Thank you very much."

"He brought out the best in his athletes . . . he worked the livin' fool out of you, and made you like it.

"His football was precision football, and he made you thoroughly enjoy doing what you were doing. And of course, he did win, and winning always is a lot more fun than anything else. It's a lot more fun than losing.

"I think he left a real impression on everyone that played for him, and I've not run across anyone that played for Sid who really didn't like Sid. We all kid about him. We kid about the things he did, about how he'd 'run that play one more time' and all that sort of thing; but we all had great respect for him. And I think we all learned a great deal — a tremendous amount — of football from him."

Paul Dietzel, Little All-America center on Miami's 1947 team, Sun Bowl champions, talking about his coach, Sid Gillman, the man he credits with attracting him to Miami and then enticing him into coaching.

V
A NEW FOUNDATION

NO MATTER HOW you slice it, Sid Gillman was the catalyst in the resurgence of Miami football during and after World War II. He was the one who beat the bushes and brought to Miami the men who first, re-established the winning tradition and second, turned their considerable talents to coaching in unprecedented numbers.

Paul Dietzel went to Duke University on a football scholarship. His wife-to-be, Ann, like Paul from Mansfield, went to Miami and became a cheerleader. And then in his first year at Duke, the military was beckoning.

"I was about to be drafted," explains Dietzel, "and I had just pledged a fraternity before I left Duke. So I dropped by Miami, and the SAEs (Sigma Alpha Epsilon) serenaded Ann. This was a big thrill for both of us then, because I was going into the service."

Dietzel enlisted in the Army Air Forces, and when he got his wings and commission, he and Ann were married. Score one for Miami. Then through his service years, he became the target of intensified correspondence from Sid Gillman, master recruiter — while hearing nothing from Duke.

"Between the combination of Sid and Ann, that was the reason I went to Miami," he relates.

Our conversation was taking place in the dining room of the Dietzel home in the mountains of North Carolina. Paul, now retired from college athletics, had spent the morning on the slopes, and Ann had warmed us with a luncheon fare of delicious home-made vegetable soup.

Not far from the Tennessee border, in the Blue Ridge Mountains, is Banner Elk, North Carolina. Next to the beautiful home on Beech Mountain is a small crafts shop, Wobbly Square. Ann and Paul Dietzel are the proprietors, and Paul is president of the Banner Elk Chamber of Commerce. That, however, doesn't keep him from serving also as a skiing instructor on Beech Mountain.

It is, to be sure, a long way from Mansfield, or Oxford, or Baton Rouge; but it is home, and teaching a deaf youngster to ski can be just as challenging as coaching the Black Knights of the Hudson against Roger Staubach and the Naval Academy.

******

Dietzel was saying that, once he settled in on the Miami campus, there were two aspects of Miami football that he would respect. One was Sid Gillman, who was to have a profound influence on his life. The other was the large amount of talent on the Miami football team.

"Very honestly," explains Dietzel, "I've never known anyone who had such a tremendous football mind, as much knowledge of the game, but most important, who worked as hard, as Sid Gillman.

"Sid Gillman knows so much football, and he's so smart, that he really talks . . . a lotta people; he's got their mind boggled because of so much stuff."

Maybe the talent wasn't the equivalent of a Big Ten school's, but Dietzel says there was enough to keep him from ever feeling secure about his role.

"There was so much competition for your job," he continues, "I'm tellin' you, you talk about fightin' for your life. Bein' late for practice? Hey, I wasn't gonna be late for practice. I would go out there hurt because I was scared as heck someone was gonna beat me out. Because I wanted to play."

At center, Dietzel earned Little All-America honors as a senior. He can still tick off the names of centers with whom he was vying: Ellsworth Nunn, Chuck Moos, Jack Faulkner.

"Ellsworth Nunn. He'd come back," says Dietzel. "He'd been All-America during the war . . . Chuck Moos was a great big rascal from Sout' Lorain, not Nort' Lorain, but Sout' Lorain, and Chuck Moos was about 220, and we had several others . . . Jack Faulkner was a young center.

"We had all these people. I was scared to miss a practice. I wouldn't have missed a practice, 'cause I knew someone would take my job and I'd never get it back. We had so much competition."

Gillman's fetish for grading films was a matter of record by the time Dietzel arrived on the campus, and coach and players alike knew it was hard to argue with what showed up on the celluloid.

"I think Sid Gillman taught more people about how to grade football film than anybody I've ever known," explains Dietzel. "A lotta people, they just check you . . . if you did your job, you got a check mark, if you didn't, you didn't get a check mark. That's the way they graded."

Gillman's system was different. His idea, according to Dietzel, was that he was going to teach a certain way, and he was going to grade according to how the player learned what had been taught. The grade also was based on "whether you got your man."

Initially, both technique and execution were weighted equally. Well, says Dietzel, Gillman discovered that you can't do it that way, "because the bottom line is 'Did you block the guy?'"

"And so then we changed to technique, one point, and execution, two points, so each play was worth three points."

Besides the competition at his own position, Dietzel observed there was considerable competition in the backfield, specifically at fullback, where Ara Parseghian was among those 1946 teammates.

"I thought we had . . . it's really an amazing thing," observes Dietzel. "Some of the names of the people we had lined up at fullback, for example. At fullback, we had Paul Shoults, Ara Parseghian, Dick Ensminger, Don Couch, Wayne Gibson, Paul Dellerba, and about eight other fellas. Actually the starting fullbacks from 1942, 1943, 1944 and 1945, and then some . . . but we had so much talent lined up at that one position . . . you just cannot believe how much talent we had.

"You know, the amazing thing . . . we had all these big, strong fullbacks and this one little, scrawny fullback by the name of H. Wayne Gibson, who weighed 155 pounds. He was not fast, and do you know what, before the season began, you know who started at fullback, don't you? H. Wayne Gibson.

"Gibby was one of these exceptional people that did everything exactly right. He kinda reminded me of that . . . you know that fella that played with Pittsburgh (Rocky Bleier) that came back from the war and he's not good enough to play and he's all beat to the devil, and they say he'd never walk, and he plays with three Super Bowl rings or whatever . . . Gibby was like that.

"He was an absolute super technician. I mean, if you grade him on technique, he'd have 100 per cent on technique, because whatever you tell him to do, he's gonna do it perfect. He will do it perfect. The little rascal could block, and he'd carry the ball pretty well, he just did everything so

Paul Shoults, now the athletic director at Eastern Michigan, was captain of George Blackburn's 1948 team.

well. He was our starting fullback."

Gillman didn't relegate people like Parseghian and Shoults to reserve roles. He moved them around, putting Fullback Parseghian at right half and Fullback Shoults at left half.

******

Harold Wayne Gibson. Like Dietzel, he started his collegiate football career elsewhere. Before the war, he had gone to Morehead State Teachers College in Kentucky. When he finally got to Miami, along with Dietzel and a lot of other veterans, he grew to like it enough to want to come back a few years after graduation, to stay.

In 1956, eight years after graduation from Miami, Gibby was brought back by John Pont as offensive backfield coach. When Pont seven seasons later opted for the opportunity to become Yale's head coach, Wayne opted to stay at Miami. He hasn't regretted that decision.

"I was around forty years old at that time," remembers Gibson. "I had to decide whether I wanted to go ahead and take a chance on getting the opportunity to be a head coach, or whether I should think about going in another direction."

At the moment, his opportunity was to stay at Miami as an assistant on the staff of the incoming coach, Bo Schembechler, with the prospect of an administrative position in the athletic department down the road.

"I thought about it a great deal and decided that was the route I would take," says Gibson. "Even though I did coach for another year, with Bo, it was pretty well understood when he came here that I would be with him only for the transition period."

The transformation from football coach to administrator has been successful. Gibson is Miami's associate athletic director, Dick Shrider's right-hand man, and he has become an integral part of the Miami-Oxford community.

His wife Phyllis, whom he met and married while coaching at Sidney, Ohio, has made her own impact on Miami athletics as an X-ray technician in the Miami Student Health Service, generally a first stop for an injured athlete.

They were selected as Miami's 1982 Parents of the Year, honored at halftime at the next-to-last game on old Miami Field, for their many contributions to the community.

Gibson grew up in the southeastern Ohio community of Gallipolis. He started college at "probably the only place I could go . . . a small, 145-pound halfback . . . finances very limited."

"I came from a big family," he explains. "My coach talked the coach at Morehead into takin' me, back in 1941, and I was fortunate enough to get a scholarship. So I went there."

By 1943, Gibby was ticketed for Navy duty in the Boston area. There he became involved in the physical fitness program for enlisted men. During this period, he began to evaluate postwar college and football prospects. He was certain he wanted to pursue a career in athletics, so he wrote to Ohio University, near his hometown, and to Miami, which he'd never laid eyes on.

Now in no way was Gibby dissatisfied with his experience at

Morehead; yet being interested only in football coaching, he figured Kentucky wasn't where he wanted to try to get a job after college.

"Luckily enough," sighs Gibson, "I chose Miami. There was something about the things I'd heard about Miami by talkin' to other students in high school, and to other people . . . it had a good reputation in those days, too."

Gibson tends to accept Dietzel's premise that Miami attracted some pretty good talent back in those days, although he begs to exclude himself from any such list. At any rate, if they weren't pretty good, they certainly were plentiful.

"In the summer of 1946, we had two hundred fifty people who were practicin' football, all summer long," marvels Gibson. And a lot of those 250, like Dietzel, and Parseghian, and Gibson, were young men who had begun college elsewhere, had entered military service, and as veterans had sought new directions at Miami.

"My feeling is that they transferred here because they either weren't satisfied with where they were," explains Gibson, "or because through the three or four years they spent in the service, they changed . . . their profession became changed in their own mind, they wanted to do somethin' else. Those particularly that had an inkling they wanted to go into coaching had a feeling back in those days that this was a pretty good school to go through.

"Some of those, because of the large numbers realizing they might never play here, because only so many can play — some of those people that had transferred here, like some of the people that were here just as students, transferred again to other schools. Maybe Miami was just lucky to get the cream of the crop. I don't know . . ."

Whatever it was, Miamians can look back now to those days as a start of something remarkable. Granted, Earl Blaik of Miami already had established himself as one of college football's premier coaches, and Paul Brown had led Ohio State to a national championship, and reputations were being forged by Weeb Ewbank, and Harry Strobel and Mel Knowlton and others in the high school ranks. One or two every so many years. But here we are looking at the time when a more spectacular Miami coaching legend was being nurtured. It would be several years yet before products of this postwar era exploded into sports prominence; and as we have seen, it would be hard to call this the birth of the legend; more significantly, it was a dramatic rebirth of the legend.

As one of those products of this era in Miami athletics, Gibby has his own theory about what brought Miami's success. He sums it up:

"If I had to pick out one short statement for all the success at Miami, in coaching or any other fields, that's what I would have to say: It's a good school, it attracts people with ability; you put both of 'em together, and you're bound to have success."

When Gibson set out to pursue the coaching career he had charted for himself after 1948 graduation, his first stop was as high school coach at Sidney, Ohio. He was there one year. Then it was on to an assistant coaching job at the University of Buffalo. Even that move was Miami related. The call was from Frank Clair, who had assisted Gillman at

Miami in 1946. Clair had gone from Miami to the Purdue staff of Miami ex-coach Stu Holcomb in 1947. As one of his first moves on being named Buffalo head coach in 1948, he had tried to hire Gibson, but Gibby had just started his Sidney job. Clair then renewed his bid successfully in 1949.

Just another year later, Clair became head coach of the Canadian professional Toronto Argonauts. He could bring with him only a playing assistant coach from the States. This was not for Gibby. His next move then was back home to Gallipolis as Gallia Academy head coach — and one year after that, he was back at Sidney for a second time. That lasted until he was summoned back to Miami in 1956 by John Pont.

Now he's the "senior citizen" around Miami's athletic department. A few months older than Athletic Director Dick Shrider, he also has either eleven years or one year of Miami seniority over Shrider, depending on whether you count his 1946 matriculation or his 1956 return. With successive retirements of George Rider, Jay Colville and Woody Wills, he became a patriarch before 60.

So how does the senior citizen feel about Miami athletics today?

"I feel great about Miami. There are some danger signs out there on the horizon for college athletics. But I'll tell you this: I believe very strongly that Miami is gonna survive in college athletics as long as anybody in the country, and that includes all the big-time schools.

"I know we'll have some money problems. We have some money problems now, but so do the other schools. But I feel confident in the reputation that Miami has as a university, and the people that we have here now, and the people we hopefully will have in the future. I can't see anything but optimism."

******

One of the pivotal games of the 1947 season, the season which was climaxed by Miami's Sun Bowl victory, was that Bradley game already chronicled in Chapter 4. And Dietzel played a pivotal role in that game. It was the quick thinking, the perfect communication between Center Dietzel and Quarterback Mel Olix which enabled Miami to salvage a victory that appeared hopelessly lost. That fourth-down sneak with seconds to play was simply a matter of two great athletes doing what they had to do.

Last-minute heroics aside, Dietzel felt the Bradley game was one of his best for Miami. Earlier in the contest, Bradley had first and goal on the five and failed to score. Dietzel as linebacker had helped repel the Braves when he led the defensive charge that stopped a second-down run and then on fourth down batted away a pass.

"To this day," says Dietzel, "I have great satisfaction from knowing that I helped our team to win. Now, it didn't say anything in the newspaper, no one came up and slapped me on the back afterwards . . . but I knew. To me, that's really important; because when you can be a part of something and you feel that in your heart you had a great deal to do with it, although no one else knows it, that's almost like doing a good deed for somebody, and the only ones that know it are you and the good Lord."

One of the reasons few people were aware of Dietzel's heroics in that game was field condition. A high school game the night before had left an already-sloppy field so muddy that jersey numbers became almost useless. And of course, on the climactic play in those final seconds, only Dietzel and Olix knew what was going to happen.

Though that particular play was a surprise to twenty other players, it was not entirely instant inspiration. Olix often had told Dietzel that in appraisal of the defensive alignment, they might catch an opponent offside; for such case, Olix had a special hand signal that would be his cue to Dietzel for the snap and the block. Olix gave that signal, and it worked.

******

Dietzel's formal football-playing career began in junior high school at Mansfield, in a program patterned after the successful program initiated at the grade school level in Massillon by Paul Brown. That career continued until Dietzel graduated from Miami.

A pre-med student at Miami, Dietzel already had his acceptance for Columbia University's medical school and had made his room deposit when he received an urgent inquiry from Gillman, who had left Miami to work under Colonel Blaik at West Point.

Blaik had suggested to Gillman that he ask one of his young graduates to come to Army to coach the plebe team.

"The medical career went down the drain," says Dietzel, "because, imagine coming right out of college and being an assistant coach at West Point."

The Blanchard-Davis era had just ended at Army, so Dietzel was walking into a high-visibility situation at West Point. Army football was at or near the top in the public consciousness, and here was a young man, on his way to medical school, all of a sudden the plebe line coach under the legendary Red Blaik. Credit Sid Gillman with an assist.

Strangely enough, Dietzel never thought about why Gillman left a head coaching position to become an assistant under Blaik.

"I feel," surmises Dietzel, "that he felt that he had gone as far as he could at Miami.

"In order for him to step into a major, major, major job . . . I think he felt that he needed to be at a major school, and of course Col. Blaik is one of the most respected people in the business. I think he thought it was a great opportunity for him to advance on up the ladder."

Blaik's Miami ties remained strong throughout his career. Ohio-born and Ohio-bred, he had lured to his Army staff first Stu Holcomb, then Gillman and Dietzel. And there were others, like Bill Gunlock, who was a product of the same era as Dietzel, although he graduated in 1951. Even today, a man with Miami connections is the coach at West Point. Jim Young, an assistant under Bo Schembechler in the Sixties, later head coach at Arizona and Purdue, took over at Army after the 1982 season. But that's another part of the story.

Dietzel was embarking on a football coaching career at the feet of a master, a man who would have a profound influence on his coaching career, at a place which would have further influence on his career.

"I thought Colonel Blaik was one of the greatest people I've ever known," recalls Dietzel of his association with the Army coach. "Marvelous integrity, a very tough-minded rascal, brilliant, very, very smart, with an entirely different approach to football than Sid, but it was great because it showed you that there's more than one way to accomplish whatever you're trying to accomplish, that there's more than one way to do things."

On top of his regular assignment as plebe line coach, Dietzel was given another important task by Col. Blaik. As everyone knows, the most important game in the Army season . . . any Army season . . . is against Navy. Dietzel was assigned to scout the Naval Academy in every game it played.

Dietzel got to know the Navy "better than I did our own team." As it turned out, that became a bit of a problem, because Navy lost every game that season, while Army remained undefeated going into the season finale.

The rookie coach was beginning to feel a little sorry for the Midshipmen when an 80-yard run through most of the Army team brought him back to earth, and at the same time taught him a valuable lesson. Army battled from behind all day and finally managed a 21-21 tie. The lesson learned: "Don't ever feel sorry for the opponents."

After that game, Gillman was offered the head coaching position at Cincinnati. Sid apparently felt that situation represented an opportunity not present at Army. Bearcat partisans were anxious to deal what they hoped would be a severe blow to arch-rival Miami.

For Dietzel, the situation produced one of a series of difficult career decisions. Gillman asked Dietzel to come with him as an assistant. Col. Blaik advised him it would be a mistake. However, Dietzel followed his old mentor and became Gillman's defensive line coach.

"Sid's idea of defense was that every Thursday night without fail, the last five minutes of practice, he'd take a card and show us where to line up on defense. That was our defensive practice — zero.

"We just had so much offense, they couldn't stop us. Our defense wasn't that good, but we'd outscore everybody."

Dietzel was responsible for Cincinnati's defensive linemen and linebackers. Although Joe Madro earlier had described Doc Urich as a "Chinese Bandit" because of his ruthless style of play, Dietzel resurrected the use of that terminology during his days at Cincinnati.

In the comic strip "Terry and the Pirates," Chinese Bandits were described as "the meanest, most vicious people in the world."

"From now on," Dietzel wrote on the locker room bulletin board, "we're gonna be known as the Chinese Bandits." As a whole culture of football-crazed Cajuns soon would learn, that would become the watchword of LSU Tiger football in a few years, but there remained some intermediate stops on the Dietzel coaching express.

Paul Bryant, who was the coach at Kentucky at the time, wired Dietzel after Cincinnati's Sun Bowl appearance and asked if he'd be interested in coaching at Kentucky. Dietzel went down for an interview but asked if he could return to Cincinnati and think about the offer.

Back with his friends, Gillman and the others he had been with since the days at Miami, then West Point, and now Cincinnati, he decided to call Bryant and say thanks, but no thanks.

"You're makin' a mistake," said Bryant. And the longer Dietzel thought about it, the more he was convinced that he was making a mistake. Col. Blaik had said much the same thing to him just a couple of years earlier, and this time he decided to heed that advice.

So he called Bryant back and said for a nickel he'd take the job if it hadn't already been filled. Bryant said, "Hell, I got the nickel; you come on down."

It was a different system and different people, but again a chance to learn something new. After a year at West Point and two years at Cincinnati, Dietzel was on his way to Lexington to coach the offensive line for "the Bear".

In 1953, Dietzel had opportunity to benefit from another significant learning experience. Army was in need of an offensive line coach, and Dietzel was summoned to fill the void. That appointment found him working side by side with Vince Lombardi, who was the offensive backfield coach.

"That was a great experience for me," says Dietzel. "I really enjoyed working with Vince. And Vince was, in some ways like Sid . . . very, very intense. I certainly didn't think he was more knowledgeable, if as knowledgeable.

"He would scrape your brains clean to find out everything under . . . I mean he was the darnedest guy just to sit there and ask you questions. And we had a great year."

Lombardi left after that year to take a similar position with the New York Giants, and that let the door open for Dietzel to be reunited with George Blackburn, who replaced Lombardi. But that association was short-lived.

Every year, from November to February, a drama unfolds around the country as coaches resign, retire or are fired, and athletic directors and others in university officialdom scramble to zero in on a replacement. A drama that Miami experiences frequently, it is the lifeblood of the Cradle of Coaches saga.

In 1955, one such plot was unfolding along the banks of the Hudson River at West Point and down near the mouth of the Mississippi at Baton Rouge, Louisiana. The chief characters were Biff Jones, Charley McLendon and Paul Dietzel.

Louisiana State University, in the capital city of Baton Rouge, had fired Coach Gus Tinsley. Biff Jones had been head coach and then assistant athletic director at Army before he was hired as LSU's head coach in 1932, ultimately to walk out a few years later after a tiff with Gov. Huey Long. Jones still was close to the LSU scene; and during Dietzel's first year at West Point, he was a direct link with Dietzel on recruiting matters, from his office in Washington.

McLendon had been on the staff with Dietzel at Kentucky. He since had moved to LSU, and his was a precarious position when Tinsley's firing came. At the same time, Dietzel by process of attrition had become the senior member of Blaik's staff. In fact, he was the lone holdover.

Bo Schembechler, second from right, was Miami's head coach when a distinguished roster of alumni returned to the Oxford campus to help conduct a clinic. From the left, John Pont was coaching at Indiana, Hugh Hindman was Woody Hayes' assistant at Ohio State, Paul Dietzel was at LSU, and Ara Parseghian was at Notre Dame.

Dietzel's call to McLendon in early February was simply to advise him of some of the changes, to let him know that, among others, Blackburn was now the head coach at Cincinnati, and Bobby Dobbs was at Tulsa. McLendon said he really wasn't interested in making a move; he'd like to stay at LSU.

Recalling that conversation, Dietzel says McLendon asked him if he knew anyone at LSU.

"I told McLendon, 'I don't even know where LSU is,' and he said, 'I'll tell you where it is.' He said, 'This is really a great place. You oughtta try to get this job.'"

McLendon persisted in finding out whether Dietzel knew anyone connected with LSU, and none of the names sounded remotely familiar. Except one. Almost as an afterthought, McLendon brought up the name of Biff Jones. Now Dietzel had a connection. And that connection, counselled McLendon, would land Dietzel the job.

It wasn't quite that simple. However, acting on the recommendation of the man who had, in effect, thumbed his nose at Huey Long, LSU was anxious to interview the Army assistant. Biff Jones had warned Dietzel about the political ramifications of the job, but then said, "Paul, if you can get that job, you oughtta take it."

Jones never had a chance to call the LSU officialdom to tell them about Dietzel. They called him. They wanted Jones to come back and become the athletic director. That post was open, too, as the previous athletic director had retired. When Jones declined, the conversation turned to the coaching vacancy. Whom would Jones recommend? When he suggested Paul Dietzel, Jones had to call Paul quickly to tell him to act appropriately surprised when he heard from LSU.

There were, apparently, a number of inquiries and applicants, official and unofficial. Ben Martin, who was to become coach at the Air Force Academy, was among those considered. So was Parseghian, who was still at Miami. But LSU had decided not to go after any head coach under contract. The choice turned out to be Dietzel. Charley McLendon was right. And he still had a job.

All wasn't a bed of roses in Baton Rouge in the earliest years, although the first two games of Dietzel's seven-year reign were memorable. LSU opened the 1955 season at home against Kentucky, where Dietzel had served just a few years before. A 96-yard kickoff return after the favored Wildcats had clawed back to within a touchdown gave Dietzel an opening-game victory, but the state of euphoria was tempered with the realization that Bear Bryant's Texas A & M team was waiting in ambush. And the Tigers were no match for the Aggies.

After those first two games, it would be two more years before the Tigers would approach the .500 level. In fact, it was only during the national championship season in 1958 that the Tigers — nee Chinese Bandits — emerged as popular favorites.

As fate would have it, LSU was a failed two-point conversion against Tennessee away from two straight undefeated seasons, and probably two consecutive national championships. And Dietzel's 1961 team, his last, was ranked fourth in the country. LSU had arrived, but Dietzel was leaving.

For a guy who got to West Point only because his road to medical school took a detour, Dietzel never tired of returning. In 1961, Dale Hall, who had been Col. Blaik's replacement, was fired at West Point. Although four years remained on his contract at LSU, Dietzel sought, and was granted permission, to speak with Maj. Gen. William C. Westmoreland, the Academy superintendent, about the vacant post.

It was hard to find much support for Dietzel's move anywhere in the state of Louisiana. His position was that there wasn't much more he could accomplish at LSU, and he always had nurtured a real desire to coach the Cadets. He might, however, have timed his reemergence on the Army scene a little better. When he landed at West Point, a quarterback named Roger Staubach was emerging at Annapolis.

As Dietzel had learned at West Point the first time, the first order of business for Army is to beat Navy. Staubach was a sophomore that first year, and he proceeded to lead Navy to a 35-10 victory.

"He put on," marvels Dietzel, "the doggonedest exhibition you ever saw. If you think he was good in the pros, you should have seen him against us that day. He put on one of the most exciting performances in a college football game I've seen."

Dietzel had to endure Staubach twice more. His junior season, Navy won, 20-16, as time ran out on the Cadets at the two-yard line. Army finally won the next year, 11-8.

South Carolina was the next stop for Dietzel, in 1966, and it was there he moved from coaching into athletic administration. Hired by the Gamecocks for the dual role of athletic director and head football coach, he hoped to phase out of coaching after a few years. But South Carolina wanted to retain the dual position; so Dietzel went to the Ohio Valley Conference as commissioner, and from there to the athletic director's post at Indiana University.

Dietzel had repeated returns to Army with success, so he saw nothing wrong with returning to LSU when that school asked him to come back as athletic director after Carl Maddox retired. Maddox had been an LSU assistant when Dietzel first arrived there in 1955.

This time at LSU, Dietzel soon began to see the politics Biff Jones had warned him about. It hadn't happened earlier, when Dietzel was riding the crest of public acclaim with winning teams and a national championship. But LSU now was struggling to regain football superiority in the Southeastern Conference and to re-establish national prestige.

In May 1982, LSU Chancellor James Wharton, at a news conference, announced the findings of an internal audit of the athletic department and reassigned Dietzel to a newly-created position in the president's office until Dietzel's contract would expire later that year.

The audit charged the department with failure to follow public bid laws and the university's own fiscal management policies. Dietzel responded by filing a $3.5 million lawsuit against Wharton, claiming the chancellor had defamed him in the news conference.

"The suit will bring out the truth," claims Dietzel.

******

As a practical matter, the main results of his removal from the athletic director's chair have been to move up by a year Dietzel's retirement from an active role in college athletics and to hasten his retreat to the mountains of North Carolina — the mountains where he can contemplate inquiries about his role in the Miami legend and what the future holds.

Dietzel was at Miami Field on that November day in 1982 when the men wearing the red and white uniforms walked off that field for the last time — winners once again. He remembers what that field meant to him, and he reasons with conviction that it meant much the same to hundreds and hundreds of Miami football players and fans, before and after.

But it was getting to the point, maintains Dietzel, that tradition was not enough.

"They (Miami) were beginning to get a little behind in one major area . . . facilities. The thing that Miami is moving into this fall, as wonderful as that old field was, and as great as it was to walk out there and sit out there, when you get that high school athlete in there and then you show him where they play football, and you compare that to the other stadiums that he goes to visit, Miami does not do well.

"The addition of that new stadium, I think, is gonna help Miami to continue to stay right where they've been."

The new stadium, Dietzel feels, will only serve to enhance Miami's chance to attract good people, which he maintains always has been Miami's strength. Those people have been winners.

Dietzel has seen first hand what it takes to sustain a program, what it takes to turn a program around, or what it takes to safeguard against turning sour. Attitude plays a big part. And Dietzel is convinced that winning attitude at Miami is all a part of the tradition.

"You know, they've got the crazy attitude that when Miami walks out on the field, it's supposed to win. I mean, Miami expects to win. They're not sure how, but they're gonna win. And that's that winning tradition."

"I'm a believer in surrounding yourself with the right kinds of people, and certainly the football team I was on was the right kind of people . . . that was what influenced me to go into the coaching profession.

"I was recruited by Sid Gillman, and when I got here Sid had left and George Blackburn was the head coach my freshman year. Then he left. I had Woody Hayes my sophomore and junior years, and of course Woody went to Ohio State, and I had Ara Parseghian my senior year.

"At the time, I didn't think it was the greatest thing in the world, because we just got used to a coach, and then he would go on. But being a coach, it probably was the best thing that ever happened to me, being involved with so many fine people and having so many diversified backgrounds from these coaches."

Carmen Cozza, Miami class of 1952, head coach at Yale University since 1965, when he succeeded John Pont, speaking at the reunion of the 1950 team, Salad Bowl victors, on which he played.

VI
THE MIAMI LEGACY

IT WAS A Monday night at Mory's in New Haven, and the Whiffenpoofs were singing, as they always do on Monday evenings. I put down my fork and just listened, as did the Yale coach, my dinner host.

Glancing around the small room, noticing the pictures of Yale captains in block "Y" sweaters, seated on the fence, the traditional pose for Yale captains, I was reminded once again of the great tradition of Yale football.

When Miami began playing football back in 1888, Yale already had been playing the game for 16 years . . . without a formal coach. Yale's first coach, the immortal Walter Camp, had been Yale captain in 1878 and '79. He began his coaching career in 1888. From 1888 through 1892, Camp's Yale teams won 67 games and lost two.

Quietly, Carm Cozza has built his own legend at Yale. His is the longest tenure of any coach in Yale's long football history. He is the winningest coach in Yale history. His record of 118 victories against 44 losses and three ties is unsurpassed. His Yale teams have won or tied for the Ivy league title nine times in 18 years.

The Whiffenpoofs finished; and as Cozza acknowledged a couple of the singers, it reminded him of a story:

"A couple of years ago, we had a pretty good tackle, a boy we were really counting on at that position because we were a little thin, and he came in after the season and said he wanted to sing. Not realizing he meant any more than singing in the shower or some such thing, I told him to be my guest. But the next year he joined the Whiffenpoofs, and there went a pretty good tackle."

Maybe Bob Kennedy knew what he was talking about. The young man who came to Yale from Florida now sings in the Metropolitan Opera.

Kennedy is perhaps representative of the interesting personalities and diverse interests Cozza has encountered in his 20 years at Yale. Brian Clarke is another one.

Clarke came to Yale as a placekicker. Cozza found out about his strange habit at the Friday practice before Clarke's first game in 1971 against Connecticut.

"We usually go over our kicking game extensively during the Friday practice," recalls Cozza, "so I sent Brian out there on the kickoff team. 'I don't kick on Fridays,' he said."

Going along with this strange behavior, but churning a little inside, Cozza somewhat facetiously questioned Clarke about his Saturday kicking habits, "since we play our games on Saturday."

Saturday came, and Clarke knocked three placements right through the uprights.

"That was his style," says Cozza, a little wonderment still creasing his brow, "so we just didn't kick on Friday anymore."

The Friday superstition wasn't the only surprise Clarke had for his coach. When the seniors finish their playing careers, Cozza calls them in individually for a chat, and to find out about their plans after graduation.

"I'm going to Hollywood," said Clarke. "You'll see, I'll make it." Cozza hinted he said it with the same finality he had observed three years earlier. Clarke's television credits so far include **The Brady Bunch** and **Eight Is Enough**, and this fall he's ticketed for **General Hospital**.

Any institution with a football heritage like Yale's is bound to number professional football players as well as opera singers, actors, doctors and lawyers among its graduates. Yale does.

Calvin Hill was in Cozza's first recruit class when he took over as head coach in 1965. When Hill graduated in 1969, he was a first-round draft choice of the Dallas Cowboys. Hill's distinguished pro career included, in addition to six years with the Cowboys, stints with the Washington Redskins and the Cleveland Browns before his retirement in 1981.

During the Miami regime at Yale, beginning in 1963, with John Pont, Pont and Cozza saw many Yalemen make it in the National Football League — players like Brian Dowling (New England and Green Bay), Greg Dubinetz (Washington), Gary Fencik (Chicago), Dick Jauron (Detroit, Cleveland and Cincinnati), Don Martin (New England, Kansas City and Tampa Bay), Chuck Mercein (New York Giants, Green Bay, Washington and New York Jets), and John Spagnola (Philadelphia).

A paragraph from Yale's press guide puts into perspective the tradition of Yale football, and Cozza's place in that tradition:

"Throughout the decades Yale football has provided a breeding ground for legends that have distinguished Yale as a paragon of gridiron glory. From the innovative genius of Walter Camp to the consummate class of Carmen Cozza; from the inspirational clarion calls of T.A.D. Jones ('Gentlemen,' he once told his assembled team, 'you are about to play Harvard. Never in your life will you do something so important') to the irrepressible charm of Herman Hickman; from the heroic (albeit fictional) deeds of Frank Merriwell to the immortal (and real-life) exploits of Dowling; from the dashing brilliance of Levi Jackson, the local hero from New Haven's Hillhouse High School, to the dominating presence of (John) Pagliaro, another favorite son from nearby Derby; and from the Yale Bowl's grand opening-day crowd of 71,000 for the Harvard game in 1914 to the throng of 75,300 fans who watched the same two teams duel at the Yale Bowl in 1981; Yale football continues to embrace a tradition that will forever keep its coffers filled with heroes and champions."

Native of Parma, a Cleveland suburb, Cozza became one of Miami's all-time great athletes. He did just about everything possible with a football. Playing three different positions, he carried, caught and passed the ball, intercepted passes and ran back punts and kickoffs.

Not only was Cozza a pretty good football player during his years at Miami, he played baseball as well. After graduation, he was signed to a professional baseball contract in the Cleveland Indians' chain. During

Carm Cozza was a two-sport standout at Miami, and as a married student, he shared an apartment with his wife, Jean, in Miami's Vet Village.

the off-season, he returned to work on his master's degree, and worked as a graduate assistant under Parseghian for a couple of years.

Baseball behind him, teaching certificate in hand, Cozza headed back to Cleveland to pick up high school coaching experience at Gilmour Academy, a small preparatory school, and later at innercity Collinwood High School.

By then, it was 1956 and Parseghian had moved to Northwestern. Cozza's college roommate, John Pont, had been named to succeed Ara, and one of Pont's first acts was to ask Carmen to join his Miami staff.

We'll talk about how Pont got to Yale a little bit later; but when John left Miami, Cozza wanted very much to be Pont's successor. Disappointed when that didn't happen, he now credits John with having helped him to get over the hurt by giving him both offensive and defensive responsibilities when he came to Yale as one of Pont's lieutenants.

Once Cozza was picked as Pont's successor, it was up to him to keep the Yale football program moving on the course charted when John had taken over in 1963. It wasn't easy. The first season resulted in a 3-6 record, and the next year brought only one more victory. But Hill and Dowling were on the freshman team, and they'd be ready for the varsity in 1967.

Yale lost the opening game that year to Holy Cross, then proceeded to rattle off 16 victories in a row before ending the 1968 season with a 29-29 tie with Harvard.

One of the characteristics of Yale teams under Cozza has been aggressive defense. That and effective utilization of the great running backs who have come Yale's way. Cozza made his mark at Miami as a defensive back, but he insists his attention to defense at Yale has nothing to do with his playing days.

"In our league, especially, you don't know if you're going to get that great athlete offensively. I've been blessed with some great running backs here . . . Rich Diana, of course Calvin Hill, Dick Jauron and John Pagliaro, to name a few . . . great backs that could play on almost any team.

"But you never know if you're going to get these kinds of people, and I realized that if you can play it real close and play tough defense, you've got a chance. And we learned that our first year here."

In the past 10 years, Yale has led the league four times in defense, and once led the nation.

"Realizing that we're not playing Ohio State and Notre Dame and people like that, by the same token we don't have the same rules that they play with, either. So we're proud of the defense we've had here," says Cozza.

On the other hand, counters Cozza, "We've had a good, consistent offense. I think offense leads to it (the defensive strength). We haven't turned the ball over as much as maybe some other people have, and I think that's helped us. We throw the football, but we try to throw it with reason."

For the most part, that offensive strategy has been in the capable hands of another product of the Cradle of Coaches, Sebastian LaSpina.

Seb played under Pont and Cozza at Miami, where he also was a weight man on the track team.

As Cozza's offensive coordinator, this 1958 Miami graduate directs the passing game and works closely with the ends. LaSpina, says Cozza, "is one of the best minds in the game, in my opinion."

People tend to credit the Yale defense, as Cozza is wont to do, but he also admits that there's a reason for that. Yale's offensive scheme is designed to control the football.

"I don't know if I could have operated without him," says Cozza of LaSpina. "He's just been fantastic."

Never in the headlines, but one of the countless Miami coaches whose role has been to provide the support for the head coaches who have built the legend.

Is he ready for a head coaching position?

"There's no doubt he's ready!" says Cozza. "We have, on a few occasions, discussed this. He's selective, and he has a right to be. He's well-established, his wife's well-established, he's got a son here at Yale. He's not just gonna take any job, it's gotta be a good one, the right one for him."

If the defense has been good, and it has been, Cozza has had coaches with Miami backgrounds to do the teaching of the defensive system. First it was Bill Mallory, a 1956 graduate of Miami who played for Parseghian and Pont. When Mallory returned to Miami as the head coach, Cozza immediately replaced him with Bill Narduzzi, a 1959 graduate who is now the head coach at Youngstown State.

During his tenure at Yale, Cozza has relied heavily on coaches with Miami backgrounds. Jim Root, a Miami teammate, already described, was his first offensive coordinator. At one time or another, he's also had Joe Galat, Miami '62, now head coach of the Montreal team in the Canadian Football League; Neil Putnam, another 1958 graduate who went on to become head coach at Lafayette College; and Mack Yoho, also class of '58, who went from Canadian football to enjoy a stellar career with the Buffalo Bills and later was lured from the banking business to assist at Yale. Yoho has returned to the banking career he forged for himself, but continues with a hand in football as coach of a semi-pro team in New England.

Most coaches, if the truth be known, look on recruiting as the least desirable of the myriad tasks that are part and parcel of their job descriptions. But very essential. To Cozza, even at Yale, it's no different. In a way, it might even be more difficult.

To begin with, the Yale coaches are looking for student-athletes who might meet Yale's strict standards for admission. As a general rule, that means board scores in the 1200 range. Additionally, the vast majority of students admitted to Yale rank in the top 10 percent of their high school graduating class.

That's not all. There are no athletic scholarships at Yale. Or at any of the schools of the Ivy League. There is financial aid, but based solely on the family's need. And that means making application no later than the first of the year to be considered for whatever aid might be available.

Recruiting, says Cozza, "is probably the most frustrating part of coaching, maybe in any league, but certainly here in view of the fact that our acceptances don't go out until the middle of April, and we have to work with a vast number of student-athletes.

" . . . And we never know . . . there isn't a cut-off . . . we never know for sure whom the admissions office is going to accept. And that's what's so difficult, because we are restricted to the same NCAA rules as everyone else is."

It is, concedes Cozza, akin to recruiting with one arm tied behind your back. But on the other hand, there are plusses that work to Yale's advantage, and Cozza is only too happy to point those out.

"The school itself," he acknowledges, "sells itself in many ways. It has a great national reputation . . . and international reputation. We've had a fine football program here for many, many years, starting with Walter Camp, and we talk about the tradition just like Miami does about the tradition that it has in football. And we have a super stadium to play in. We seat over 70,000 people. We've led New England (in attendance) ever since I've been here, and I'm sure far beyond that."

"So we've had some good things to sell here," he continues. "but the thing we can promise our youngsters is that they're gonna get a top education, and the thing I brag about the most . . . and I've done very little to help, if anything . . . and that is, we don't lose anybody."

Only four former Yale football players, of the more than 2,000 Cozza has recruited and coached in his career, have failed to graduate. If it's biochemistry, or political science, or pre-med, that is a record that the head of any department, at any university, can cite with pride.

Having said that, it seems unfair to ask Cozza to compare Miami with Yale. But as he himself points out, both have traditions of excellence of which they are justifiably proud. And the Miami man didn't shrink from the challenge.

"People asked me, when I first came up, about the difference in football in the Midwest and here in New England, and I said about 620 miles. Kids are kids. We have some real talented kids like we had at Miami, and some kids that play with a lotta heart with lesser abilities, and we had some very bright kids at Miami who were excellent students. We had a few that we had to push a little bit. But Miami's a fine academic institution, and I'm very proud to have played there and also coached there."

Cozza continues, "Here all the kids are bright. You can do a lot of things with them mentally. Not all of them react like you'd like them to on the field on a given day. By the same token, the commitment during the season is no different than it is at Miami."

Off-season, Yale players under Cozza have a weight-training and conditioning program which is not mandatory. However, the coaches seem to know who's there and who isn't. And they are very much aware that, with the absence of spring practice in the Ivy League, a significant number of Yale football players play a second sport.

Or they're involved in another activity completely apart from sports . . . singing groups, drama . . . wherever their interests lie.

"They're gifted in other areas," concludes Cozza, "and I feel that's why they choose a school like this, so they have these options . . . so that they in fact will be able to do the things that they've always wanted to do in their life."

All these thoughts came into sharper focus for Carm Cozza on October 1, 1977, when Miami traveled to New Haven and defeated Yale, 28-14, in the Yale Bowl. It was a season when Yale won an Ivy League title, finishing with a 7-2 record, and Miami won a Mid-American Conference championship, losing only once in 11 games. Carm Cozza was hurting inside, but being the Miami man he is, he was there after the game to mingle with the Miami celebrants. He, as much as anyone, understood.

"The people that I played for and played with," explains Cozza, "were so highly motivated and dedicated. I mean it was their life, and they were bright individuals who had goals in life. It was more than a game with them, it was a way of life."

Those Miami teams of the late Forties and early Fifties, Cozza believes, were a part of a "family atmosphere that's hard to explain unless you were a part of it."

One senses Cozza has tried mightily to bring that same sense of family to Yale. He has succeeded, because he cares, and he understands. He understands that he is, first and foremost, a teacher; and being a good teacher means being able to relate well to people.

"You know," he says, "I'm naive (enough) to believe that they learn more in football than they do in these great classrooms here at Yale. They learn how to deal with people, they learn how to deal with adversity, they learn how to cope with some very difficult situations."

Through their football experiences, Yale players, and players everywhere, are learning things "that you really can't learn in a book," points out Cozza.

The teacher-coach is the one who makes those things happen, and Carmen Cozza has proved to be one of the best. Understanding people and relating to people are among the attributes which permit Cozza to stand above many in his profession.

He explains his philosophy of coaching: "There's only so many ways you can go off tackle. There's only so many ways you can throw a football. There's only so many ways you can defense an option. Everything else is getting into that young man's head. And making him feel that he is the best that he can possibly be and motivating him to be the best he can possibly be."

Commitment to excellence is a two-way street, as Cozza sees it, which means in the player-coach relationship the lines of communication need to be wide open.

"The way I find best for me," says the man who served as president of the American Football Coaches Association in 1978, "is to let 'em know you're genuinely interested in everything they do, without sort of having a watchful eye over their shoulder every minute."

After nearly 20 years at Yale, Carmen Cozza is in a unique position to observe the academic and athletic traditions of an institution which from its earliest days has held pre-eminent rank in American higher education.

At the same time, he has developed perhaps an even deeper feeling for his Miami heritage. Unquestionably, he says, the Miami tradition of excellence will continue indefinitely.

"You know," he says, borrowing a phrase from today's students, "I feel so strongly about that University. I just think it's always gonna attract great people, and I don't think they'll ever have a problem getting a top-flight football coach there.

"I think because of the beauty of the campus and the way the school is situated, the recognition it receives, the credibility it has in the academic world . . . it's always going to be strong. I want to believe that, anyway. I know as long as I live I'm going to try to make sure it stays that way.

"I hope they always keep their standards high, and that they shoot for the best, because in my opinion they are the best . . . we're different type schools, here and Miami, but in many ways we're also similar. This school has a great deal of respect, and so does Miami. You have to earn

John Pont and Carm Cozza . . . Yale's coaches since 1963.

that. You don't buy it. You don't turn a switch on and it happens. It comes through years of hard work and dedication. Miami has achieved this with some great, great people, and they've had great, great teachers."

While drawing comparisons between Miami and Yale, Cozza had a final thought . . . one which says a lot about the Miami football player of his day and is an eloquent testimonial to their ultimate success.

"I think one of the reasons for my success here," observes Cozza, "is the quality that I have. On this team here, I have 57 high school football captains, 83 high school National Honor Society students, 16 valedictorians . . . real quality."

That's why Yale wins, says Cozza, and Miami was no different during that glorious period which began in the mid-forties.

"I really believe that's why we won. We had some great human beings on those teams in those days, and they've all gone on to better things."

******

Speaking of better things, let's take a look at Tom Pagna. He dreamed of Notre Dame, this product of Akron, Ohio. Notre Dame became an integral part of his life, but Miami came first.

Ara Parseghian was something of a hero in Akron when Pagna was growing up. Pagna was from the east side of town, and Parseghian from the south side, but by the time Pagna had graduated from bantam football to a high school career, Parseghian was Akron's hometown hero on the fledgling Cleveland Browns, Paul Brown's team.

Even before that, Pagna knew about Parseghian. It was the early days of television, and "I saw Miami play Case on very localized television in basketball, and Ara Parseghian was the left-handed guard."

Pagna recalls that in the days of his recruitment, there were perhaps 50 to 60 schools in the Akron area to canvass, and it was the winter of 1949 when Freshman Coach Parseghian stopped by Pagna's high school to talk with him and to watch him play basketball.

When Pagna came down to Oxford for a visit, he remembers he sat in the end zone, and "there were names that loom up at me . . . Doc Urich, Al Maccioli, Norb Wirkowski, Johnny Pont, Jerry Beckrest, Boxcar Bailey . . . I watched them . . . saw Beckrest make a fabulous run."

The die had been cast. Pagna knew then he was going to wind up at Miami. He was enamored of Parseghian. Besides both being from Akron, they had similar builds.

"Anyhow," he says, "there was a tie. I had dreams of playing for the Browns and everything, and I really liked Ara and respected him.

"To make a long story short, when I went there, I kinda went because of Ara. And then of course when you get there, you get there because of Miami. Uniquely different. Fell in love with the place."

Freshmen weren't eligible for the varsity when Hayes' 1950 Miami team was carving its special niche in Redskin lore. But Pagna learned early about the Miami rivalry with Cincinnati. And he was destined to leave his own impact on Miami football before it was all over.

"You had to play freshman football," says Pagna of his formal introduction to Miami football. "They played a four-game schedule, and the first game that Ara coached in, and the first game they had scheduled that year, was Cincinnati. That was a big, big rivalry. And of course, we didn't know that. We walked into it, like, you know, just another game, that's all. But we learned . . . Cincinnati - Miami . . . that's war."

Made more so, no doubt, in those days, by the fairly recent defections from Miami to Cincinnati of Sid Gillman, and George Blackburn, and Joe Madro, and Jack Faulkner, who remained on the Cincinnati staff.

Pagna became the first Miami back to rush for more than 1,000 yards. He did that in his junior season, 1952, when he totaled 1,044 as the Redskins went undefeated through eight games before losing the finale to Cincinnati.

That same year, Pagna scored 78 points. Both his season point total and yardage were Miami records at the time, to be eclipsed later as schedules expanded. Be that as it may, he remains sixth on Miami's career rushing list with 2,078 yards, and his 151 career points is equal to Tirrel Burton in sixth place. Pagna averaged 6.4 yards per carry for three years, captained the team his senior year, and in 1974 joined his Miami coach, Parseghian, in the Miami Hall of Fame.

When it was all over, Pagna could look back on a lot of memories, but few of them topped the impact of that freshman game at Cincinnati.

"It was a game like I've never been in before, or since," remembers Pagna. "Played pro football, and never was in one as punishing as that one . . . we didn't realize that we were in a grudge fight, not between

Tom Pagna crosses the final stripe to score during Miami's 20-7 victory at Dayton in 1953.

teams, but between coaches.

" . . . We didn't realize that there was such a feeling between the coaching staffs, Sid Gillman and Woody . . . Sid Gillman and Ara . . . there was a lot at stake, but we didn't understand that. But when we went on the field we understood."

The youngster from Akron picked up a lesson outside the classroom when, as a sophomore, he was on the traveling squad for the season's opening game at Wichita. Not only was he on the traveling squad, he was slated for the starting backfield, along with Boxcar Bailey at fullback, John Pont at the other halfback and Jim Root at quarterback.

"In the hotel," says Pagna, "they were not going to let Bailey in, because he was black. Ara made a stand, and I'll never forget it. He told the guy, 'If he doesn't stay here, none of us will,' and in Wichita in those days there wasn't any place else to stay. We'd have stayed in a hayfield."

Obviously, Ara won that battle, and Miami won the war the next day on the field, but it wasn't without its casualties. Bailey was bothered by the fuss, and even more bothered when he was booed when Miami came on the field. And the incident opened the eyes of a naive sophomore from Akron.

If a single game sticks in Pagna's mind from that memorable season when he rushed for his record-breaking total, it was a game one night in Milwaukee when the Redskins rallied to eke out a 22-21 victory over Marquette.

"There were a couple of things that happened," recalls Pagna. "One was — and I'll never forget it, because in those years you didn't have sidewinder kicks, and Paul Sautter, who was a 128-pound field goal and extra-point specialist, kicked it straightaway . . . I think he's a pilot and maybe a colonel in the Air Force today — he kicked one, and I swear it was off-target 20 yards, and the wind caught it and swept it through, and we won 22-21."

The other phenomenon Pagna recounts from that game is a catch Clive Rush made lying flat on his back. It kept the winning drive alive.

Yet Pagna doesn't boast of still another bit of heroics, unforgettable to anyone who saw that game: his own contribution of 212 yards and two touchdowns in 25 carries.

It was harder to get into coaching once he graduated from Miami than it had been to make the decision which brought him to Miami in the first place. Because of the Korean conflict, many students had been funneled into Miami's Air Force and Navy Reserve Officer Training Corps units. Qualified for a commission at graduation, Pagna knew he faced an Air Force stint sooner or later, and so did Paul Brown in drafting him for the Cleveland Browns.

Pagna hung on with the Browns until the last possible moment, but he was traded to Green Bay. He played for the Packers that 1954 season; but by February he was headed for Mitchell Air Force Base where, because of his background, he played and coached.

That was alright for background, but it didn't prepare him for what he was about to face when he returned to Akron: there wasn't a job in sight.

Pagna thought he had a better idea. He'd go back to Paul Brown and ask for another tryout. Brown asked him what he really intended to do with his life. Pagna's reply was that he really always had wanted to coach. Brown gave him a pretty good piece of advice.

"He said," as Pagna remembers it. "'Then, for God's sake, get into coaching, and the sooner the better, at any level.'"

With two children, nearing age 30, Pagna listened. His first stop was a junior high school in the Akron area, and from there he went to Akron North High School. He didn't think he had a shot at that job because "people were standing in line"; however, I think maybe the Miami of Ohio influence and a phone call from Ara helped."

In 1959, two years later, and five years after graduation from Miami, Pagna was hired by Ara to be his freshman coach at Northwestern. It was a coaching relationship that was going to last for as long as Parseghian remained active in coaching, and a friendship that would last forever.

Friendship aside, it was obvious from those early days in Akron that Parseghian was to be a dominant influence on the life of Tom Pagna. Conversely, in his role as loyal assistant, Pagna had to feel he had a role in Parseghian's success.

There are a lot more assistant coaches than head coaches, and yes, they are a factor in any team's success. What, I asked, does it take to be good at that job?

"That's a loaded question, and a good question," came Pagna's response. "I don't think anybody really asks that of anybody else. To be a good assistant coach, I think the first thing is loyalty. That was what Ara asked of each assistant coach. He'd say, 'I want loyalty.' And then he'd elaborate on it."

The thoughts on loyalty are not Pagna's alone, but he has obviously considered them carefully and has accepted them.

"Loyalty is an easy thing to give when things are going good . . . and it's a very difficult thing to give when things are going badly."

"That's what he'd ask of a staff member," says Pagna of Parseghian. "Because he knew, and he was smart enough to know . . . and I gleaned this from Ara. I was always psychologically forming my own thoughts about . . . you know, I may become a head coach tomorrow, and if I do I want to remember this . . . and I'd take notes . . . I've got notes and theory and ethics and philosophy stacked in my closet at home. And in my mind closet also."

Listening to Tom Pagna talk about loyalty, one realized also that enthusiasm is a big part of a successful assistant's bag of tricks.

"He's runnin' through the streets of Akron, Ohio, and all the little farm districts, and he's lookin' for that guy that picks the plow up and points. He's gonna recruit the All-American. And you've gotta have that. You've gotta have the youth and the enthusiasm to beat the bushes."

On the other side of the coin, and the reason coaching from the assistant's perspective can get old, the head coach-assistant relationship is, according to Pagna, "as near to a dictatorship as there possibly can be."

"If you're lucky enough to work for a benevolent dictator, that's good," continues Pagna. "He's the last word. He's the captain of the ship. If he says sink, you sink. If he says fired, you're fired. And you're answerable to him, and if he says we're workin' 15 hours today, you work 15 hours. So when he said loyalty, he said it all."

With that request for loyalty, there was the head coach's unwritten promise to return the favor. The head coach's commitment extends from such private matters as helping in times of family troubles to giving a young coach a boost up the ladder.

Pagna never climbed that top rung. Maybe it was his loyalty as much as anything that kept him at Ara's right hand. Or maybe it was his belief that if Ara ever left, he might be considered for the top spot.

"I never thought he'd leave the way he left," says Pagna of Parseghian's resignation at the end of the 1974 season. "I never thought it would happen that way. And I really thought it would not be cut and dried, which we found out later on it was.

"Had I known that the job was already promised to a Dan Devine, to hell with it, I don't stay as long as I did. I suppose, though, I'd probably been loyal to Ara in any event. I know I would have."

The truth is, these two guys from Akron were loyal to one another, and remain so. Parseghian knew Pagna like a book, and knew he thirsted for a head coaching opportunity. Had Pagna said he was ready, Ara would have been on the phone in a minute. Pagna never asked. When Parseghian asked for loyalty, that's what he got.

Today, Pagna is living a life apart from football as General Executive of four YMCA branches in and around the South Bend area. Like Parseghian, he has settled in an area in which he and his family are entirely comfortable.

He had a brief fling after Ara's resignation as Director of Alumni at Notre Dame, but he found he just wasn't suited to a life of complete academic regimen. So he worked for a while with Ara Parseghian Enterprises and at the same time, with Ara's blessing, fulfilled some speaking engagements and did the color for Mutual Radio's broadcasts of Notre Dame football.

It was also during that period that he began working on a book with Bob Best of the Notre Dame sports information office. **The Era of Ara** was published in 1976. Once finished with that, and while still with Mutual, he realized "that I had a lot to give, and a lot to offer" in terms of associations in the world of football.

He picked up the phone and called somebody he didn't know, Marv Levy, then coach of the Kansas City Chiefs. In 1978, Levy had an opening as an assistant coach, and signed Pagna to a five-year contract. He was back in football again.

But the illness of his wife interrupted that plan after a couple of years, and he returned to South Bend, where, as he remembers the admonition of James A. Gordon, Miami's Director of Physical Education, he "walks proud."

Gordon, the same Jim Gordon who caught the passes from Paul Brown and was an Olympic finalist, had a breakfast for all the physical education majors the morning of graduation. Pagna recalls their conversation that day:

"For the first time I saw James Gordon as, instead of Old Ironface, as a real mellow, wonderful man. And he said something to me. He said, 'Tom, do you owe anybody anything?' I said no. He said 'Does anybody owe you anything?' I said not that I know of. He said, 'You got an education here, in more ways than one. Walk proud.'"

Pagna says he wasn't sure at the time what Gordon meant, but today he knows. He's carried Gordon's words with him, and from the vantage point of 20-20 hindsight, he can see "that's exactly what happens."

"You go there," explains Pagna, speaking for the hundreds and hundreds of Miami athletes who shared the experience, "and you get humbled. And you work for everything you get.

"At the time, waiting tables was . . . every athlete. I don't care if you were the superstar in any event . . . you just worked, that paid for your room and board, and that's it. And you played, and you played your sport, and you were one of many.

"And you attended class, and if you didn't attend class, and you know those crazy assemblies . . . you had to go to four assemblies, whatever they were . . . if you didn't get all that in, you didn't graduate. And it was a bona fide degree, and I felt very proud about it when I walked out of there with it. Yes, I paid for this, in body and soul and in mind. But in turn, I was paid."

Pagna talks about his Miami education in terms which have real meaning in light of his career shift and the tendency, in some circles today, to ignore the classroom.

"Wherever you go, if you don't study and apply yourself, you're not gonna be educated. But I know this, that nobody at Miami of Ohio ever patsied his way through because he was a great athlete."

Well, I think having talked to a lot of other people . . . and this is not a soap box . . . people at a lot of other schools, they talk about people they know and work with; but I think here, there's a meaningful relationship . . . there's no put-on, there's no come-on, or anything like that. They know what their families are doing. They know the trials and tribulations of each other. They maintain contact. And you see a person you haven't seen for five years. It isn't as if you haven't seen him for five years, it's as if you just talked with him yesterday.

I think there's a closeness there. And I think part of that stems from the University, in that the University . . . the people here . . . created an atmosphere that the people here were not bigger than the University . . . you're a part of it.

At some institutions I've seen people who felt that they **were** the institution. At this place, you're **part** of it. You've created the folklore and what have you. You're part of the scene, you aren't the main act, and people accept this at Miami.

**John Pont, Miami's football coach
from 1956 to 1962,
describing Miami's impact on him
and other coaches as he looks
back on three decades
in college football.**

VII
JERSEY NUMBER 42 . . . RETIRED

THE FIRST TIME John Pont saw Miami, Sid Gillman told him to go get a steak, and he'd talk with him when he grew up.

As far as Gillman was concerned, it wasn't love at first sight when John took a first look at Miami. Fortunately for Miami, John took a second look.

Pont had been a 149-pound offensive and defensive guard, an all-state performer, at Canton Timken High School when Gillman in 1945 invited him to visit Miami. Pont was philosophical about meeting Gillman, and about the coach's reaction.

"If I were in his shoes, I wouldn't recruit a 149-pound guard either," observes Pont. "But, I fell in love with the place, and if someone would say, 'What did you like about it?' I would simply say, I like the place."

Without a scholarship offer, Pont opted for the Navy, serving with a submarine squadron based in San Diego, and learning to be a running back.

"When I got out," he recalls, "I worked for a year and then, with the GI Bill, a couple of people from Canton and I decided, 'Let's try college.' And I said, there's only one place I want to go, and that's Miami."

When Pont was in service, his sub squadron included a doctor who was a University of Minnesota man. The doctor was impressed by the skills Pont had developed as a halfback. Asking whether Pont would be interested in playing football in the Big Ten, the doctor said he believed a scholarship to Minnesota could be arranged.

"For whatever reason, I said no, if I go to college, I'm going to Miami," Pont recalls.

Gillman, who had put him off in 1945, wasn't even around when John finally got back to Miami in 1948. George Blackburn was coach. And by the time Pont reached sophomore status and varsity eligibility, Gillman and Blackburn had become reunited at Cincinnati, and the Miami coach was Woody Hayes. Hayes got a nice surprise when Pont wore a Miami game uniform for the first time.

Miami's opening game in that 1949 season — also the first game of Hayes' two-year regime — was at Wichita. The Redskins were receiving the kickoff. Hayes had his stubby neophyte running back at the deep position when the Shockers kicked off.

Pont didn't field the kick cleanly . . . in fact, he fumbled it. But when he did get a handle on the ball, he carried it all the way to the end zone . . . 96 yards for a Miami touchdown, the first time he officially touched a ball in collegiate competition.

Considering that he weighed only 149 pounds as a high school senior, it's not surprising that Pont hadn't started to play football until he was a junior at Timken. Son of Spanish immigrants, Pont says he always figured he would follow his father, Bautista, and work in Canton's steel mills.

However, says Pont, "football was a way of life in the neighborhood, and like 90 per cent of the guys, I was an athlete. I considered high school as a step to a job, not to college."

Football, and Sid Gillman, intervened.

Pont's career as a Miami halfback was the stuff from which legends emerge. Starting with that opening kickoff return, Pont went on to establish yardage and scoring records which weren't surpassed until freshman eligibility produced four-season careers. His jersey, number 42, was the first ever to be retired by his alma mater.

In three years as an All-Mid-American Conference halfback, Pont scored 27 touchdowns, gained 2,390 yards in 340 rushing attempts and returned 33 kickoffs for 874 yards. It was a career which, coupled with coaching success at Miami and Yale and then selection as 1967 Coach of the Year at Indiana, earned election to Miami's Athletic Hall of Fame. He became one of its eight charter members in 1969.

I never saw John Pont play. I only wish I had. The stories about his playing field feats have been told over and over by Miamians of the era.

With the ball tucked under his arm, John Pont was always a threat.

The kickoff return, of course, is memorable. And Woody Hayes and everybody else on the 1950 team remembers his performance in the famous "Snow Bowl" game in Cincinnati. But when I was in the press box at the University of Dayton for a Miami-Dayton game during John's coaching reign, they were still talking about his performance there in 1951.

Miami trailed, 20-7, beginning the fourth quarter. Pont already had raced 31 yards for Miami's first touchdown, on his way to 108 rushing yards for the afternoon. Now, with Miami in a hole, his 40-yard kickoff return, which almost went the distance, sparked the rally.

Pont's pass to freshman Jay Ansel, after faking a sweep, pulled Miami within six points of the Flyers. His third touchdown of the game, and the one which set up Paul Sautter's winning conversion, came when he took Jim Root's pass in the flat and ran 30 yards through what appeared to be the entire Dayton team.

"I think it's fair to say Johnny Pont inspired that rally," said Coach Ara Parseghian in his post-game remarks. "But the whole gang caught the spark. Every man did everything I could expect of him in that fourth quarter. There's absolutely nothing I could say that would be too extravagant for Pont's performance. On the other hand, I don't want anybody to forget that we'd had been sunk if Paul Sautter had missed any one of those after-touchdown place-kicks. Imagine the pressure on him for that third one!"

In Bob Howard's account of the climactic fourth quarter drive, the Miami publicity man said this: "The final touchdown had been set up shrewdly — the Root-Pont flat pass first gaining nothing but setting up a subsequent play on which Pont whipped a forward to John Zachary for 15 yards, which in turn made Dayton's defense cautious enough to help Pont get underway on the same setup for the touchdown three plays later."

Howard later was to comment about Pont's passing exploits during that game when he found Ansel in the end zone. "Hell, no, he couldn't pass. His hands were too small to grip the ball. He just laid the ball in the palm of his hand and willed it to Ansel."

Of such stories are legends, and retired jerseys, made.

"The finest thing about the win," Parsehgian had said after the game, "was the fact our players didn't let up when they were behind 20-7 in the last quarter. That determination to win is one of the finest things college football can develop or demonstrate."

If ever a phrase described John Pont, that was it. His determination to win, be it football, handball, golf or bridge, was never camouflaged. Yet through it all, he was and is, one of the most sensitive, caring human beings I have ever met.

My first meeting with Pont came on the way to an earlier game at Dayton, in 1954. He was the freshman coach. I was a freshman writer on **The Student**. (This was even before my introduction to Parseghian). Miami's freshman team was playing that night at Dayton, and after the varsity practice, Pont was driving to Dayton to be with the team, which had bussed up earlier.

It was the first of countless such trips, either by car, or bus, or heaven forbid, airplane, which Pont and I would take to and from Oxford, and later to and from Evanston, Illinois. Mainly, it served to break the ice in a relationship, personal and professional, that has spanned almost 30 years.

Reference was made, in the preceding paragraph, to airplane travel. There are few things in this world that John doesn't enjoy doing. One of those is flying. It is one of the costs of doing business in his chosen field, but this former submariner doesn't like it. In fact, there are times when he'll try to avoid it at any cost.

In our days together at Northwestern, when he was the athletic director/football coach, and I, as his associate director, was making the travel arrangements, it appeared we could avoid the drudgery, to say nothing of the cramped conditions, of a long bus trip to Iowa City. I suggested a charter flight.

Pont had a better idea. Since the players hadn't begun classes yet (Northwestern started late), we could leave a day early, practice Thursday and Friday at Iowa, have the players well rested, and save money. To say nothing of John's mental state.

But we're ahead of the story. We should go back to 1955, when Parseghian's Miami team had ambushed Northwestern as part of a 9-0 season, and ex-Miamian Stu Holcomb had lured him to Northwestern. Then it was left to Miami Athletic Director John Brickels to find a successor. Brickels turned, almost immediately, to Parseghian's freshman coach, John Pont. At 28, Pont became the country's youngest major-college head football coach.

******

Pont had been drafted by Green Bay after his Miami senior season, and he signed to play for the Packers "for a bonus of twenty dollars at the airport in Cincinnati." He was pleased with his performance at Green Bay, yet still didn't survive the final cut.

Pont played the rest of that 1952 season instead, in Canada. He was all set for a second year when something happened which Pont describes as "unique to Miami."

"I was signed for the second year up there," says Pont, "and then Ara called in July and said, 'John, would you come down and be the assistant coach, freshman coach in football and basketball?' I said, 'Ara, I'd like to try playing football, how long can you wait?' And knowing Ara, I'm even more indebted to him for having patience. Because I said, 'Ara, can you hold off?'"

This "on-hold" situation lasted about five weeks, until Pont finally decided to give up his playing dream and accept Ara's offer.

"I must admit," Pont now spoofs in reference to accepting responsibility for basketball as well as for the sport in which he had demonstrated skill, "I probably was one of the greater basketball coaches Miami has ever had who knew nothing about basketball."

Pont's hesitation was apparently the result of anxiety over his readiness, not to leave the playing behind, but for coaching.

"To be honest," he says, "I really didn't think I was ready, but by spring I had changed my mind. I found coaching was fun, and my assistants (the graduate assistants) were a tremendous help. I was hooked."

Three years later, when Brickels tapped him, he was hooked for sure. Now the entire burden of being the head coach was on his shoulders. If he wasn't ready before, he needed to be ready now. He was, more than anything, because of a basic Miami strength.

"I don't think there's a university in the country," maintains Pont, "where a young man who wants to go into football . . . we're talkin' about football now . . . as a profession, can learn more about the basics of administration of a football program than Miami.

"And that started way back with, in my lifetime, with Sid Gillman, Woody, what have you. I was always impressed with the administration

This is John Pont's first Miami staff. That's Pont at the front of the wedge. Flanking him are Woody Wills, left, and Wayne Gibson, right. To the rear, left to right, are Jay Fry, Carm Cozza and Ernie Plank. Interestingly, four of the six live in Oxford today, and a fifth, Plank, lives between Oxford and Cincinnati in Milford.

. . . the notebooks, the detail. I think every coach who left here did the same thing. That can be learned. What can't be learned is a people thing. That has to be for real."

Not long after John became Miami's head coach, I became sports editor of **The Student**. My first year in that role would be John's first year as head coach. We shared a lot of highs and lows over the next several years, as he grew in his coaching responsibilities and I graduated from two years as sports editor of **The Student** into a job as Miami's sports information director.

I learned quickly what Pont meant when he talked about "the people thing." Player relationships were important to him then and remained so throughout his career. It was something which emerged from the feeling of closeness that was so much a part of that 1950 team, and it stuck with him.

When you were around John as much as I was in those days, some of those special moments he shared with his players are forever stamped in the recesses of your mind. They were at times joyous, sometimes sad, occasionally humorous, always poignant. One such moment comes to mind.

Before practice, some players had gathered to congratulate a teammate on the birth of his child. Everybody knew the couple had intended marriage, but they'd actually made it to the altar only a few days before the baby's arrival. The teammates knew that, too.

As Coach Pont approached, the group suddenly grew silent. He, too, offered congratulations, then broke the tension: "You know, he's the only guy I know who could get married one week and be a father the next."

In another context, Pont had a daily routine which may have helped players take pressure for granted. He'd picked it up from Ara — engaging the placekickers in friendly competition before and after the day's team workout. One of those kickers in Pont's tenure was Bob Jencks.

Jencks, a rangy, 6-5 end, was the nation's leading kicker in his senior year. Over three seasons at Miami, he converted 46 of 53 extra-point attempts and kicked 17 field goals. He also caught 50 passes for 862 yards and 13 touchdowns.

But every night at practice, he was humbled, needled, cajoled . . . anything to break his concentration . . . as Pont tried to beat him out of a milk shake or two. And so long as the distance didn't get beyond Pont's limit, there was plenty of competition between the two.

Pont didn't confine his practice field antics to just place-kicking. Many was the time when he would jump into the backfield for demonstration purposes. Nobody really dared to take a shot at him, but there never was any question that he still had all of the moves which had endeared him to the Miami fans a few years earlier.

******

Pont's first season as a head coach would be considered a resounding success by most standards, but for him it had to be exceedingly frustrating. The record was 7-1-1, the only blemishes a 7-6 loss to George Washington in the opening game, and an agonizing 7-7 tie at Bowling

Green.

As I recall, opening game jitters and all, Miami didn't play extremely well in the George Washington game. However, a fourth-quarter rally did put the Redskins in a position to tie. In fact, everyone thought the score had been tied at 7 when Don Smith's conversion attempt split the uprights. But one of the officials detected holding on the Redskins. When Smith tried it again from 15 yards farther back, he came up short.

Pont on occasion has had a short fuse, and after the game with Bowling

On the sidelines, Pont was fiery.

Green, he exploded. Miami had been leading that game by a 7-0 score when the Falcons broke through to block a Redskin punt. The resulting touchdown and conversion produced the 7-7 tie. It was early the next week before Pont recovered. I know he still was seething when the team bus stopped at Findlay for the players' post-game meal. Pont didn't eat, and talking to him was out of the question.

"That probably was the toughest of all the losses," recalls Bill Mallory, senior captain of that team, who was to become Miami's coach himself 1969-73. "Tyin' Bowling Green meant that we would lose the title (Mid-American Conference championship) because we played one less game than Bowling Green."

When Mallory speaks of "all the losses," he's talking about two. In three years at Miami, he played in only two losing games: a 20-12 loss to Dayton the week after Miami beat Indiana in 1954, and the 1956 George Washington squeaker which was Miami's first loss under Pont. Yet under the circumstances, the 7-7 tie felt like a loss.

"He had tough feet to follow," says Mallory of Pont. "Even though he inherited a pretty experienced ball club, I don't think we were as good a team as the two previous years."

Miami had won two consecutive MAC championships under Ara and was expected to win a third under Pont. It was a bitter pill for the first-year coach, and he took it hard. At the time, there was no consoling John; but that experience at Bowling Green did lead to a series of classic confrontations between the Redskins and the Falcons, an intense rivalry which continues unabated to this day.

The first of those confrontations took place the very next year. A scheduling quirk dictated that the Redskins return to Bowling Green for a second consecutive year, but it mattered not. This was one of the times at Miami when Pont knew his team was ready.

"You always wonder how prepared you are — whether you've done everything you can," Pont has conceded. "But sometimes, because of the situation and the way the players react in practice, you know the team is ready to play."

For this 1957 Bowling Green meeting, Pont's team was more than ready, and even he was confident. Final score remained to be determined, but Miami would be on top.

That confidence underwent a severe test, but the suspense isn't the only reason I remember that game so vividly, recall my emotions as if it were yesterday.

It was my senior year in college. And as senior sports editor, I felt I was entitled to assign an underling to cover the game while I watched from the stands, for a change — with some friends, including the girl who later would become my wife.

We had great fun: fine football, fierce hitting, delightful companionship. But by halftime of this contest that looked so safe, the score still was tied, 7-7. Sound familiar?

Wondering whether my understudy was getting along all right under the developing suspense, I excused myself to visit the press box, promising Marian I'd return in plenty of time for the third quarter.

But I paused on the sideline to catch some action as that quarter started. That was my undoing. I was caught up in the excitement, my proximity to superb action, my fascination with the surge of play and indeed with the intensity of the coach as I paced the sidelines a few yards behind him.

I'd never admit I forgot the girl in the stands, but I have good reason now to believe she thought so.

Every time the ball changed hands, I determined to return to my seat in the stands. But there'd be another loud pop, another great play, another tense moment. And I'd pace some more.

Twice in that third quarter, Bowling Green penetrated to Miami's 24 — first to miss a field goal and later to have its leading ball-carrier stopped cold on fourth and one.

Miami had fumbled the ball away between those two threats. Now, with time winding down in the third quarter, Miami began a relentless march. Dave Thelen carried ten times, with additional rushes by Curt Gentry and Bill Miller. Play moved into the fourth quarter. After 13 plays, Miami had reached BG's four. Thelen managed only a couple in two tries. Pont sent Halfback Hal Williams inside, and he made the one-foot line. Then with everyone massed inside, Pont sent Williams wide for the score. However, a missed extra-point attempt left Miami clinging to a precarious 13-7 lead with 10 minutes left. I wasn't about to leave the sidelines.

Bowling Green battled back to manage first and goal at Miami's ten. But on fourth down at the one, Mack Yoho, the guy who had missed the extra point, led the charge that stopped the Falcons cold. In the five remaining minutes, I was pinned to the sideline by three more crises: BG forced us to punt from the end zone, it drove to our 20 before a penalty helped us stop them, and John Baker intercepted a pass to end another threat. Only then did I decide I could leave it to the Redskins and scramble back to find Marian.

She wasn't particularly overjoyed, but it could have been worse. It could have been a year earlier.

******

And yet another highlight of the Pont years, and this time it's a reminiscence of Nick Mourouzis, Miami '59, and wouldn't you know the subject is yet another Miami-Bowling Green game:

" . . . and finally we had a 21-14 lead, and there was about a minute to go or so . . . I can't remember the exact time . . . I know we called a quarterback sneak just to kill the time, but they were in a game or something. They veered the middle guard one way, the linebackers were blitzing, and the middle was just wide open. I'm not the fastest guy around, and I know I stumbled down to about the two-yard line, and we scored again to make the final score 28 points."

Mourouzis was Miami quarterback. These days, as head coach at DePauw University in Greencastle, Indiana, he still remembers that 1958 meeting with BG. After the previous season's thriller, now gunning for a second consecutive Mid-American Conference championship, the Redskins had fallen behind at the half, 14-0.

This time, Pont didn't wait until game's end to get mad. He had a few things to say at halftime. A quarter-century later, relaxing at his home overlooking the golf course at Greencastle, Mourouzis remembers:

"He spoke to us, and after he spoke to us, he must have hit on a nerve there, because inside the locker room, it was something that I'll never forget. I remember Willie Narduzzi (now a coach at Youngstown State) and several others . . . we were goin' around just about hitting one another . . . we really were. We were getting so fired up, and you could just feel the electricity and you could just feel that something touched us off on something that John told us . . . I can't remember the exact words now.

"When we went out on the field, on the sideline right before the kickoff in the second half, we were literally bangin' one another. We were throwin' forearms into each other's shoulder pads, and I'll never forget that. You talk about emotional peak, it was unbelievable."

Now the head coach at Youngstown State, Bill Narduzzi played for Pont, and was the prime initiator of the Cradle of Coaches Association.

Doyt Perry, the veteran Bowling Green coach, the dean of Conference coaches at the time, maintained that his team grew too conservative, trying to protect the two-touchdown lead. But Mourouzis remembers the emotion of the moment, and realizes even now, as he did then, that Miami was a team of destiny in the second half. The Redskins tied the score on their first two possessions of the half and built the lead to 21-14 early in the fourth quarter. That set the stage for Mourouzis' "sneak attack."

******

When Nick Mourouzis was a seventh-grader in Uhrichsville, Ohio, a teacher asked him if he would coach her fourth grade team. "I just really enjoyed that," he says. "I just felt that I'd like to be in charge of a group of young men, and from that day on I've always wanted to be a football coach."

That dream of being in charge of a group of young men was only a dream for a long, long time. Mourouzis was 44 years old, an assistant for 23 years, when he finally got a chance to do "what I always wanted to do."

It was his high school coach, Milan Chovan, a Miami grad, who introduced Mourouzis to Miami and persuaded Parseghian and Pont to take a chance on a quarterback who had been injured during the second game of his senior year and didn't play anymore.

Never a particularly gifted athlete in terms of speed or obvious physical attributes, Mourouzis was nevertheless a leader. He became team captain, president of Tribe Miami, the letterman's organization, and Outstanding Senior Athlete. Omicron Delta Kappa, leadership honor society, tapped him for membership. The Department of Physical Education named him its outstanding senior.

Obviously a man who has applied himself unfailingly to learn his craft, Mourouzis at Miami was impressed by the preparedness of men like George Rider, who even in the twilight of his coaching career, was a stickler for every detail.

The speed with which Rider's track class transpired, the notebooks of Parseghian and later Pont; these are memories of Miami which Mourouzis carries with him to this day.

"It was just a great school that prepared you well to become a teacher and a coach," says Mourouzis of Miami. "That's the philosophy, I guess, of the University and of the Department. I think they had outstanding teachers and coaches, and that rubs off on you. There's no question . . . you want to be like them. And everyone that leaves there hopes that some day he would coach there. They have fond memories of the place, and a lotta loyalty to Miami University."

This chronicle at this stage is dealing with coaches who were my schoolmates: Mallory, Mourouzis, Narduzzi, Yoho, LaSpina, Burton, Tom Dimitroff, Neil Putnam, Jerry Ippoliti, John Drew, Jerry Hanlon . . . Because we were students together, I viewed them then not as future coaches, but as contemporaries whose athletic feats became part of a winning tradition at Miami. It didn't dawn on me until much later that many of these people — like Parseghian, Pont, Cozza, Pagna and others before them — came from similar background and shared a common trait.

In the best sense of the word, that trait was toughness. Not crudity; just aggressiveness, resilience, ingenuity in a genuinely competitive nature. Mourouzis has a logical explanation:

"I'll tell you one thing. Most of us, when I look back on that era, were people from lower-income families. My folks came from the old country, and most of these people — our teammates that we played with — were from tough-background environments, and people that had a lotta pride and people that wanted to go on and succeed, and their parents looked up to them.

"We had . . . I'd call it ... a lotta personal pride to go on and do the best job you can and try to strive and work and climb the ladder, so to speak. We were tough, I'll tell you . . . not we were, but our teammates were a very tough breed."

When Nick Mourouzis sneaked through Bowling Green, he wore high-type shoes to protect the broken ankle he suffered as a junior.

Made tough by a burning desire to succeed, and their environment. These men were attracted to Miami first, not by the beauty of her autumn afternoons, nor by the pretty coeds who strolled the campus, but by others who were mainly products of similar environments.

Mourouzis' road to DePauw took him from Miami to Ohio University, where he helped in football as a graduate assistant while earning a master's degree. He next became football coach at Fairmont East High School, Kettering, Ohio. Then he went back to Ohio University as an assistant, and from there to Ball State University, Muncie, Indiana, again as assistant.

By 1965, Pont had returned from Yale to coach at Indiana, and Mourouzis was there to coach the defensive backs and pass defense when the Hoosiers went to the 1968 Rose Bowl. He stayed with Pont through the hard times at Indiana and the hard times at Northwestern. He was still at Northwestern when DePauw beckoned in 1981.

"I always wanted to be a head coach," says Mourouzis, "and felt I could be a success; but I never knew if I was ever going to get the opportunity."

He was considered on several occasions, and often was told he came in second. "But it's not like getting the job; coming in second is just like coming in last."

Now that he's top banana, he has a chance to reflect on his Miami experience, and to realize that Miami was at the top of the heap in those years because of the people recruited by Parseghian and Pont, and others before and after.

"One thing I've learned being an assistant all those years," maintains Mourouzis. "You're only as good as your own assistant coaches and your players. You've gotta have good players . . . there's a high correlation between recruiting and success."

Plus a bit of luck and the right timing. When he finally was annointed at DePauw, it was Mourouzis' second chance at the job. His predecessor, whom DePauw chose instead of Mourouzis two years earlier, left him plenty of talent when he departed for Penn. It was enough to give the first-year head coach, at age 44, as great a thrill as he has had in coaching.

There are big traditional games in college football every year. Texas-Oklahoma is one. Harvard-Yale is called The Game. On the West Coast, Stanford-Cal packs the same impact. In the Midwest, we hear of Michigan-Ohio State and Purdue-Indiana.

But in central Indiana, The Game matches DePauw against Wabash for the Monon Bell. They've played since 1889, second year of the Miami-Cincinnati rivalry.

DePauw entered that game, the last of the season, with eight victories and a single defeat. Wabash, on the other hand, was trying to extend a 24-game unbeaten string. When the stirring game ended, DePauw had stopped that streak by making a third-quarter touchdown stand up for a 21-14 victory.

To Mourouzis, it mattered not that the game did not mean a Big Ten championship, or the Rose Bowl.

"The coaching is the same. You have just as much fun at this level as you do as Division I — believe me. The thrill is just the same. When you win the key games and you stop a winning streak like we did two years ago against Wabash . . . when the stadium seats forty-five hundred and we had ten thousand seven hundred there . . . it was unbelievable.

"I mean when they're five or six deep around the field, and there's emotion with each play, it's unbelievable. And the intensity by the players . . . these players, there are no scholarships holding them out there so they're out there because they enjoy the game of football. And as long as you're playin' . . . as I tell 'em, 'It's the key thing. The football field's the same size here as it is at Ohio State or Notre Dame or Michigan, and the idea is to be playin.' And these young men have the same intensity, the same competitiveness, they hit just as hard . . . the only difference is that they're maybe an inch or two shorter and don't weigh as much and maybe are a step or two slow. But other than that, we have some tremendous football players."

And will continue to have, if Mourouzis has his way. His goal, and that of his players, is to win the Division III national championship, "to go to a bowl game."

To do that, Mourouzis knows he's going to have to recruit, and that obviously doesn't frighten him.

"It's easy to recruit here," he says, "because we have a great product. We've got a great academic school and fantastic facilities, and it's a friendly place, and with the winning tradition we have now in football, where we're striving for . . . we're pursuing excellence . . . it is easy to recruit, believe it or not."

Mourouzis, like Carm Cozza at Yale, sees similarities between Miami and DePauw. One of his advantages, which isn't possible at Miami, is that the number of recruits at a Division III school is limited only by the availability of uniforms, and the student's ability to meet DePauw's tough admission standards.

******

No matter what you might think, Miami football during the Pont coaching regime didn't revolve solely around Bowling Green. There were, as always, the traditional rivalries with Ohio University and Cincinnati. And there were great games; like the game against Purdue in 1962 that thrust Miami once again into the national spotlight.

During the Parseghian years, there had been other big Miami games, like the victory over Indiana or the win at Northwestern. But those paled when compared to the impact of Miami's 10-7 upset of Purdue.

Miami warmed up for its appearance at Ross-Ade Stadium in West Lafayette, Indiana, by beating Xavier, the Quantico Marines, Western Michigan and Kent State. At the same time, Purdue also was undefeated, but the most notable of those triumphs, over Notre Dame, had vaulted the Boilermakers into the top 10 in the national rankings.

Remembering how Parseghian had surprised Indiana under similar circumstances eight years earlier, I asked John how he wanted to play it when I made some media stops in Indianapolis and West Lafayette early in the week.

Coaches, as the media folk know, tend toward the conservative when asked to give a realistic assessment of their team's chances. Pont, though never one to pass up an opportunity to promote Miami football, was no exception. I was surprised, but pleased, when John decided to be very up front about Miami's hopes for victory.

"Tell 'em we'll show up," said Pont. "We have the talent, but we're not as deep as they are. We might not win, but if we don't wear down, we should be in the game."

It was fun to tell the newspapers about the 1962 Redskins. They were big, and they were talented. And they had a sophomore quarterback, a left-handed fellow named Ernie Kellermann, who was as brash as he was exciting.

All the publicity about the Miami team resulted in one of the largest gate sales in Purdue history. Nearly 50,000, the most people to see Miami play up until then, were there. The Indian summer weather didn't hurt. But the hot, humid day caused Pont to worry about the Redskins' staying power.

Miami drew first blood, when Jencks, the most productive placekicker

Bob Jencks (kicking) and Ernie Kellermann manufactured all 10 points in Miami's upset of Purdue in 1962.

in collegiate football that season, kicked a 31-yard field goal in the first quarter. Purdue came right back to take a 7-3 lead. Miami wasn't finished, though.

In fact, Kellermann and Jencks were about to collaborate on a play that will long be remembered in Miami football. Miami received the ensuing kickoff and immediately got backed into a corner. After a penalty, the Redskins faced a second-and-long situation from the 12-yard line.

The conservative approach called for a running play followed by a punt. Pont had other ideas, and he had a quarterback who didn't mind taking a chance. After the game, Pont would refer to "intelligent recklessness."

The play called for the left-hander to option to the left and for Jencks, at end, to try to sprint past the defense. If Jencks did gain the advantage, Kellermann's pass should hit him in full stride.

It worked so well that the only problem was whether Pont, who was urging Jencks to hang onto the ball as he passed the Miami bench, could stay out of Jencks' way as he provided escort service down the sideline. Jencks kicked the extra point to make the score Miami and Jencks 10, Purdue 7. However, more than 30 minutes remained and nobody, especially Purdue, expected that score to stand.

Throughout the second half, Purdue threatened. Courageously, Miami threw back every challenge. The huge Miami linemen, led by Tom Nomina, were beginning to wilt in the heat, resting only occasionally against the fresher Purdue troops. But one of the many heroes of the afternoon, Vic Ippolito, the senior quarterback who had lost his job to Kellermann, continually punted the Redskins out of trouble.

Scott Tyler, Miami's best running back through most of the day, still made his biggest contribution on defense. Twice in the closing minutes, he made plays that prevented a reversal of Miami's 10-7 margin: choking off a pitchout for no gain on fourth and two at the three-yard line, and then intercepting a pass at the 13 on the final play of the game.

As Miami fans poured out of the stands Nomina, bathed in sweat, found his coach, wrapped him in a big embrace, and with a knowing grin across his face, shouted, "For a minute, there, Coach, I thought they were gonna upset us!"

The celebration which began in the Miami locker room continued unabated well into the evening. By the time the Miami caravan — two buses and a couple of station wagons — reached College Corner, on the Ohio-Indiana line, a police escort took the Redskins into Oxford and a welcome home ceremony in Withrow Court. Celebrants poured out of the fraternity houses on Tallawanda Road and other students made their way down High Street from a night of partying.

With the aroma of Oxford's infamous 3.2 beer filling the old gymnasium, the student body saluted their conquering heroes for what would be acknowledged at year's end as college football's "Upset of the Year."

All of that failed to impress the Redskins' next opponent, as Miami fell to Ohio University, 12-6. Fortunately Miami regrouped, and on the strength of that upset of Purdue, earned an invitation to the Tangerine Bowl in Orlando, Florida.

When the game ended in West Lafayette, it was a signal to remove the goal posts from Miami Field and set them up in the middle of High Street, effectively limiting north-south traffic on Route 27 through town. When the Redskins returned to Withrow Court, Lowell Caylor displayed a souvenir and big Tom Nomina just grinned.

That turned out to be perhaps Miami's most humbling experience since the Wilton era, as the Houston Cougars saw Miami take a 7-0 lead, then roared back to score five touchdowns in the first half. The final score was 49-21. Miami licked its wounds and went home, but the impact of the Purdue "moment" wouldn't be forgotten.

******

It was Sunday night in Oxford, winter beginning to fade, spring on the way. On Melissa Drive in the Southern Knolls subdivision, four couples were gathered for bridge and conversation at the home of Jim and Wanda Goldey. The ringing phone interrupted the conversation.

Wanda called John Pont to the phone. He excused himself and the game continued. In the background though, I thought I heard John making travel arrangements. Immediately, I was more intent on eavesdropping than on the cards.

The telephone conversation ended and John returned to the table. As we all would admit a week or so later, everyone at the two tables had a pretty good idea what that phone call was all about, but nobody dared say anything. Least of all John.

The story of how John came to receive that Sunday-night telephone call which confirmed his selection as Yale's coach actually began a little more than a month after we returned from Orlando. In late January, Jordan Oliver quit as Yale's football coach. About two weeks later, John Brickels received from Delaney Kiphuth, Yale's director of athletics, a letter: might Pont be interested in the coaching position vacated by Oliver, and if so might Kiphuth have Brickels' permission to talk to him?

About the same time, Clint Frank was writing to Kiphuth. Frank was the third winner of the Heisman Trophy, and he remains one of Yale football's legendary figures. He also was one of my dad's best friends.

Clint Frank and Wallie Kurz, both active in the Chicago advertising community, golfing partners and sports enthusiasts, talked casually about the Yale coaching situation. Before long, Clint Frank began to take an interest and was suggesting to Kiphuth that he might want to look into this Pont fellow from Miami of Ohio.

That obviously had been Kiphuth's intention for some time, but it didn't hurt to have an endorsement from Clint Frank. By mid-February, Pont was on his way to New Haven to talk with the search committee chaired by Kiphuth. Pont was one of ten who had been invited.

Over lunch at Mory's, Pont told the assemblage something they wanted to hear. According to William N. Wallace, writing in **The Saturday Evening Post,** one of the interviewers wondered why John was even interested in the Yale position, as opposed to something in the Southeastern Conference or even the Big Ten.

"Those places stress what I don't like, recruiting, and play down what I do like, teaching." There were obviously other things which impressed the committee about John Pont, but Yale being Yale, his emphasis on teaching was most convincing.

The thing that impressed Pont about the interview was how relaxed and comfortable he was made to feel, how easily the conversation flowed. He still remembers how the history professor who was on the committee

In the basement of Withrow Court, John Pont packs his coaching gear for the trip to New Haven.

was extremely interested in Pont's evaluation of Purdue's Golden Girl.

"For God, for country, and for Yale." With white handkerchiefs waving, the Yale football team emerges from the tunnel of the 70,000 seat Yale Bowl to that chant, and Pont says that's an overpowering emotional experience.

There was another emotional experience during that 1963 season, Pont's first at Yale. As the coaching staff readied for the final practice before the first meeting with Harvard . . . The Game . . . news came from Dallas that President Kennedy had been shot. The game was postponed until the following week. One week later, despite the anguish felt by many, Yale achieved its first win over Harvard in three years, and the adulation for the newcomer from Ohio increased.

The next year marked the 600th victory in Yale's storied football history, a 54-0 whitewash of Lehigh. But the 1964 season, his second in a row which ended with six Yale victories, was to be John Pont's last in New Haven. He didn't know it at the time, but Carm Cozza was soon to have his turn.

******

Pont really had to struggle when Indiana University officials approached him about taking over the coaching reins at the Big Ten school. He was really enjoying life in New Haven, and he found the player-coach relationships with his Yale football players stimulating. And he knew that to survive in the Big Ten, he'd have to make a commitment to recruiting, the part of the game he least enjoyed.

On the other hand, he argued with himself, it was the Big Ten, and being a Midwesterner, he knew what that meant. And the Hoosiers were throwing down the gauntlet. Indiana was prepared to make a commitment to improving . . . to winning.

This time, it was the Oxford contingent that initiated the late-night telephone call. His Oxford friends knew the day of decision was approaching, and we were anxious, as we had been two years earlier. We could tell he was being challenged, and we knew that John Pont never backed away from a challenge.

The challenge was to restore some respectability to Indiana football; and as the football world would discover in 1967, Pont had the answer to that challenge. Feeling his way through the first two seasons while digging into recruiting in earnest, Pont was ready to make a move, with a big assist from three gifted offensive football players, Jade Butcher, John Isenbarger and Harry Gonso. From the very beginning, these three provided thrill after thrill for Hoosier fans, and heart-pounding, dramatic moments for Pont.

It was Cinderella in Cream and Crimson football uniforms. It was a series of miraculous, down-to-the wire finishes that captured the imagination of football fans in the Midwest, and later, around the country. The opening game, a 12-10 win over Kentucky, only whetted the appetite.

Four times in the next six games, Indiana won by five points or less, each time coming from behind. But with an undefeated record on the line in a game at Minnesota, the Hoosiers tripped on the way to the altar:

Minnesota 37, Indiana 7.

So it came down to the Old Oaken Bucket game against Purdue. Win and share the Big Ten title with Purdue and Minnesota, and earn a trip to the Rose Bowl. Or lose, and wait patiently, as Hoosier fans had been doing for a long time, 'til next year.

Purdue was favored, so Indiana reverted to its pattern of suspenseful finishes. This one was a dandy. Indiana knew it had to stop Purdue's All-America running back, Leroy Keyes, and they did. Offensively, Pont figured Purdue would be set to stop Indiana's outside game, which featured Isenbarger's sweeps, Gonso's run-pass option threat and Butcher's acrobatic pass-catching. So Indiana attacked inside and took a 19-14 fourth-quarter lead.

But the game was still in doubt when Isenbarger, who often through the course of the season, caused Pont's heart to flutter when he dared to run from punt formation, dug Indiana out of a hole with a 59-yard punt. His effort preserved the victory and touched off near-hysteria in Hoosierdom. The Cinderella Kids were going to the Rose Bowl, and much of the country celebrated.

Indiana succumbed to Southern Cal and O. J. Simpson, but the storybook season didn't diminish the brilliance of the star shining over John Pont. The American Football Coaches Association, and almost everyone else, named him 1967 Coach of the Year. He was on tour for Kodak and the AFCA when I ran into him in Dallas that winter.

He was relaxed and confident then; but over the next several years, Pont's coaching career would never regain the luster it had known in 1967. Less than a year later, when students everywhere were rising up in indignation, several blacks on Indiana's team, many of whom had played in the Rose Bowl, refused to practice or play until Pont agreed to certain demands. The protestors were demanding more playing time.

None of the charges ever was proven. It all didn't make much sense to Pont, and still doesn't. Mourouzis was on Pont's staff then.

"I remember this vividly," recalls Mourouzis. "Harry Edwards (civil rights activist and university professor from California) spoke across the country that year, and wherever he spoke . . . he spoke at our place two weeks before we had the boycott . . . it was just unbelievable times.

"At that time, if they weren't playin' it was because they were black. Basically, if you're objective from that standpoint, and you play the best player . . . that's the only way you could do it. If someone didn't see it that way, then he should quit. And of course, there were some guys that stood up for the cause and walked out, and tried to be the martyrs."

Those weren't the best of times for a lot of college football coaches. There were only a few bright moments in the rest of Pont's Indiana career, and when factions within the University began to erode his backing and that of the football program, he started looking.

What he found was Northwestern. It was looking for a successor to Alex Agase, who had accepted a similar position at Purdue. University support for football . . . athletics in general . . . hadn't changed much at Northwestern since the Parseghian years, and Pont never succeeded in effecting a change in his eight years at the school.

Pont came to Northwestern with the unofficial understanding that he would be in line for the athletic director's position. Ironically, the pro-Pont faction at Indiana had hoped that he would fill that role there, but it wasn't to be, as Mourouzis explained:

"I think John should be the athletic director there, no question he should've gotten it. But there's some petty jealousies in the upper echelon of the alumni and the administration that forced the change, there's no question. I still think to this day that John Pont should be the athletic director at Indiana University."

One year into his Northwestern tenure, the retirement of Athletic Director Tippy Dye opened the door for Pont to inherit that job, while retaining the coaching spot. One condition of the appointment was to bring in his own associate director, someone to handle the day-to-day administration of the department. He lured me from Texas to help him, and I was proud he asked me.

Like Ara Parseghian several years earlier, we weren't prepared for the woeful situation at Northwestern. When University president Robert Strotz told me he hoped Northwestern wouldn't get in the habit of going to the Rose Bowl because it might tarnish the University's academic image, I threw up my hands in despair.

To his everlasting credit, Pont never stopped working to bring winning football, and winning teams, to Northwestern. And in many areas, women's basketball, men's and women's tennis, and women's basketball, he succeeded. In football, he didn't.

But he did close out his coaching career the way any coach wants to . . . with a season-ending victory over an arch-rival. When Illinois fell to Northwestern on a dark November day in 1977, it brought down the curtain on 22 years of college coaching.

It's tough to hold the dual position of head football coach and athletic director. At Northwestern, it turned out to be virtually impossible. And I hold myself partially responsible.

John just laughed when I suggested that maybe I forced his retirement from coaching and caused him to devote all his energies to his administrative duties. A serious illness forced me to the sidelines for a year, and there was no one to pick up the slack.

After that enforced absence, my role had been altered, and I really had no choice but to resign from a situation which I regarded as hopeless almost from the outset. But if I thought it was hopeless, imagine how John felt when they asked him to leave two years later.

He handled his dismissal with class, but he was bothered and remains troubled by the obvious commitment on the part of the Northwestern administration to make up for past neglect.

Life, however, does go on, and life in Oxford has always been good to John Pont. So that's where he has chosen to live, where he and Weeb Ewbank can join the audience at the weekly Tomahawk Club luncheons, and root for his favorite team.

Like the man who preceded him at Miami, he's been in the insurance business, and he's president of a company that is manufacturing and marketing specialized athletic training equipment for development of the hamstring muscle.

You might guess who the corporate spokesman is. Fellow named Pont who wore number 42 when he wrote the book on running with the football at Miami of Ohio.

" . . . the last school that will drop it (football) will be Miami, and do you know why? Because if it gets down to the nitty-gritty, there'll be a helluva lot of us there knockin' on the door, and whatever has to be done will be done. We will have football. You know that."

Bo Schembechler, Miami class of 1951, head coach at Miami from 1963 through 1968; coach at the University of Michigan for 14 years and 1983 president of the American Football Coaches Association.

VIII

HIS NAME IS BO ... YA GOT IT

IT WAS SUNDAY afternoon in Ann Arbor, Michigan. The day before had marked the end of the first week of spring practice for the 1983 Michigan Wolverines. Sunday would be a good day to talk, Bo said, because he'd probably be in his office watching films of Saturday's scrimmage.

He had been napping when he escorted me into his spacious office on the second floor of the administrative offices which are a cornerstone of the enormous athletic complex at the edge of the Michigan campus. His suit jacket was flung over the back of the couch because after church, he'd come directly back to the office.

The situation was altogether too familiar. Bo Schembechler's life revolves around football. In the spring, and in the fall when it's time to practice football, diversions are not acceptable. Occasionally they need to be tolerated, but he'd rather they'd go away.

Millie, Bo's wife, and their 13-year-old son, Shemmy, understood. Shemmy's two-week spring vacation had just begun, and knowing Dad would be preoccupied anyway, they had headed South. So there was time, as a winter snow storm paid a final visit on the first day of spring, to talk about Miami and the Cradle of Coaches.

There's reason for concern, cautions Bo as we visit, because high school football faces serious problems . . . problems which are a reflection of our troubled economy.

"I'm producing no coaches, Bob," says Bo. "I don't produce coaches like I used to. First of all, there are no high school jobs out there. The declining enrollment at the high school level . . . the teacher unions will not allow them to hire coaches . . . it's not the game it used to be . . . The problem, particularly here in the Midwest, is that the emphasis on high school football is declining because we can't place the coaches . . . so that particular era may be over."

For emphasis, Bo points out the case of Pioneer High School in Ann Arbor, a school of 2,500 enrollment, with only one coaching position available, and that for a man who teaches just a half-day. "Every other coach they got, they pick up off the street."

But what really hits home is the realization that Barberton High School, back in his old hometown in northeastern Ohio, is perilously close to dropping football as a varsity sport.

"The town's almost a ghost town," moans Bo. "They've lost their industry. And they've had four or five consecutive millage failures."

Parenthetically, Schembechler acknowledges that he personally addresses his own placement problem by retaining recent graduates who are interested in coaching on his staff as graduate assistants, then trying to move them into college coaching positions as spots become available. But at the high school level, it's a dead-end street.

And what does that mean as far as the Miami coaching legend is concerned?

"That classification of school such as the Mid-American Conference, that level of competition, is in trouble financially. I mean they don't have the resources. And people don't go to the games. A lotta the students don't go to the games," says Bo. "They can't fill their stadiums.

"That's particularly true in sports other than football, because football still is the greatest spectator sport there is. I mean that is a happening."

And as far as Bo Schembechler is concerned, it will always happen at Miami.

"I mean of all the places where we're gonna have football, we're gonna have it at Miami," admonishes Schembechler, who is seldom at loss for words. "But the problem is . . . right now it's a sectional problem in the Midwest. The economy is the thing that's really hurting us now, but there are a million little things that are involved there."

Not the least of those little things which Bo sees as a threat to the game which has been so good to him, the game he loves so much, is the problem of protective equipment. He points out that the number of helmet manufacturers has dwindled from twelve to two.

There have been liability suits, and helmet manufacturers are going out of business. "They will not even guarantee you helmets in '84," says Schembechler.

"No matter how you add it up," he continues, "there will be nine to eleven catastrophic injuries in football . . . nine in high school and two in college . . . And they'll blame it on the helmet. The helmet doesn't have a damn thing to do with it."

Schembechler maintains it's not possible to play a game that's as rough as football and avoid injuries. The problem, he says, goes back to understaffing at the high school level, with a result "there are unqualified people to teach a game like this."

However, counters Schembechler, "for every football player that's hurt, there will be 27 catastrophic injuries in automobiles . . . for the same age group that would be playing football. But people don't understand that."

When Schembechler speaks out like that, it's in his role as chief administrator of one of the most successful intercollegiate football programs in the United States. It's a role he is comfortable with, but he is well aware that "I've got too many irons in the fire . . . I'm runnin' too big an operation."

In spite of the enormous demands on his time, the responsibility for a much larger staff, with specialists for every conceivable function, he still enjoys it.

"The alternative," he says, "is to not be able to do any of the coaching, and you live for the coaching. Just like now. Spring practice . . . what a joy . . . what a joy. We had scrimmage in the stadium . . . had fun . . . Saturday . . . ya know. And that's still fun to me.

"And you're always around kids. You've got thousands of problems with 'em today. Seems like kids have a lot more problems today. What was the alternative if you didn't stay out for football at Miami? You had to go home. What else were you gonna do?

"Do you realize that we went through school and never even . . . probably never discussed dope. Did we? I don't remember it even being discussed. The only thing I ever remember is drinkin' a barrel of 3.2 beer."

Football . . . the practice and the games . . . is Schembechler's escape from the pressures of molding the successful Michigan teams which have won or shared in 10 Big Ten championships in 14 years, have never won fewer than eight games in a season, and in the decade of the Seventies, won 96 of 109 games, losing 10 and tying three, the best record in the country over that span.

It's a pressure that he has been able to cope with, even after suffering a heart attack on the eve of the 1972 Rose Bowl and subsequent successful heart by-pass operation. But there's no doubt he sees his job in a different light today than he did in his early years in coaching.

"The demands today, Bob, make it (coaching) a lot less attractive than it used to be when I first started. With the tremendous exposure and the emphasis on fillin' your stadium, a coach today . . . he's gotta be able to fill the stadium, he's got to stay within the rules, he's got to graduate every single guy he brings in . . . he's gotta do that . . . it's an impossible task.

"He's got to be morally better than any faculty person on the campus. His players have to be morally better than any other students on campus. And you gotta be a great p.r. guy . . . you know representing the university well, and all of that. . .and then you gotta win all your games."

That seems a harsh way of looking at it, but Schembechler sincerely believes that the coaching fraternity is being backed into a corner.

"Sad, but true," he says. "I mean, you're almost in a no-win situation . . . you're almost at that point."

His record as a coach . . . never a losing season in 20 years . . . and his stature among his coaching brethren give Schembechler license to speak his mind on many issues relative to his profession. It's a responsibility he doesn't take lightly nor shirk.

As we talked, Schembechler was reminded that on the preceding Thursday, he had had to leave practice to attend to one of those administrative duties which rankle him so. As president of the American Football Coaches Association, he had been called to Washington to testify before the Senate Judiciary Committee investigating the so-called Herschel Walker Bill.

Schembechler doesn't need a prod to plead the case for college football. Indeed, he is most outspoken on the virtues of the game and what it can mean in later years to those who play football as undergraduates.

His message on behalf of college football was simple and to the point. The mission of coaches like him and Joe Paterno of Penn State, who also testified, is not to develop professional football players. The task is to develop the student-athlete, to prepare him well for a productive and meaningful life after graduation. It's a mission Schembechler and others in the Miami tradition have long understood.

For those like Herschel Walker who might come along and be urged to leave the college campus before their class graduates, Schembechler and Paterno were seeking protection from the "unscrupulous agents who swarm all over the college campuses."

After Paterno and Schembechler had testified for a couple of hours, Ed Garvey, executive director of the National Football League Players' Association was the next to testify.

"I had to grab my bags and leave the room," explains Schembechler, "but I heard him as he got up there. Do you know what his first statement was? 'I want the committee to understand that when you listen to Joe Paterno and Bo Schembechler you're not listening to the typical college coaching situation . . . that most of the colleges are basically minor league pro teams. They are recruited with the idea that they will make them into professionals and the coaches use that as a . . . and he goes on and on because he's against the bill."

Schembechler bristles when he even thinks about agents and Herschel Walker. He has made it clear that agents are not welcome on the Michigan campus . . . at least until a player's eligibility has been completed and his graduation has been assured.

Without question, Schembechler will use his term as president of the AFCA to sell the virtues of college football to those who would dare to cast a dissenting vote.

"College football," he says, "has been such a tremendous draw because, Bob, of all the athletic spectacles . . . the sports spectacles . . . To get up and drive on a college campus and have a tailgate picnic and go into the game . . . there's a different caliber crowd at a college stadium than you find in the pros.

"And the bands, and the enthusiasm, you're not gonna match that . . . college football is excitement. Even if I were to retire tomorrow, my fall weekends would be in college stadiums, not pro."

Schembechler is angry about the recent developments in professional football, and as president of the AFCA, he seems determined not only to make waves, but to take some action. In 1969, Bo was recognized by his peer group as Coach of the Year. He seems unconcerned about that when he says:

"The American Football Coaches Association has been a nice, docile group of guys . . . that have a clinic every year and roll over and play dead. This is the first time in 50 years they took one of our undergraduates . . . pulled him right out, unceremoniously. Can't deny he didn't wanna go. The agent put him in such a position that . . . he couldn't compete, no matter what he did . . .

"He doesn't wanna be there. If the truth were known that kid doesn't wanna be there. You pay a guy a million dollars, if he doesn't like where he is, I don't give a damn, that isn't gonna make him happy. That does not make him happy." The words came staccato from his lips, for emphasis.

"So don't think you did him a great favor," Bo continues, "by sendin' him to the pros, because that kid was havin' a great career and enjoyin' himself in college."

Obviously, Bo doesn't blame Walker. He blames the system which has allowed the agents to capitalize on the young man's, and the system's vulnerability.

"It's time," he says, "that we confront these people, and let 'em know in no uncertain terms . . ."

But there's a rub. Any tough-guy posturing is tempered by the vulnerability of many in the organization which Schembechler leads.

"There's so many guys out there coaching football with skeletons in their closets that can't say anything . . . they can't shoot their mouths off . . . because they can't draw a lotta attention to what they're doin'.

"Because if somebody were to go in there and pry . . . like for example . . . the reason they don't come out and get mad as hell on the Herschel Walker issue is because somebody's gonna come out and check to see what the hell they're doin' academically in their program and find out they ain't doin' anything.

"That's just like when there's a lotta cheating and things goin' on, coaches don't get up in arms because there's too many of them with skeletons in their closets that can't afford to do it. And so we've been the type of group that hasn't been very forceful . . . hasn't been very tough. And I think that should change."

Will it? Can it? One wonders. Schembechler has some ideas, but one man alone isn't likely to be able to affect a change. Bo understands that.

"See what we have to do," he begins. "We've got $2.7 million in our treasury we never use . . . just draws interest. What we gotta do is hire a public relations firm. We gotta hire lawyers, we gotta have lobbyists . . . we gotta have guys that are ready to go in there when somethin' like this is pulled, and we need some legislation in Washington . . . let's get some guys in there doin' somethin' for us.

"I can't do it. I've got a job here. I mean, it can't be done unless we hire some outside help."

The question is: How is that best accomplished? And all of a sudden Bo finds himself confronted with the docile nature of the AFCA and the passive posturing of those members who have skeletons in their closets.

Remember Charley McLendon, who was on the LSU staff when Paul Dietzel came to Baton Rouge?

"Well, we have an executive director, Charley McLendon," says Bo, "who's a nice guy, but Charley went down to . . . I set him up, I said 'I'm not goin' to any meeting with liars.' So I said, 'Charley, you go in and talk to 'em (the United States Football League people), and make no agreements with 'em, and you tell 'em we are bleeped, that they are in trouble.'

"He goes down there and lays over . . . rolls over dead. 'We have an agreement', McLendon told me. 'They're not gonna do it again.'"

Schembechler just chuckles: "See what I mean? He doesn't know how to be tough. He doesn't know how to . . . you know, you've got to make an ass out of yourself sometimes, because you gotta make 'em say, 'Hey, remember one thing. If you do that, you gotta deal with that son of a bitch.' You can't be Mister Nice Guy. I mean they're gonna walk all over you."

Schembechler has one more thing to say about the evils in his sport, and this time it's more personal.

"Let me ask you this," he says rhetorically. "Where would I have fit in at Texas A & M? If I'd gone to Texas A & M, I would have gone to become a millionaire. Period. No other reason in the world, because there's no . . . That would have been a tragic mistake."

How seriously did he consider moving?

"I had a ten-year contract, without all the perks, at a quarter of a million dollars a year." Sure, he considered it. And he stayed at Michigan.

******

It's a long way from Barberton's east side to a chance at millionaire status, especially if you're an offensive lineman wearing #74, instead of a running back wearing #34. Bo's journey started in seventh grade at Oakdale Grade School.

He wouldn't be ready for high school competition for two more years, but in the seventh grade he went down to the high school and "got those guys to let me go out for football."

"I used to get out of school in the seventh and eighth grade, and I would run and jog and walk fast at least five miles to get to football practice down at the stadium. I did that all the way up until basketball practice started at the grade school . . . so by the time I got to high school, the guys all knew me. The coaches knew me, everybody knew me . . . I made sure I played."

There was some justification for Bo's daily venture down to the stadium, since Oakdale didn't have a junior high team. And until he got to the high school, indeed as a freshman, he was a wingback in Barberton's single wing formation.

By the time his sophomore year rolled around, Bo learned from his coach, "a great old, tough coach . . . a Heidelberg guy," that he wasn't fast enough to play in the backfield. But Karl Harter said he needed some help in the line.

"I said, "Where in the line do you need some help?" He said 'I need guards.' I said, 'Well, put me down as a guard.'"

Bo played guard as a sophomore and junior, but then Miami intervened. A Miami graduate, Harry Strobel, replaced Harter as coach, and moved Schembechler to tackle. The other tackle was a fellow who went on to Notre Dame and starred professionally with San Francisco. His name was Bob Toneff.

Harry Strobel was a Miami contemporary of Paul Brown, and he was a strong influence when Sid Gillman came to Barberton in 1947 to offer Bo a scholarship. Bo had been recruited by Ohio State, but "as a marginal player, because of size, and on the visit there, I could tell that."

When Gillman was talking to Schembechler about Miami, Harry Strobel was there. "I told Harry, 'Coach, I don't know anything about

Miami.'"

"He said, 'Miami's good. You go down to Miami.'"
"And then my mother said, 'You go to Miami.'"
"So I got on the bus and went down to Miami."

Bo did pay one visit to the campus before he actually enrolled, and he remembers being housed in a third floor room of the old Phi Delt house, right on High Street, "and every guy in the house came in drunk that night. It was a wild night."

George Blackburn, who was later to succeed Gillman as Miami's head coach, showed Bo around the campus and introduced him to Joe Madro, who became Bo's first line coach at Miami. Bo feels he was a part of what may have been one of the biggest, and perhaps best, class of freshman football recruits at Miami.

"Now that year," recalls Bo, "Sid had brought in, my God, unbelievable . . . I mean we had like two-three hundred on the freshman team. Figure it. It was right after the war. A lotta of the guys gettin' out of the service."

Obviously, not all of those who came stayed. But Gillman, in his own way, had a lot to do with that. Because when he wound up at Cincinnati two years later as the Bearcats' head coach, he staged a recruiting raid that lured some of his 1947 Miami recruits to the Cincinnati campus.

Others, like Tom Pagna, and Ara Parseghian, and Wayne Gibson, have referred to the intensity of the Miami-Cincinnati rivalry during those years, particularly after Gillman defected. Here's how Bo puts it:

"Half (of that class) ended up playin' for Miami and half for Cincinnati. See, he took that group and split us . . . Sid came back and recruited us, and half of 'em went to Cincinnati. And then when we played my senior year, it was Miami against Miami.

"Danny McKeever was Miami, Jimmy Driscoll was Miami, Jack (Bear) Campbell was Miami . . . all the guys who played for UC were on our freshman team. It was an inter-squad game . . . and it was a war . . . an absolute war. That was the "Snow Bowl" game . . . ya got it."

It's probably one of his teaching techniques. When Bo wants to make sure one of his student-athletes fully understands the lesson he's trying to impart, Bo seeks affirmation of total comprehension. 'Ya got it' is a frequently-used phrase in any conversation with Bo.

The "Snow Bowl" game is one of those memories of Miami that Bo will cherish forever.

"It was so unique," recalls Bo, "it wasn't funny. That was a very, very special game. Ya' know, all the time that I coached at Miami, when we used to play Cincinnati at Nippert Stadium, I'd always think about when we went down to that game on the bus, and the snow was fallin', and you know, we got in there in time to play the game and everything and then we couldn't get out of there. Nobody came back home. You couldn't get back home. We spent two days in Cincinnati."

You will recall Woody Hayes' reference to that game in an earlier chapter. Schembechler certainly remembers the penalty called on him on the draw play that took away one of the five touchdowns Miami scored in the first half of that game. But it was the circumstances and the setting

. . . and the stakes . . . that made the game memorable.

There was the bad feeling brought on by the wholesale transfers, and finally Miami's awareness that Cincinnati already had a Sun Bowl invitation and Miami, in spite of an 8-1 record, was out in the cold . . . and on this late-November Saturday . . . the snow.

"We had nothing"' recalls Bo. "We went in there, and we went in with great resolve. And we beat the daylights out of 'em, and came out of that game with the Salad Bowl bid."

When Woody recalled that Snow Bowl game at the team's 30th reunion a few years ago, he made mention of the little man who "played like a madman" that day. Bo says that John Pont **always** played like that.

"Pont was our horse," says Bo. "Ya' see, we had Pont and Bailey (Boxcar) in the same backfield. Pont, of all the players I've ever seen . . . of the guys I've ever seen play football as a back, you know, like the horse, the guy you're gonna rely on to win it for you, was the greatest competitor I ever saw. Ever saw.

"I never saw a man in coaching . .. now maybe it's because I was a kid myself, too, and I looked at him . . . one kid lookin' at another, not necessarily looking at him from the coaching standpoint . . . but I've never seen a guy get ready for a game mentally like he did, or play it like he did."

The amazing thing about Pont, as Schembechler remembers his playing days, was that he did it every game. He'd get off to himself, Bo recalls, and just concentrate on the task at hand.

"I've never seen him play it any other way."

That intensity carried over into coaching and, thinks Schembechler, demonstrates a trait of Miami-trained coaches that is admirable.

"Nobody . . . nobody . . . is a moralist more than John Pont. Nobody. I mean if this is green," says Schembechler, jabbing his finger at the desk, "it's green and it isn't any other shade of green, or if that's black, it's black. Am I right? I mean we ain't wavering six inches from one side to the other. That's it. That's the way it is."

With that salute to the man he succeeded at Miami, Schembechler was pointing out an important characteristic of the men who have maintained the Miami coaching legend over the years. Each, in his own way, has been unwavering in the primary mission of the college coach, the complete education of the players who come under his influence.

Bo, I'm sure, alluded to such characteristics in his testimony in front of the Senate Judiciary; but talking about Miami in his office that Sunday afternoon in the spring of 1983, the clarity of this man's belief in his Miami associates, near and far, before and after, was unmistakable.

"It's interesting from my standpoint," he began, "because I think the guys that have, in the time span that I coached there and played there and have coached since . . . when you talk about coaching with Woody, or Ara, or John. or any of the guys that have come out of there since I've been there . . . Bill, Dick, Tom Reed . . . all of those guys have been strong character people.

"Never bending the rules, player-oriented type coaches that are interested in the people that they coach, academically-oriented guys . . .

not, you know, keep 'em eligible, play 'em and forget 'em . . . and I believe all of that is important.

"Because when they came out of Miami as a player, and then usually have been associated . . . their careers were spurred on by other Miami guys . . . I mean they were hired by other Miami people ... when you stop to consider . . . you see I worked with Ara, I worked with Woody . . . then you develop an attitude toward coaching that is wholesome.

"No matter how big-time you get, it's still a game, and it's in a college setting, and it's important that the guys that play have a meaningful experience. In other words, as we all relate back to Miami, we relate to some of the greatest years of our lives.

"The guys we played with, the teams we played on, the people that coached us, and all of that has had a tremendous effect on the way we coach. Regardless of how big in college football you got, you always wanted it to be that type of an experience for the guys that play, and you never short-changed the academic aspect of it.

"Now I believe that . . . I honestly believe . . . I'm sure I'm right . . .

Paul Schudel, a tackle who played for Bo, works for him now on the Michigan staff.

that almost all of those guys feel that way. If Tom Reed, for example, after coming out and coaching with me, did it any other way, I'd kill him. I mean if he's not that kind of a coach. Now whether you like his personality, or the way he coaches, or what kind of system he runs . . . that's not important. The important thing is does he coach the game the way it oughta to be coached?"

Schembechler, outspoken advocate of student-athletes earning degrees, often is criticized by his detractors and others for what they call a holier-than-thou attitude. He remains steadfast, if for no other reason than it is the way he was taught.

When he returned to Miami as head coach in 1965, Schembechler was his own academic counselor. He advised his athletes on courses which would lead to graduation and, when necessary, called a professor or two to learn whether those athletes were progressing satisfactorily.

Even before that, when he was single and an assistant coach at Presbyterian and Bowling Green and Northwestern, and finally at Ohio State, he counseled the athletes in their academic pursuits. So when he got to Michigan, he knew what his priorities would be.

"When I came here, he says, "I knew that I'm not dealing with a school that is going to be tolerant of a big-time college program that doesn't emphasize academics and graduation. That some day, they were going to come to me and say, 'Well, what are you doing academically to help these youngsters . . . proper counseling, how many are getting degrees?'

"For ten years, Bob, nobody ever said a word to me. Nobody ever did a thing. For ten years, I kept right on doing . . . havin' the transcripts here, checkin' the graduation rate, callin' guys back that went into pro ball, havin' to get them some assistance if they didn't have any money, and, you know . . . not all of them graduate but a helluva lot more, percentage-wise, than the regular university . . . and I did all that until, just this last four years, there's been all this emphasis on how many you graduate . . . ya got it . . . so I was prepared. I mean there isn't any way they could get me, ya' know. There's no way they could say this guy played for four years and didn't even . . . well, he's not close to graduation.' And so that has paid off."

Recalling Tom Pagna's Graduation Day breakfast conversation with Jim Gordon, I was wondering if Bo, in his playing days at Miami, and later as a coach, ever had any occasion to doubt that a player was there to pursue a degree.

Granting that times are different, and it may be like comparing apples and oranges, Schembechler says that most of his contemporaries, with a few notable exceptions like Pont and Cozza, and earlier Parseghian, went directly from Miami into coaching. But they did graduate.

Schembechler points out that at Miami, unlike Michigan, a player is not likely to be looking at a career in professional sports.

"If you don't get a degree, where are you gonna get a job?" he asks.

And, surmises Schembechler, Miami's graduation rate in his days, like Michigan's today, is extremely high.

"I don't know what their (Miami's) graduation rate is, but I'll guarantee you it's very, very high. It was with the players on our team, I know that."

Schembechler notes the scarcity of blacks on the Miami teams of that period. Boxcar Bailey, the great running back from nearby Hamilton, was a rarity, a point which did not go unnoticed when Parseghian made his stand in the Wichita hotel in 1951.

"Let's go back, first of all, to where Miami was recruiting when they first started," continues Schembechler. "You see Miami . . . when I was there, for example, never did a lot of heavy recruiting in disadvantaged schools. They never brought a lot of black players to Miami.

"Boxcar Bailey and Billy Harris were the only two guys that I can recall on our teams. Then, following the Fifties, they started to recruit heavily in areas where they had some disadvantaged kids."

That changed to a marked degree once Parseghian, and then subsequent Miami coaches, brought to the campus athletes like Tom Jones, the great tackle and NCAA shot put champion, or Sherman Smith, the Seattle Seahawks great star, and Bob Hitchens, the running back whose number 40 rests beside number 42 in the Miami trophy case. Hitchens is a Miami assistant.

One early recruit in the Fifties was an Oxford home towner, Tirrel Burton, who returned from four years in the paratroops to become one of Parseghian's great ball carriers during his three Miami years. Burton's 84 points in 1955 make him, along with Bob Jencks, the second highest single-season point-producer in Miami history. With Tom Pagna, his 151 career points put him sixth on Miami's all-time list.

Burton has long been a trusted aide of Schembechler, serving on his Miami staff and now at Michigan. He is one of three Miami graduates on Bo's current staff. The others are Jerry Hanlon, a 1956 alumnus, and Paul Schudel, a 1966 graduate who played on Bo's Miami teams.

Those three are but symbols of one of Schembechler's strengths as a head coach. At Miami, and at Michigan, he has surrounded himself with assistants, both Miami graduates and others with promise, who have moved rapidly up the coaching ladder. While there may be some truth to his claim that his production of coaches has reached a dead end, there is no denying that coaches with the Schembechler stamp out of Miami are legion.

It all started with his early Miami staffs, which included Dave McClain (son-in-law of Bowling Green Coach Doyt Perry referred to in an earlier chapter), who went from Ball State to the University of Wisconsin; Jim Young, a highly successful coach first at Arizona, then Purdue, and now beginning his first year at Army; Dick Tomey, now head coach at Hawaii, who Bo predicts is soon likely to land a prestigious position on the mainland, and John Mackovic, Kansas City Chiefs skipper.

There was Jerry Wampfler, a 1954 Miami graduate who coached at Colorado State and is now an assistant with the Philadelphia Eagles; Larry Smith, now the head coach at Arizona; Chuck Stobart, coach at Toledo for several years and now head coach at the University of Utah; Joe Galat, 1962 Miami graduate who now coaches the Montreal Concordes in the Canadian League; and of course the two Miami graduates who followed as head coaches at Miami, Bill Mallory and Tom Reed.

Weeb Ewbank and Paul Brown, among others, early on identified this as how coaching becomes a fraternity unto itself. Bo tells a story about Michigan's loss to North Carolina in the Gator Bowl in 1979 that serves to illustrate further the feeling of brotherhood. He was reminded of the incident as he remembered that two of his Miami players, Denny Marcin and Jack Himebauch, were on Dick Crum's Tar Heel staff.

"It's funny," he relates, "we got one guy here . . . real negative guy . . . writing, you know . . . always on me about somethin', tryin' to find somethin' wrong. Well, we played North Carolina in the Gator Bowl that year . . . Dick was coaching there and Denny Marcin and Jack Himebauch were up in the press box (on the phones) and they beat us.

"And so he comes running into the interview and he says, 'I heard the North Carolina coaches on the press box elevator comin' down. They were laughin' at you. They were laughing that they beat you.' I said, 'You are absolutely insane. Those kids played for me. You think they're not excited about beatin' me? You gotta be outta your mind. They're not laughin' at me.' I said I think they still have great respect for me and

Bo Schembechler's early Miami coaching staff included, from left to right, Jerry Stoltz, Dave McClain, Jack Hecker, Joe Galat, Jerry Wampfler, Jim Young and Bo. All but Stoltz are still in coaching. McClain is the head coach at Wisconsin, Young is the new head coach at Army and Galat is the head coach of the Montreal Concordes in the Canadian Football League.

Denny Marcin, now on Dick Crum's staff at North Carolina, listens to Bo on the sidelines during Schembechler's first game as Miami's head coach.

everything. They're just excited about beating me. 'No, no, they were laughin'.

"And so those guys heard that from other newspaper guys that were around there, and Marcin and Himebauch were upset . . . what the hell, like they were gonna make fun of me. See, guys that weren't involved in that kind of association would never understand."

******

Once Schembechler got to Miami as an undergraduate, there was never a doubt that he was going to be a coach. That was why he was there. Sure, he'd been a pretty good southpaw pitcher for the Redskins until he hurt his arm playing football, but he was at Miami to pursue his dream of becoming a football coach. And the pursuit of that dream was an adventure.

First, he tackled an advanced degree at Ohio State, and was the first of Woody Hayes' graduate assistants. Then he got caught up in the Korean Conflict, and spent a couple of years in the Army at Fort Rucker in Alabama.

The first year, he was a player-coach, and by making himself middle linebacker so somebody else would "keep all those guys off me," made All-League. But he was ready to give it up the second year, when the Chief of Staff got wind of the fact that he wasn't planning to play a second year.

"The next thing I know I'm before the Chief of Staff," says Bo, "to explain why I'm not playin' football. I said, 'Well, my knees are bad,' and he said, 'Well, you can coach, can't you?' and I said, 'Yeah, I can coach.' He said, 'All right, you coach.''

It was on the way back from being released from service early . . . the war had ended, the post was being shuttered, and he had less than six months left on his tour of duty . . . in June of 1954 that a bizarre combination of circumstances led to a unique coaching and cultural experience.

"Not anticipating that I'm gonna get out," explains Bo, "I had no job. So I had an old wreck of a car down there in Alabama . . . and I threw all my gear in the car and I'm drivin' north alone, whistlin', man, "I'm out of the service,' and feelin' good, see.

"I said, 'Well, I'll stop in and see my old buddy Arnsparger.'"

Schembechler and Bill Arnsparger, you will recall, had been teammates on the 1950 Miami team, and Bill was an assistant to Blanton Collier at Kentucky. Bill had been Collier's high school coach at Paris, Kentucky, before Collier went on to assist Paul Brown with the Cleveland Browns. Now teacher and pupil were reunited in Kentucky, this time at Lexington. And an ex-serviceman wandered in unannounced.

Schembechler had come to know Collier earlier on visits to Paris with Arnsparger. The three would spend an afternoon at Collier's house talking football, with the two undergraduates demonstrating "some of the basic techniques that he (Collier) knew were from the Gillman notebook."

As the three visited again that June afternoon in 1954 in Lexington, Bo was explaining that he didn't expect to be separated from the Army until

August, and he was without a job. Collier interrupted.

"He said," remembers Bo, "'Well, wait a minute. I know a guy who's lookin' for a line coach at Presbyterian College in Clinton, South Carolina.' I said, 'Oh, my God, I'm goin' back to the South.'"

Bill Crutchfield was Collier's friend who needed an assistant at Presbyterian. The only other football assistant was the basketball coach, Norm Sloan, who eventually went on to coach at North Carolina State and Florida and Bo says "he never helped us a lick."

So Bo continued north to Barberton, said a quick hello to his folks, packed his bags and headed for Clinton and "the absolute best deal in America."

And, like it was yesterday, Schembechler proceeds to recall his first full-time collegiate coaching experience, one that resulted in a 6-3 record after a decade of losing. But that's only a part of the tale.

"When I went in there," he begins, "I'm single, and I'm lookin' for a room. The town's like ten thousand people. The banks, the cotton mill, the college and everything . . . it's all the Bailey family . . . Well, Mrs. Bailey, and her daughter, Mrs. Marshall, whose husband was deceased, and her daughter, who was a teen-age girl, all lived in Boxwood Gardens, this huge, southern home in town.

"They had these boxwood trees . . . you could hit a five-iron and not get it out of the yard . . . and they had all the servants . . . the butler and the maid and the cook and the gardener and all that . . . well, I'm lookin' for a place to stay, they're lookin' for somebody, some man, single man, that teaches at the college, to live at the house, just so it's known that there's a man livin' at the house."

Bo called and was invited over to take a look. After "tea and crumpets" and socializing, Bo asked if he could see the room, which he says was "a delight. Everything was beautiful."

The room was thirty dollars a month, explained Mrs. Bailey, and finally after some more small talk, Bo got up to leave. As he was driving away, Mrs. Marshall leaned over the porch rail and said, "Mr. Schembechler, for you, it's twenty five dollars a month."

Bo laughs. "She let it be known I'm the choice."

He went out to move in, and the butler appeared.

Bo continues: "He unloads all of my stuff, puts it in the drawers, shines my shoes, takes the dirty clothes down to wash 'em . . . and I sit there and have supper with the ladies . . . the three ladies. I come down to give 'em the check, she tears it up. They don't take the money . . . ya got it.

"Then, I'm invited to breakfast. 'Would you like to eat breakfast? You're leaving just as we're ready to eat at 7:30 in the morning . . .' I said, 'Sure,' so it ends up I come down every morning during the week and I sit at the head of the table . . . and the teen-age girl was beautiful, she was usually away at a private school . . . and Mrs. Bailey and Mrs. Marshall, her mother . . . and the Bible is open to the passage that I'm to read.

"So I come down every morning and I read the Bible to the ladies, and we say our prayer, and we have our breakfast, and they say 'Goodbye, Bo' and I say goodbye to the ladies and I'm off to work. Every night I come home, the refrigerator has my sandwich and milk and everything ready for me."

Then there was the brand new car that Mrs. Bailey bought, a Chrysler New Yorker, and was worried about breaking it in, so she asked Bo to do it for her. Not wishing to hurt her feelings, he obliged. And there was the time when the ladies became concerned about Bo's social life, and decided to throw a party for him.

"'We just don't feel,' said the ladies to Bo, 'that, you know you're single and handsome,' ya' know, they're givin' me all this, 'We want to throw a party for you.' I said 'Ah,' and they said 'Well, let's do that.' OK, so we throw a party.

"The elite from Spartanburg and Columbia and Greenville, South Carolina . . . they're all drivin' in in their Cadillacs." By now, Bo is laughing so hard telling the story, he can hardly keep the words coming.

"I'm standin' there at the door. 'Oh, come in, come in . . .'" and finally he just has to stop.

Schembechler took that first job for $3,400 and free run of the cafeteria. He had a choice of $3,600 and no meals at the cafeteria, but, as he explains:

"I never paid any rent. Every meal I ever ate was taken care of."

He wound up saving money and enjoying a different culture and a 6-3 record to boot. It was too good to last.

Schembechler left the relative tranquility and obscurity of Clinton, South Carolina, to hook up with another Miami teammate, Bill Gunlock, on Doyt Perry's Bowling Green staff. It was 1955, and Parseghian and Miami were headed for the first undefeated, untied, season since 1921. Bowling Green, and then two of the neighborhood rivals, Dayton and Cincinnati, stood in the way.

"We're goin' in to play 'em, at Miami, for the title," remembers Bo, and you can almost see him reliving the pre-game locker room scene in Withrow Court, where both teams dressed before heading into battle. "And you gotta figure by that time I'm a tiger anyway. We're goin' to Miami, and Bill and I are . . . and we're playin' Ara and the gang and Miami . . . you know, this was really somethin'.

It was a scene that Bo will "remember for the rest of my life," as Perry called on the two Miami guys, Gunlock and then Schembechler, to say something, and neither one of them could respond with anything more than gutteral sounds, so emotionally wound up were they.

"We poured outta that locker room," recalls Schembechler. "We put in a new defense for Ara, and we did one great job, but they beat us, 7-0. I mean it was a helluva game . . . it was the only game we lost that year."

Although making another move, his third in three years, seemed an unwise course to follow after that 1955 season, that's exactly what Schembechler did. Collier had a place for him at Kentucky, Pont asked him to come to Miami when he succeeded Parseghian, and Ara invited him to Northwestern. He chose Northwestern.

The first year was a success, as we have learned earlier, but the second season, when Parseghian's Wildcats lost every game, was trying to say the least.

"I learned more that year, I think, as an assistant, than any of the successful years we had," marvels Bo, "because Ara was superb. He kept the staff together. No backbiting. No animosity. No 'your fault, my fault' deal. I mean everybody was solid."

Besides the Miami coaches on Parseghian's 1956-57 Northwestern staff . . . Bo, Doc Urich, Paul Shoults and Bruce Beatty . . . there was an assistant who would go on to succeed Ara at Northwestern, to coach later at Purdue, and then become athletic director at Eastern Michigan. Today, Alex Agase is on Schembechler's staff at Michigan, providing the same sound counsel he did for Bo after that 1957 season.

Nobody likes to be remembered for deserting a sinking ship, and that was Bo's dilemma when Woody Hayes asked him to return to Ohio State to replace Bill Hess, who had been named the top man at Ohio University.

"Believe it or not I debated," remembers Bo, "because I didn't want to run out with an 0 and 9, and Alex is the guy that told me, 'Bo, you're outta your mind. You gotta go. It's time for you to go.' And so, in 1958, I went back to Ohio State."

And that's where he stayed until 1962, when the Old Blue of Yale made the call to Bo's old Miami teammate, John Pont.

******

Part of the Schembechler brain trust on the sidelines during the early years at Miami. That's Dave McClain in front of Bo, and John Cocanougher, a graduate assistant, on the phone. Wayne Gibson is to the rear.

Bo Schembechler's astounding coaching record . . . 171 victories, 45 losses and six ties . . . in 20 years as a head coach, is in contrast to the fact that he got off to a really rocky start in his first year at Miami.

It was the third game of the season before Miami recorded its first victory under Bo, a 27-19 triumph at Western Michigan. The Redskins' first victory at home in 1963 was a 40-8 rout of Toledo . . . in the season's eighth game. It took a 21-19 victory over Cincinnati to insure a winning (5-3-2) season.

Considering his often stubborn refusal to accept defeat, Schembechler is extremely candid about his first two years at Miami . . . indeed his six-year tenure as Miami's head coach.

"Like most head coaches," Bo admits, "when you get your first head coaching job and your primary emphasis as an assistant was as an offensive coach, you fail to teach the most important single fundamental of the game, and that's defense.

"Although our offensive teams were acceptable enough, and we could move the ball, and they were good-lookin' teams, and they could get you on the scoreboard, and they could do all those things, my defense was not good enough to win championships."

In six years, Bo's teams won two Mid-American Conference championships, both co-championships, back-to-back, in 1965 and 1966. He remembers with special fondness, the players on those teams and he remembers too, the disappointments.

"While I was there, although I only won two championships, and I didn't do a great job . . . I mean I worked awfully hard . . . night and day . . . I drove myself hard."

Any discussion of the players who played for Schembechler begins, but doesn't necessarily end, with Ernie Kellermann, whom Bo inherited from John. I have remarked that I didn't see John Pont play, but always wished I had. I did see Kellermann play, and sometimes I can't believe I saw him do the things he did.

One of his exploits, the touchdown pass that beat Purdue, has been well chronicled. I like to remember how he broke into the starting lineup.

There really was not much in Ernie's background to suggest he would make the splash he did on the Miami scene. He wasn't heavily recruited out of the tiny high school, Chanel, in suburban Cleveland. By any standards, he was small. And he was a left-handed quarterback who, because of a high school injury that lingered on, didn't do much in spring practice except punt a little on the sidelines and work his way into non-contact defensive drills.

Fall practice began, and all the conversation centered around the returning senior, Vic Ippolito, who was the son of the Cleveland Browns' long-time team physician. But all of a sudden in practice, Kellermann began to display some of the God-given athletic gifts which made him such an exciting player.

Pont and his coaching staff outwardly maintained that the two, Ippolito and Kellermann, rated about dead-even in practice, giving a slight edge to the senior's experience. But inwardly, they knew who they thought should get the job, so they devised a little scheme to test their theory.

The Saturday before the opening game of the 1962 season, a night game in Cincinnati against Xavier, Pont scheduled a final scrimmage under the lights at Oxford's Talawanda High School. In most practices during that week, Ippolito and Kellermann had been alternating at quarterback with the first team.

Pont gathered the team together after calisthentics for a few words of wisdom, then began by pairing the first offensive unit against the number two defense for the first series. Without waiting for a word of instruction from the coach, Kellermann jumped into the huddle and listened for Pont's first play.

That was what the coaches had noticed, and wanted to test. Not only did Kellermann have the athletic tools, he had a sort of charismatic leadership quality. Charisma wasn't the overworked word in those days that it has become today but no matter. Kellermann had it, and he used

Kellermann's back to throw, as Schembechler looks on from the sidelines. Note the attire of the student spectators.

it to lead his flock of Redskins.

It didn't take long for Kellermann to establish why Pont had chosen him to start the season at quarterback. Directing the team flawlessly, running the option play with reckless abandon, and passing well enough to keep Xavier off guard, he led Miami to a 23-14 victory in his first collegiate game.

The turning point came late in the first half. Working against the clock, Kellermann moved the Redskins into scoring position. With time running out and Miami inside the Musketeers' 10-yard line, Kellermann worked the option play to perfection. Faking to the fullback inside, then working his way to the left side, he maneuvered the defensive back to cover Miami's halfback, and headed for the end zone. Xavier never recovered.

******

The Xavier coach that night in Cincinnati was a Miami alumnus from the class of 1953. Ed Biles is a native of the Cincinnati suburb of Reading and had cut his coaching teeth at Cincinnati's Woodward High School. In 1956, he joined the Xavier staff, and in 1961, he was named head coach.

Size and injury had cut short Biles' playing career at Miami, but he did catch the coaching bug when he served two years on Parseghian's staff as an undergraduate assistant helping with the freshmen.

His Xavier record was good in his eight years at the helm . . . 39-28-3 . . . including two losses to Pont-coached teams, three victories and a tie in six matches with Schembechler's teams. But by the end of the 1968 season, Biles could see the handwriting on the wall.

That 1968 season, a 6-4 mark, was the Cincinnati school's last winning season. By 1973, the Musketeers abandoned football, bringing to an end the "unofficial" four-team battle which many referred to as the Miami Valley championship.

For years, Miami, Dayton, Cincinnati and Xavier had waged physical, media and fan warfare for football supremacy in southwestern Ohio. First, Xavier went belly-up in football, then Dayton opted for Division III (non-scholarship) status.

"It became evident to me," Biles told the **Cincinnati Enquirer's** Bill Ford almost ten years later, "what was going to happen. It would become increasingly difficult for an independent like Xavier to compete."

What Biles really wanted to do in 1973 was hook up with Paul Brown and the then-fledgling Cincinnati Bengals. Ever since his days at Miami, when he felt Brown's presence everywhere, Biles dreamed of one day working with the man from Massillon. And with the advent of pro football in Cincinnati, Biles thought his dream might come true.

"I can't tell you why," Biles told Ford, "but I've always idolized Paul Brown. When I went to Miami, Paul Brown wasn't there, of course. But his influence was everywhere. John Brickels, the athletic director, had been an assistant under Paul Brown. Ara Parseghian, the coach, had been directly influenced by Paul Brown.

"Even Bill Rohr, the basketball coach, had played high school football for Paul Brown at Massillon. Brown's philosophies and talent for organization were everywhere."

Biles talked to Brown about a job. "But he reasoned," Biles suggested

Air-bound on the way to play Northwestern. That's a pensive Ernie Kellermann in the foreground and a relaxed Jack Himebauch in the background. The two were to play vital roles in Miami's victory. The bottom photo shows Ernie's ball-handling. He's about to hand off, or maybe he's going to roll to the right. Note the blocking. Or maybe he'll throw. With Kellermann, one never knew.

to Ford, "that if I left Xavier for his staff, it would present a public relations problem in Cincinnati. So he wouldn't hire me."

Instead, Biles got into pro football via the New Orleans Saints. He served his professional apprenticeship under Tom Fears, then under Weeb Ewbank with the New York Jets, and finally under Sid Gillman at Houston. That was 1974, and the next year, when Gillman left and Bum Phillips replaced him, Biles became the Oilers' defensive coordinator. Since 1981, when Phillips was fired, Biles has been the Oilers' head man.

******

Schembechler remembers well that one of the blessings of his first season was the offensive talent he inherited from Pont. And Kellermann was a big part of that talent. The game Bo remembers most, though, was the game at Northwestern in 1964, Ernie's senior season.

The year before, Northwestern had humbled Miami, 37-6. Kellermann, as I recall had been injured going into the game, and eventually had to take a permanent seat on the sidelines. The rest of the Redskins didn't fare much better, and the plane Miami took back to Dayton resembled a hospital ship more closely than it did one carrying young athletes.

But the next year Miami, and Kellermann, got even.

"Ask Alex Agase (then Northwestern's coach)" demands Bo, "about when we beat 'em up there 28-27. Were you with us then? Hey, he did that alone. He beat a Big Ten team . . .ALONE. All by his lonesome. I mean they blitzed him, and he got out of the blitz and hit Himebauch and he just . . . I mean that guy did it alone . . . 28 to 27. Remember that game?"

Who could forget it? Kellermann hit 11 of 18 passes for 245 yards, with no interceptions. He scrambled ingeniously and ate the ball courageously in the 17 rushing attempts credited against him for a net of 10 yards. And his two touchdown passes were phenomenal.

The blitz Bo recalled had helped put Northwestern into an early lead by forcing Kellermann to fumble on his own 24. Kellermann responded two possessions later with the 54-yard touchdown pass to Jack Himebauch. Glenn Trout converted, and it was 7-7 with 12:08 gone. Northwestern moved 72 yards in seven plays from the kickoff to lead again 13-7.

Then Kellermann, pinned back to the Miami 13 by a penalty, launched an 87-yard drive with a pass to Frank Dwyer covering 34 yards. He kept Don Peddie and Joe Kozar alternating on the ground through the next five plays, Kozar scoring over right tackle from the three, to put Miami ahead 14-13. A Northwestern fumble gave Miami the ball at its own 31, and six plays later a Kellermann pass to John Erisman was good for 54 yards and a touchdown. Miami led 21-13. After a scoreless third quarter, Northwestern ground out 92 yards in 22 plays to make it 21-19; Miami's Ed Philpott batted down the pass attempt for a two-pointer.

Northwestern's onside kick was captured by the Redskins at the Northwestern 45. Kellermann passes to Himebauch and Erisman were good for 12, 12 and 8, Peddie slanting at left tackle for a touchdown, and Trout's placement made it 28-19 Miami. Northwestern came right back with a 66-yard scoring drive and a two-point conversion, just a point shy at 28-27 with 38 seconds left. Kellerman nursed the ball through four remaining downs after the kickoff, to preserve that winning margin.

Ernie in 1965 was drafted by the Cowboys, and I was in my first month with **The Dallas Times Herald** when he came to Dallas from the Cowboys' training site in Thousand Oaks, California.

He had some bright moments during the pre-season schedule, so it was a sad moment, and a surprise, when he called to tell me he'd been the last one cut. He was down then, but anyone who knew Ernie knew of his resiliency. He'd find a way to get what he wanted.

What he wanted was a chance to make it as a defensive back in the National Football League. Dallas had drafted him for that position, and he was sure he could make somebody's team. When Ernie called Bo to see what he could do, Bo immediately thought of Blanton Collier. Arnsparger's former coach was now head coach of the Cleveland Browns.

Collier suggested to Bo that he have Ernie come to Cleveland to meet with him and Art Modell, the Browns' owner who had wrested control of the club away from Paul Brown. Kellermann was signed to a contract with the Browns and went on to grab a starting strong safety position, a role he played with his customary gusto from 1965 until 1972.

******

"When a guy gets that job," says Schembechler of the job he held from 1963 to 1969, "he doesn't realize what a great job he's got, because if he's successful, he's going to have opportunities . . ."

Schembechler was contacted, he says, by everybody that had an opening, and he maintains that happens at Miami to this day. Pittsburgh, Vanderbilt, Kansas State, Tulane, Wisconsin . . . that's a partial list of schools that were interested in Bo when he was at Miami.

"But then," says Bo, "Michigan called. And this school is a big Miami, is what it is. It's got a marvelous reputation academically. It's never been one of those schools that's been investigated. Its reputation has been impeccable, ya' know. It's been that kind of a situation.

"So, when Bump Elliott called me here, I took this job for one thousand dollars more than I made at Miami. That's a fact. And I never asked any questions, never had a contract, never have had a contract here."

It seemed strange to me that Bump Elliott, who had preceded Bo as coach, would have been the one to contact him.

"Canham (Don) told him to do it," says Schembechler. "Canham is the AD; he told Bump to contact me. But that's after he couldn't get Parseghian, he couldn't get Joe Paterno, he couldn't get all the big names, see." And Schembechler laughs.

"So then he comes to me. And I came up here and he hired me. Never met a committee. Talked to one man. Canham. That was it."

The only other Michigan man he met before he was hired was the faculty representative, Marc Plant. And he discovered at that meeting that Plant already had seen Bo's teams play, because the Michigan law professor had a daughter who attended Miami.

Schembechler can tell the Michigan man exactly how the Miami Magic works, because he, like Miami men everywhere who have wound up on other campuses, has seen it from both sides of the street.

"There's a strange loyalty there, you know," he says, "Guys that have come outta there . . . I don't think there are many of them that just turn their back . . ."

Tim Rose will carry on the tradition in grand style, maintains Schembechler. "I think they got a good football coach," he says. "I think that guy's good."

And the tradition passes from generation to generation.

"I keep tellin' Shemmy. 'You're gonna go to Miami . . . Get your grades up, son, you're goin' to Miami.' And he comes back, 'I don't wanna go to Miami just 'cause you went there.' See, he doesn't like to be around any place where I am, where they're makin' some fuss over me . . .'"

And the father-son debate continues. But there's no argument, especially since Shemmy and Millie are on their way to Florida.

"As I sit in this chair, he's goin' to Miami. Now the only thing I'm worried about," laughs Shemmy's dad, "is I go down there and submit his credentials and the guy says 'Hey, can't take him,' and I say, 'Oh . . . don't tell me that.'"

Loyalty? It's there. It's made Miami a winner.

"I think that is kinda expected there at Miami. You know, you're there five years or so, and you have success, it's time for you to step out, and let somebody else step in. Frankly, I'm probably one guy that could have stayed there.

" . . . Had it not been, again, the tradition and what was expected there, I might still be coachin' at Miami. But when I went in, I think I was like anybody. I was conditioned to the fact that . . . I wasn't going to be there the rest of my life.

"So . . . five years or whatever, ya' know, and you've had success, opportunity knocks. It was just expected, and I was kinda conditioned that was the way it was gonna be."

Bill Mallory, 1957 graduate of Miami and the Redskins' head coach from 1969 to 1973, reflecting on his move from Miami to the University of Colorado.

IX
NEXT IN LINE

WHEN ARA PARSEGHIAN was recruiting Bill Mallory, recalls Bill, the Miami coach had something to say to Bill's father. Guy Mallory had been a high school coach, so the elder Mallory had some idea of the impact of his message.

"When I came in," says Bill, "I remember this. He said to my dad, 'You give me a boy now, and in four years, I'll return you a man.'"

However long it took, Bill Mallory is quite a man. Guy Mallory must've been quite a man himself. Bill was his first son, but Tom and then Dave, followed. For an entire decade, from 1953 through 1963, one of Guy Mallory's sons was playing for Miami.

They played for Ara, and they played for John Pont, and they played for Bo.

Miami, in Schembechler's first year, was 2-3-1 going to play Bowling Green, which was 6-0 and had one of Doyt Perry's better teams. Dave Mallory was Bo's captain, and on the opposite side of the field wearing the headphones, was Bowling Green's defensive coordinator, Dave's brother Bill.

Dave "couldn't run a lick," says Bo, but "was as tough as anybody you ever met . . . and we played a helluva game. I mean we went after them . . . beat 'em solid. But the most interesting play, and this is an absolute true story:

"We had this defense where we overshifted and covered the guys over on the weak side, and Dave's playin' middle backer . . . and he made a lotta plays. Well, there's one play that went out of bounds . . . right at Bill's feet.

"He's got the phones on and everything . . . and here comes Dave . . . the whistle blown, the play's over . . . zoom," and Bo provides the special sound effects. A late hit if ever there was one.

"And Bill's standin' there," continues Bo. 'Call it, call it, call it,' and Dave jumps right up in his face and says '—— ——', and runs back out on the field."

Intensity. The Mallorys had it in big doses. Today, while older brother Bill toils on the sidelines, now as head coach at Northern Illinois University, younger brother Tom, '61, is one of the country's outstanding orthopedic surgeons and owner of Joint Implant Surgeons, at Columbus; youngest brother Dave, '64, a dentist at Loudonville, Ohio.

At Dr. Dave's office in Loudonville, an Ohio State assistant coach stopped to pay a visit. Again Bo picks up the life and times of the Mallory clan.

"You know, I have two of Bill's sons here . . . Mike Mallory, a linebacker, is here (at Michigan), and Doug, his younger brother, a defensive back, is coming this fall. Mike Mallory . . . this is an interesting story . . . is being recruited by Ohio State, Michigan, a lotta people.

"The coach who is recruiting him for Ohio State stops in at Dave Mallory's office . . . and he sits down and he's tryin' to get Dave to get Mike to come to Ohio State. And he sees on his desk a picture of his family.

"He says, 'Is that your family?'

"And Dave says, 'Yeah, that's my family.'

"And he says, 'Boy, that little guy's a nice lookin' guy.'

"And he says, 'Yeah, you know what his name is? . . . His name is Bo.'

"He says, 'Well, uh, I think I've wasted my time here. And Dave says, 'Yeah, you have. If I have anything to say about it, he's gonna play for Bo.'"

******

When the Mallory brothers were knocking people down and then picking them back up for Miami in the Fifties and Sixties, Northern Illinois University was struggling for football identity. Membership in

Dave Mallory was a four-year letterman at Miami, captain his senior year, and tough as they come, and all the Mallorys came tough. Here he is in a softer moment, with Bob Jencks, center, and Scott Tyler, visiting the Shriners Hospital in Orlando during Tangerine Bowl week in 1962.

the Mid-American Conference was but a dream.

In the three years, 1954 through 1956, that Bill Mallory played for the Redskins, Miami lost two games and tied one. Among the victims, as we already have learned, were Indiana and Northwestern.

On the other hand, during the same period Northern Illinois won but three times. Its only three victims were Beloit and Southern Illinois in 1954 and Wheaton in the opening game of the 1956 season.

Less than ten years later, in 1963, Northern Illinois won ten straight games and acclaim by the National Association of Intercollegiate Athletics and the Associated Press as College Division national champion.

That success paved the way for even higher aspirations, and in 1973 the Huskies passed the entrance exam and gained admission to the Mid-American Conference. Northern's efforts in the MAC have been fraught with frustration, a 4-3 league record that brought a third-place tie with Miami in 1960 being the high-water mark.

Mallory and his Huskies marked a milestone, however, when on November 13, 1982, at DeKalb, they managed a 12-7 upset. It was Northern's first win in three tries against Miami.

Bill Mallory catches a pass and turns upfield during action at Miami Field. Miami players in the background are Stan Jones (67) and Tirrel Burton (40).

Huskie Stadium, seating 30,000, is one of the more impressive in the Mid-American Conference. It is a major element of a physical plant which serves Northern's needs well.

In relaxed conversation at his office in that stadium, Mallory gives little indication of the competitive fires that burn within him. Physically imposing, he still looks like an athlete who would be named All-Mid-American Conference second team as a junior and All-MAC first team as a senior in 1956. Temperamentally, he seems calm, low-key.

It wasn't planned, of course; yet when Dick Shrider and Miami's student-faculty-administration Athletic Advisory Board tapped the 33-year-old Ohio State assistant to replace Schembechler in 1969, they couldn't have realized how many similarities these men possess. Granted, the outspoken Michigan coach is more brusque, more volatile. Yet he and Mallory share comparable philosophies.

"Bo's a fiery guy," begins Mallory, "but he operates the way I believe in . . . a disciplinarian, he cares about his kids, wants them to get a good education, does a good job of dealing with his people, an excellent coaching staff.

"They always talk about the so-called blue-chips, but . . . but I think he's one who's also taken kids who've had pretty good character and good work habits and made 'em darn good football players; so I like that too about him."

We had been discussing Mallory's decision to leave Miami and take up residence in Boulder, Colorado, and he was expressing not regrets, but second thoughts.

"My second thoughts were not so much that I'd never be leaving . . . I knew I would . . . it's just whether this was the right thing, and of course what was tough for me to leave was the fact . . . I had good people there and I knew a lot of time and effort had gone into it, and I wasn't too anxious to leave it. I was hoping to maybe reap a little bit more from it and enjoy it, but it was just that opportunity knocked . . . and it was time that I go and let somebody else have a crack."

Even though Mallory's 13-year head coaching record at Miami, Colorado, and now Northern Illinois reads 89-50-1, a .639 winning percentage, it's easy to tell that he's at home at Northern Illinois, as he was at Miami.

He says candidly, "Miami is my kind of school. Here, too. I like the small town. I like the school itself . . . it's my kinda school. It's the kinda situation I could be very, very happy with . . . and the Conference, too. I've always liked the Conference because I think the Mid-American Conference makes a lotta sense."

Particularly in comparison to the Big Eight, where he saw many things, especially as regards recruiting, which tended to "bug" him, things which "I never encountered recruiting in the Mid-American Conference."

Mallory doesn't talk much about his Colorado experience, and his expressed feelings about Miami, Northern Illinois and the Mid-American Conference would seem to indicate why. Dick Crum, the man who succeeded Mallory after the 1973 Redskins produced the best record

(11-0) in the school's history, offers this insight:

"Well, that was kind of a scary situation, really, because Bill was approached about goin' out there, and I really didn't think he was all that crazy about goin,' and I told him that. To be honest with you, I'd heard too many things about Eddie Crowder (the athletic director) that bothered me.

". . . I was really concerned about goin' out there, and I told Bill. I mean I always told Bill what was on my mind. I didn't play games with him. But . . .

"So they came back after him again. And you know, he asked a lotta people about that job, and a lotta people said, 'Oh, that can be a great job, and so forth.'"

Apparently, the pressure from Colorado intensified. In January 1974, Mallory and Crum were at the annual meeting of the American Football Coaches Association (AFCA) in San Francisco and, says Crum, "they were working on him pretty hard to get him to take the job.

"He decided to take it and, I mean, it was a real shock to my system because . . . it was about 11 o'clock at night and I was in the room . . . I was lyin' on the bed watching TV and he came back in and he said, 'Well, I'm going to Colorado and you're going to be the next football coach at Miami.'

"And I said, 'I'm glad I'm lyin' down, buddy, I'll tell you that.'"

It wasn't quite that simple. Having hired Crum and observed how effectively he handled his assignment as the defensive coordinator, Mallory had urged Athletic Director Dick Shrider to appoint Dick Crum as his successor.

No matter how logical that might appear on the surface, at Miami nobody "automatically" inherits the position of head football coach. It's a job maybe like no other, as Bo Schembechler had learned; and as we will discover in the next chapter, sentiment had its day before Crum was picked.

So Crum didn't need to be worried about going to Colorado after all. The concerns were all Mallory's, and as luck would have it, Crum's reservations were all too real.

Trying to fight the good fight, without sacrificing his principles, Mallory persevered for five years at Colorado. He won five and lost six the first year, but in 1976 a 9-3 record earned a trip to the Astro-Bluebonnet Bowl. The next year, Colorado won its first ever Big Eight championship and a berth in the Orange Bowl.

Evidence of the pressures on Mallory to win at all costs, and affirmation of Crum's earlier fears, were apparent when John Pont's Northwestern team paid a visit to Colorado early in that 1976 season. The Wildcats seemed hopelessly overmatched against the Buffaloes; yet as the score mounted, so did Colorado's apparent determination to keep right on scoring. It didn't seem like a good way to treat your old coach, but Pont discounted the incident, citing external influences beyond Mallory's control.

Despite his five-year record of 35-21-1, Mallory was fired by Colorado in 1978, apparently to make way for the New England Patriots' Chuck

Fairbanks, who had forged so many successes at Oklahoma in the Big Eight.

******

Mallory traces his interest in coaching back to his father, who coached at Canal Winchester and at Brown High School, outside of Delaware, Ohio, before becoming a school administrator, and his interest in Miami back to his high school coach, Robert E. (Jeff) DeHaven, 1932 Miami graduate, another Paul Brown contemporary.

"I feel as I look back," explains Mallory, "I'd have to say it was an idea that I entertained most of the time. It would go back to my dad, who had a lot of influence on me and whom I had a tremendous amount of respect for.

"When he was coaching, as a kid I used to tag along, and I kinda grew up with it. Even though he did eventually get out of it, athletics were such a big part of my life. So I think the fact that he was a coach, and athletics is something that I enjoyed so much, when that day came . . ."

Mallory pauses to reflect on his career in coaching and on some advice that he has carried with him since the very beginning.

"You look at coaching, and if it's something that you feel you can do without or do it on an entertainment or part-time basis, fine, go some other direction.

"But if it's something you feel you can't live without, something you want to be a part of all the time, or most of the time, you ought to pursue the coaching profession. That's the advice I took, and I've never been sorry."

Native of Glendale, West Virginia, Mallory is one of the few members of the Cradle of Coaches not born in Ohio. But Ohio is where he was raised, and he learned to play football at Sandusky High School. Indeed, when his parents moved to Hillsboro before his senior year, he stayed with another Sandusky family so he could finish high school where he started.

Jeff DeHaven knew Mallory wanted to coach, so it wasn't surprising he was pointed in Miami's direction.

"He (DeHaven) thought this would be the perfect situation for me," says Mallory. "So it was through his recommendation that I was able to have a good opportunity to at least be looked at, and they came around and talked to me, and I went down and visited."

On that visit, Ara suggested to Bill that, when he went home to Hillsboro for the summer, he and his dad should come back for another visit. It was on that visit that Mallory received his scholarship offer.

Parseghian always will occupy a special spot in Mallory's treasury of memories, because he personifies "class," as Bill puts it.

"He was a perfectionist," adds Mallory. "He used to have that air about him that . . . I had a lot of respect for him. He was quality . . . he was a winner. He was a very classy individual. I thought he handled us well on his team . . . seemed to say the right things, do the right things . . . and in a classy fashion."

Mallory was just beginning his collegiate career as a sophomore when I arrived on campus. He was on the team that went into Bloomington and upset the Hoosiers. And he maintains that "was a masterpiece of getting a team ready."

You recall the story . . . how the "ragamuffins," as Mallory refers to his Redskin teammates, came out on Friday wearing muddy practice gear in full view of Indiana. When I suggested to Mallory that Parseghian himself downplays his role as a master strategist that weekend, he says quite matter-of-factly:

"I know he does, but I . . . you talk about catchin' a team off guard . . . you talk to any of the other players . . . Dean Porter or any of 'em . . . he's probably dealt with so many teams through the years that that probably doesn't stand out . . . but it was a masterpiece of strategy."

Mallory laughs self-consciously when he recalls that and other examples of Parseghian's timing in getting a team ready. There was, for instance, this incident at halftime of the Miami-Cincinnati game, also in 1954.

This was a pressure game for Miami. Its final three games of the season had been the upset of Indiana, then the one-touchdown loss to Dayton the week after that upset, and now the oldest rivalry west of the Alleghenies. Cincinnati had beaten Miami three years in a row. The Parseghian-Gillman personal rivalry remained as intense as that between the two teams. And now at halftime, Miami trailed the Bearcats 9-0.

"He's talkin' at halftime," whispers Mallory, as if he's still in that steamy locker room, "and all of a sudden, he starts yellin' at Sid. 'I know you got this locker room wired, and you can hear everything I'm saying!' and of course . . . I don't know how many there were — forty-some tryin' to get out the door at the same time . . . and we went out and cleaned their clock that second half."

For the record, the final score read Miami 21, Cincinnati 9, and the Redskins had completed Ara's second 8-1 season in three years.

"He had a way . . .," marvels Mallory of his first collegiate coach, "his timing was good . . . he knew when to put it on and when to come off. He did a good job in that way . . . of really gettin' 'em ready. We felt well-prepared . . . just went into a ball game and you had a lot of confidence in what the heck you were doing, and he was able to insert a few things here and there that kinda get you right to your peak."

"I don't know today," wonders Mallory, "whether that has much effect on kids . . . whether we weren't very intelligent, or naive, or what."

That loss to Dayton, sandwiched between the season-ending victories over Indiana and Cincinnati in 1954, was the only time Mallory experienced defeat during his two varsity seasons under Parseghian. What was it like after losing, to come to practice on Monday?

"Hell!" and Mallory chuckles. "It was tough . . . you hated to go to practice. It was rough . . . it was tough to lose there. You dreaded losin'. You played hard not to lose. Those were tough weeks."

Weeks? I thought there was only one. But so rare were those occasions that he remembers how it was when he was a freshman.

"I got that real quick, back when I was a freshman player and they let Ohio U. beat 'em, and I remember we had to practice against the varsity.

And that made us all aware that, by golly, we better hadn't be losin' very often."

Not only was it physically tough, it was mentally demanding. Mallory says the prevailing attitude among the players was to get the week over and get back to playing the game on Saturday, because certainly that would be easier.

"I'll say this," he concludes. "I feel sorry for those guys that had to play us after a loss . . ."

It may come as no surprise to the reader to learn that the loss to Ohio University to which Mallory refers was not actually a loss, but a 7-7 tie. But in all my years of following Miami football, I don't recall a player or a coach, or even a fan, who regarded a tie as anything but a loss. There were no moral victories.

When Pont took over from Parseghian ahead of Mallory's senior season, Mallory and the rest of the players already knew about the young man they would be playing for, because all had played for John as freshmen.

Enthusiasm and hard work were among the traits Mallory thinks John brought to the job. And emotion. Parseghian was an emotional person, but "John even more so."

Pont is "a person I had a lot of respect for . . . cared about you . . . I thought he had a good feel for his players. Probably you got a little closer to John . . . he was one who was easy to get to know."

******

Coaching stints at Bowling Green and Yale and then Ohio State were a part of the apprenticeship that Mallory served before returning to Oxford in 1969 to launch the career as head coach which has taken him also to Colorado and Northern Illinois.

The high water mark obviously was the undefeated season in 1973, and to get to that point Mallory refers to "the hard work . . . to assemble what I thought was a pretty talented group of players."

Mallory speaks with obvious deep feeling of the team which began the season with a 32-0 victory over Dayton and ended it with a 16-7 triumph over Florida in the Tangerine Bowl.

"We just had a good group of young men and the type of people that I believe in . . . good character individuals, they cared . . . football was important to them, and there was talent. We had — not to brag or anything — a group of young men that were the kinda people you could win with . . . when we took the field, you just had a feeling about it, they did, that they would win.

"A lotta pride . . . a great group of young men, pride-wise. They just . . . boy, they'd just fight ya' right down. I mean, you know, if you're gonna beat 'em, you're gonna have to work to do it, because they just didn't believe that they could be beaten.

". . . That year we went undefeated, that senior class was just a good, determined bunch. They were bound and determined that they were gonna be champs and be good, and we had an air about us that when we took the field, we just had confidence."

Bob Hitchens, Miami's all-time rushing and scoring leader, both for a single season and for his career, provided much of the senior leadership on that team. But people like Dick Brown, Dave Cripe, Dan Cunningham, Bill Driscoll, Herman Jackson, Pat Leahy, Mike Monos, Andy Pederzoli, Dan Rebsch, Stu Showalter, Jerald Tillman, John Wiggins and Tim Williams also did their part.

"But we didn't have just seniors," adds Mallory. "We had good juniors

Bill Mallory stalks the Miami sidelines.

and sophomores, too, that were in there, and they all seemed to come out of the same mold."

What made this group of Miami athletes so special . . . winners . . . in Mallory's eyes?

"They were tough kids . . . tough in a good way . . . they weren't 'bummish' kids . . . I think the kinda kids I have seen Miami have. Miami has, I think, always been known . . . bein' on the other side, coachin' agin 'em, whether it's here or back when I was coachin' at Bowling Green . . . they're tough, but yet they're clean, and they're classy."

Mallory harkens back to his playing days under Ara, and how the Armenian pushed the pride factor. He used to say, remembers Mallory, "By golly, we don't lose here. We're a winner, and we're expected to win. That's our role."

Adds Mallory, "That's the same way I presented it to my teams when I was there: 'This place is deep in tradition, and it's a winner, and we're gonna carry that type of attitude.'"

A quick review of that 1973 season is appropriate. Not only was it the best season, record-wise, in Miami's long football history, the way it was accomplished is indicative of the pride of which Mallory, and others, speak.

After the opening shutout of Dayton, the next stop on the trail was Purdue. Miami had faced the Boilermakers once since the 1962 upset, and that had been a 28-0 Purdue victory in the opening game of the 1965 season.

"They were sayin' we had no business bein' over there," remembers Mallory, "and we ended up gettin' them."

Indeed. Dick Crum, Mallory's aide, remembers the Redskins trailed, 19-10, in the second half, "and we came back and got 'em. That gave us the momentum."

Miami 24, Purdue 19.

The very next week, the Redskins had a return engagement with South Carolina, a team Miami had beaten the year before, 21-8.

"You know, you're down there in that South," notes Mallory. "The people are really rabid football fans. We went back the second time . . . they were sayin' it (the first victory) was a fluke . . . they'd get us the second time around . . . Dietzel was there coaching, and it was disturbing to him to lose the second time."

Miami 13, South Carolina 11.

Marshall, which had left the Mid-American Conference in 1969, was the next victim, 31-6.

Among the continuing Mid-American members, a pattern had been emerging over the past several years. Toledo, under the wing of Quarterback Chuck Ealey, had won 35 consecutive games, dominating the Conference. That streak had ended; yet Miami, in spite of non-conference victories over the likes of Maryland, Pacific and South Carolina during Mallory's tenure, had not been faring as well in the MAC.

This time, a sweep of Mid-American opposition — Ohio University, Bowling Green, Toledo, Western Michigan and Kent State — gave the Redskins the MAC title for the first time since 1966.

Defense was the key to Miami's success. No Conference team scored more than one touchdown against the Redskins. Toledo, for the first time in a long while, didn't manage a point. Crum, having been the defensive coordinator at the time, especially relishes that. But, he observes, there had been plenty of frustration on the way to that moment in the sun.

Remembers Crum: "We had two super great games with them. The first one was in Oxford in 1969, and they beat us, 14-10, and the whole second half, they never had the ball outside their own 40-yard line. Our possessions started from their 40 in, and we just couldn't get it in the end zone. And that was a good Miami football team.

"And then the next year, they beat us up there 14-13 right at the end of the game. And then the next year, they killed us in Oxford. They beat us, 45-6, I think. The next year, with that contingent being gone up there, we thought we'd get 'em. We went up there and got beat again, so we lost four in a row to Toledo."

Crum was trained to teach mathematics. In fact, it was his math teaching background which got him his first coaching opportunity. It must have been statistics. His recitation of the scores and detail of these games of more than a decade ago was given without aid of any old scrapbook . . . without thumbing through media guides. It was simply his personal recollection.

Having disposed of the Conference foes and earned a berth in the Tangerine Bowl, all that remained in the way of a perfect 1973 regular season was traditional rival Cincinnati, and for the first time in 75 years the game would be played in Oxford.

"We ran the opening kickoff back . . . Larry Harper ran it back 95 yards for a touchdown," remembers Crum. "And that stood, 6-0, the whole game. They scored once, and had it called back, and that's the way the game ended . . . 6-0."

So Miami went to Florida and played the Gators in the Tangerine Bowl. Even though the Redskins had beaten Purdue of the Big Ten and independent South Carolina from Atlantic Coast Conference territory, the proud representatives of the Southeastern Conference showed little or no regard for the champions of the Mid-American Conference.

Mallory takes up the story of the undefeated season from here: "They kinda looked down their noses at us, and our kids . . . I could tell, boy, it was . . . I didn't have to say anything before that game . . ."

The final score was 16-7, and it was convincing. Nobody was proclaiming national championship status for this team from southwestern Ohio, yet there was almost universal recognition that Miami in 1973 was more than the home of the Cradle of Coaches.

It had, as John Brickels, the athletic director of years past, used to love to say, "earnt the right." Earned the right to be acknowledged among the country's better college football teams. And the Redskins did it, maintains Mallory, because they believed in themselves and had intense pride.

"It's something that you . . . when you get there, it's there. It's something, I think, that probably just exists. People you're around . . . people you meet . . . people come back, you know, that played there. It's an air that exists.

Mallory disputes the notion that the players who brought the "love and honor to Miami" . . . words from the school's fight song . . . just wandered in because there was no other place to go. While acknowledging that it would be foolish to think Miami could go head to head, toe to toe, in the recruiting wars with the likes of Ohio State or Michigan, he prefers to point out that, in certain situations, Miami might win a battle or two.

"Maybe on Carpenter," says Mallory. "I got him. Woody wanted him, but there's a little story on that one. And then maybe on Hitchens, Ohio State wanted Hitchens, but again . . . Chuck Brockmeyer, his coach (who was also a teammate of Bill's at Miami), was the reason why Bobby came to Miami.

". . . In the Mid-American you recruit a kid who you feel has good potential, that down the road can develop into a so-called 'big-time' football player. We were able to uncover and bring in people whom we worked in, but they did develop and had good potential."

The Carpenter story was one of exhaustive recruiting on the part of Mallory and one of his assistants, Milan Vooletich, and Carpenter's desire to play close to home, where his family could see him play, and to

Mallory . . . pushing the pride factor.

play early in his career.

Sherman Smith, who has enjoyed a sparkling career with the Seattle Seahawks of the National Football League, and Randy Walker, the magnificent Miami fullback of those days, who now works as an aide to Dick Crum on the North Carolina staff, are others whose recruitment was a key element in Miami's three-year surge.

Smith, says Mallory, was a "gangly 16 year old" who was overlooked, but had obvious talents, and Walker, who chose Miami over Northwestern, did so because he wanted to be a coach.

Coaching . . . that's really what **Miami of Ohio: Cradle of Coaches** is all about. And in a young man like Randy Walker, Miami has a graduate who not only has achieved coaching success at an early age, but aspires to a major head coaching position.

And there are others on coaching staffs throughout the country who have the same aspirations. Two of them, Gary Durchik and Joe Novak, are on Mallory's staff at Northern Illinois.

Both played for Bo Schembechler, who recruited them out of Mentor, Ohio, when Dick Crum was coaching there. Novak, the Huskies' defensive coordinator, assisted Crum at Miami from 1974 through 1976; from 1977 through 1979 he was an assistant coach at Illinois. Offensive Coordinator Durchik has been on Mallory's staffs 10 of the past 11 years, serving the other year at Illinois.

What coaches like Novak and Durchik have to understand, points out Mallory, is how Miami alumni are vying for that one head coaching spot at Miami every five or six years . . . whenever the incumbent moves on. Only one is selected, but that does not necessarily mean that the others are any less qualified. Both Durchik and Novak are "well qualified," says Mallory.

In his quiet way, Mallory suggests that Miami's coaching legend will continue regardless of Schembechler's warning about the shortage of coaches. Bill concedes his predecessor at Miami makes good sense, but he sees more and more evidence that the worm is starting to turn, that coaching and teaching are indeed becoming viable career options again.

"I think it can, as long as they don't take it for granted." Mallory's response to the question of whether Miami's coaching magic will live on is direct.

"Miami doesn't dare allow (itself) to become spoiled or complacent. I think they need the stadium badly. It's been too bad, really, it's been so long coming, because football has been awfully good to Miami.

". . . It goes hand in hand. It's something that should have been done before now. I know it hasn't been easy, and money's a problem and the longer it was put off, the tougher it was to get because of the cost. I understand that. But I do feel that stadium is something that's very important, and should have been done sooner.

Miami, with its recently regained Division IA classification after a year in the minor leagues, along with several other Conference members, perhaps is facing some of its toughest hurdles in the next several years, as Mallory sees it.

"The schedule that they have . . . they're playin' Washingtons and

Houstons and LSU . . . they're playing some awfully good people. I don't feel they can live off yesteryear or yesterday and expect to be continually successful.

"I think they have to keep feeding into that program and making sure that it's constantly done, because it would be a shame to ever let it deteriorate. I think it's done an awful lot for the University."

Considering he's running the football program at one of Miami's Mid-American Conference rivals, Mallory's comments amount to fair warning. But also understand that, while he may be coaching the Northern Illinois Huskies, his feeling for his alma mater has always run deep.

"I think probably what was a little funny was two years ago I went back and I was over on the far side. I don't know, that kinda was a strange feeling, that I wasn't over on the other side."

To Mallory, competitor that he is, Miami now represents the "other side." But he hasn't forgotten that he traces his roots in coaching to those undergraduate days when he learned directly from Parseghian and Pont

Co-captains of the 1969 team, Kent Thompson (10) and Merv Nugent, present a game ball to Fred C. Yager, the Miamian whose bequest led to the Yager Stadium complex which is being unveiled in 1983.

and found out what it means to feel the Miami tradition.

"First of all," says Mallory, trying to explain what he has been an integral part of, "Miami being a quality institution as it is, attracted good, quality people . . . people I think that would have been successful no matter whether they'd gone into the coaching profession or what profession when you look at it.

". . . I think coaches like Ara had a great influence on me, and they're the reasons why I wanted to go on and continue coaching, because I came through such a classy program. It sorta had the same effect on others. It got in their blood. They liked what they saw, and we were trained, I thought, well.

"We were so far ahead of everybody back in those days."

Miami's mission is to stay ahead. Mallory's mission is to see to it that doesn't happen. Because he's been there, he knows how tough that is.

"My biggest concern . . . I wasn't so worried about coachin' kids, I knew I could do that . . . but my biggest concern was that I wasn't a Miami graduate. And there was a lot of flack over it. I tell you. Things . . . I'd say 99 per cent of the Miami people were really great, but there were some people that didn't like that happening."

Dick Crum, Miami coach from 1974 through 1977, recalling the apprehension he felt upon being called to succeed Bill Mallory.

X
AND STILL COUNTING

DICK CRUM was a teenager at Boardman High School near Youngstown, Ohio, in 1950 when Woody Hayes coached his final season at Miami. Twenty-three years later, Crum became the first Redskin coach since Hayes who didn't have a Miami bachelor's degree. He had earned a Miami master's degree while on the staff.

In the minds of many, and I include myself among the many, it had been the Miami alumni from Parseghian to Mallory who had given the Cradle of Coaches story its special meaning.

But that overlooks the very message the people who are the heroes of this real-life drama are spreading, wherever they go. Miami . . . the University . . . it's the common bond, the thread that ties everybody together.

"Many are called, but few are chosen." This conclusion to two parables from the Bible also expresses what happens every time Miami is in a position to select a new football coach. Those wishing to be chosen are numerous. Those chosen to be interviewed are few. More often than not, their earliest training, usually as student-athletes, has been at Miami. And of those interviewed, only one is chosen.

Crum was chosen Miami's 27th head football coach on January 20, 1974, just eight days after Mallory told him he was going to Colorado. Two days after the announcement, here is how Bob Howard, from his vantage point in Miami's Office of Public Information, viewed Crum's appointment. Wrote Howard, in a letter to me:

"From where I sit, much as we cherish the sequence of authentic alumni, Crum is an extremely good pick.

"There's every reason to believe he's a completely sound coach who will tackle the entire job as astutely as he carried out his particular responsibility with the defense. He's intelligent, he gets along with people, he has a quiet, almost sly sense of humor which delights, and he will not be imitated by Jonathan Winters.

"His comments are those of a man who already has thought out what he wanted to say, who expresses in his own language just what he means, and says it once. He does not wander, does not repeat himself, and does not talk in bromides . . ."

Other than playing the game, which he didn't do much of anyway, Crum was well grounded in Miami football. As a coach at Mentor High School, he made an early determination to recommend Miami to many of his graduating seniors.

". . . I always thought Miami was a pretty good place for kids to go, not only because they played good football, but they had an academic reputation which I think was maybe as good as any I'd heard of, and I always felt that if a youngster went there, he could not only play in a good football program, but he could get a good education."

Bo Schembechler was the Miami coach when Crum first began bringing some of his better prospects down to Miami for a look-see.

"I thought highly of Bo," says Crum. "I used to go down there and watch them practice in the spring, and of course, Bo being Bo, the kids, when they were practicin', didn't think he was very funny; but he really did have a sense of humor . . . he was somethin' to watch.

"If it (Bo's sense of humor) was not directed at you, it was kinda humorous; but if it was directed at you, why, it wasn't very funny at all."

But we have digressed. In the Schembechler and Mallory years, Dick Crum was very much a part of Miami football. Sentiment for a Miami graduate notwithstanding, his selection was the right choice. As the next two years would prove.

******

Miami partisans would cast a dissenting vote, claiming their beloved Miami Field with all its charm, was college football's most picturesque setting. There is, however, nothing quite like Kenan Stadium on the campus of the University of North Carolina

Nestled among the tall pine trees in the middle of Carolina's campus, Kenan Stadium is hardly visible until you're there. And when you get there, it nearly takes your breath away. At the closed end of the stadium, Kenan Fieldhouse, a stucco and Spanish tile structure resembling a clubhouse at an exclusive golf club, houses dressing rooms, training facilities and offices.

Not surprisingly, the office of the head football coach at North Carolina looks out over the stadium. Even on a gloomy, rainy winter afternoon it looked like a pleasant place to work. On one wall of Dick Crum's office are mementos of Miami. One plaque, I thought, was especially significant. The heading was inscribed, "Little Turtle, Chief of the Miamis," and read:

"Little Turtle was born in Indiana in 1752 and died there in 1812, but both his fighting and his peace-making were centered in Ohio. The principal village of his tribe, the Miami, had been Pickawillany, near what is now Piqua. His braves frustrated the arduous campaigns of Generals Harmer and St. Clair through the dense forests and swamps of the Miami and Maumee valleys in 1790 and 1791. He led an attack on Fort Recovery three years later, but he foresaw that the invaders would win in the long run and counseled peace. He sat among the chiefs around the council fire at Fort Greene Ville and said of the treaty. 'I am the last to sign it, and I would be the last to break it.' Mild-mannered and courteous, Little Turtle became a great favorite with Americans and was presented to President Washington in Philadelphia.

As the rain pounded on the window, I learned more about how this quiet, introspective man grew from high school mathematics teacher to one of the country's most successful football coaches. In nine years as a collegiate head coach, his teams have won 11 games twice and ten games three times. Going into 1983, only five active college coaches, including one of the men he studied, Bo Schembechler, had better lifetime winning percentages than his .750.

Football really was Dick Crum's game, even though he didn't play it much until he got to college. And even then, whether it was at Muskingum, where he played for two years, or at Mt. Union, from which he graduated in 1957, he was by no means a star.

"And I think," says Crum, "one of the things that kinda helped me down the road in coaching was . . . you know, I knew what it was to be on the scout team and be one of those guys that went to practice every day and knew you really didn't have a whole lot of chance of playing in the game on Saturday afternoon."

But he liked the game, and he wanted to coach. So he turned to teaching as a means to that end.

"Really," he explains, "I think I got my first coaching job because of what I could teach, not because of coaching. At that time, there was a shortage of math teachers, and I could teach math . . . and physics. So I went over to Boardman and taught and was the jayvee coach.

"One of the things that I'd always thought about was, you know, had I graduated from a school like Miami, maybe my coaching career would have moved along a little more quickly than it did. But in looking back on it, I think I kinda came along at the speed I needed to, because I was an assistant in high school for six years . . ."

Actually, Crum spent two years at Boardman as an assistant, one year at Sandusky and three years at Warren Harding, before he got his first head coaching assignment at Mentor High School in 1963. His six-year record at Mentor was 50-9-1. His team was champion of the Freeway Conference two years and the Greater Cleveland Conference one year. In 1968, when Mentor ranked second in the state of Ohio and went undefeated, Crum's team defeated Massillon, 19-0. During his tenure, Mentor had two undefeated seasons and had a 38-2 record for the last four years.

Crum became acquainted with Miami and Schembechler during his pilgrimages from Mentor to Oxford. During those years, he also met another coach who was to have even more influence on his career.

"The other guy that I got to know," remembers Crum, "was Bill Mallory when he was at Ohio State. He recruited our area for Ohio State and we spent a lotta time talkin' football."

In 1968, Ohio State was preparing to play in the Rose Bowl . . . it was the year after John Pont had led Indiana to Pasadena . . . and Bo Schembechler was on the way to Michigan. When the Buckeyes returned to Columbus, and Mallory was named to succeed Bo, Crum had a thought.

"When Bill came back," says Dick, "I talked to him. And I told him, 'If you're looking for an assistant coach, I'd be interested in goin'. So, time passed and in mid-January, he called and wanted to know if I'd be interested and I said 'Yeah.' I jumped at the chance.

"It's kinda funny, because when I was an assistant in high school at Warren . . . well, I've gotta go clear back . . . the first year I was out teaching and coaching. I made $3700. I taught six classes, guarded the lunchroom, started the wrestling program and was the jayvee football coach. And, you know, was happy to make $3700."

The last year at Warren, he had progressed all the way up to $6500, but when he took the head coaching job at Mentor, he had to start at $5800. But his salary level progressed nicely throughout his years at Mentor, to the point he had reached approximately $13000 in annual earnings.

"I got the opportunity to go to Miami, and I knew I'd have to back up to go," he recalls. "I mean I expected to do it, and was willing to. I went to Miami for ten-three. But, you know, that's been one of the things I think that's kinda been the Miami attitude, because they're notorious for really not payin' all that well.

"But . . . they've got a lotta people wantin' to go there, and I felt the experience there would be well worth backing up some. So I really didn't have much reservation about going."

He went, and stayed for nine years. As we talked, as Crum described his journeys back and forth to different high schools in the northeastern quadrant of the state, it struck me as it hadn't before. So much of the story of Miami football, no matter where it leads, has been written in Ohio by people with roots in Ohio.

"You just look around the country now," explains Crum, "and a lot of the people who are very, very prominent in college and professional football have their roots in Ohio . . . no question about it.

"And the thing about it is: I'm sure some of our guys (his North Carolina assistants) are gonna go out of here and be head coaches and, with the exception of Bobby Cale, who had played for us the first year I was here, every single guy is from Ohio."

Three of those seven are Jack Himebauch, a native of Rocky River, who played as a tight end under John Pont and Schembechler and has been with Crum since 1977; Denny Marcin, a Cleveland native who was a year ahead of Himebauch in school and has been Crum's defensive coordinator at Miami and North Carolina, and Randy Walker from Troy, who played on the Miami teams from 1973 through 1975 that had a record of 32-1-1. All of Walker's coaching experience has been under Crum.

Of those three, Crum feels Walker is the most likely candidate to be a head coach. Marcin, thinks Crum, "just doesn't wanna be a head coach," and Himebauch, having passed age 40, seems, with his family, to have settled into the North Carolina lifestyle. But Walker should be ready soon, if not now. And remember, he's the one who came to Miami because he wanted to coach.

"Randy will be a good head coach," maintains his boss. "He'll be a fine head coach some day. He'll be a guy that'll perpetuate things."

Walker, who played tailback, wingback and fullback during his three years, is the ninth-leading career rusher in Miami history with 1,757 yards. He was drafted by the Cincinnati Bengals after being named Miami's Most Valuable Player following his senior year, but returned to Miami as a graduate assistant. Contemplating Walker's future, which is bright, Crum realizes what others who have enjoyed Miami's riches in coaching background have realized.

Says Crum: "There are not as many Miami guys from . . . I'd say, like . . . '69 on that are out in coaching as maybe, you know, prior to that. I think a lot of that has to do with the economic situation in Ohio. They're cuttin' back on teachers. They're not hiring coaches. It's tough to get a coaching job today."

It wasn't always that way. Particularly among the Miami coaching fraternity. Crum remembers Himebauch as a specific case in point. Crum needed an assistant and he asked Bo who might be available. Schembechler suggested Himebauch, who was then an assistant at Fordham University and had high school coaching experience in Darien, Connecticut.

How does Miami do it? It continues to be a burning question, and when one considers what has happened in the nearly half-century since the coaching school made its debut, and what has happened and is likely to happen to people like Dick Crum and Randy Walker, that question also demands an answer.

"With mirrors," replies Crum. "I think I heard maybe Paul Dietzel say it once . . . 'When you're coach at Miami, when you don't know what you haven't got, you don't miss it.' And you know, when you leave there and

Randy Walker turned down Northwestern to come to Miami because he wanted to coach. Here he runs for good yardage against Eastern Michigan in the 1975 season opener.

you go to some of these other programs and see the things that they make available to you . . .

". . . when you've been operating on a real tight budget. I think maybe that's why some of the guys can do as well as they do, because it's . . . you just have so much more to work with. You know, you come in and you're not worrying about the equipment budget and you're not worrying about how many guys you can take on the road when you play . . . just a lotta things like that."

One wonders, reflecting on some of the meager beginning salaries of the Miami coaches and strained budgets, if that isn't a part of the learning process. It's not a part of any official coaching curriculum, but like the lessons learned by the athletes who worked in the dining halls, the lessons in frugality never seemed to do any irreparable damage to a Miami coach. And maybe, just maybe, it made it easier to teach the mental toughness that has contributed in large measure to Miami's winning attitude. Restrictions, such as they were, tended only to add to a Miami coach's resolve. And it would never dull his sense of humor. Crum explains:

"I'll tell you. The first year we were there, we could only take 40 guys when we played on the road . . . 40 players. And of course, you had to take some extra offensive people, and I think we only took either 16 or 17 defensive players. I know when the defense would run on the field, I'd look around and boy, it was lonesome there. You and a couple guys," he laughs, "and that was it."

Crum pauses, then continues with another story about the Miami traveling squad in those days.

"And then, we always laugh about it, because the NCAA made the rule that the minimum traveling squad was 48. I always tell people, 'When they went to that, we went up eight.'"

As he referred to Miami's four-year struggle with Toledo recounted in the preceding chapter, Crum was voicing some of the frustrations which Miami faced within the Mid-American Conference in the late Sixties and early Seventies.

"During that period of time," he says, "we could always beat Western Michigan. We had trouble with Kent State. We had trouble with Bowling Green . . . that was really about the last time, football-wise, Miami had had trouble with Bowling Green . . .

"It was really funny because, with those teams . . . you know, we beat South Carolina, and we beat Maryland . . . we'd go outside the league and really do the job. Boy, we'd get in the league . . . and we always had trouble with Toledo, Bowling Green and Kent. And of course, Ohio U. That was a traditional dog fight."

But in 1973, all those frustrations ended with the perfect season. Crum describes what made that team winners.

"We were playin' good defense . . . we wound up Number One in the country in defense that year . . . and just really had a good total football team, because the defense was strong, we had a good kicking game and the offense did not turn the ball over. We didn't beat anybody, blowin' 'em out . . . the games were all reasonably tight. But then, if you were ahead of somebody, 14-7, you knew you had 'em. That was a good football team. Conservative offensively, and a very good, aggressive defense."

******

The 1973 Miami football team was Bill Mallory's. But in 1974, the team had a new leader, a man who inherited the burden of not only duplicating the greatest season in Miami's football history, but also of dealing with the fierce loyalty of those who had come to believe that the job of head football coach at Miami was a Miamian's birthright.

Doesn't the Masters champion always inherit the green jacket at Augusta? Ever since Parseghian, there had been a Miami graduate waiting in the wings. And when called, each one had delivered.

"Why change?" asked the critics.

Dick Shrider, the Miami athletic director who introduced Crum to the media at his first press conference, put it this way:

"We have again reached into the Cradle of Coaches Association," said Shrider in January 1974, "to select our new head football coach and he is Dick M. Crum. The Cradle of Coaches is a fantastic organization and has done so much to promote our great athletic heritage and tradition here at Miami.

"To all of us it is a very sacred organization. Perhaps it would be advisable for me to read to the members of the news media a part of the Constitution of the Miami University Cradle of Coaches Association that pertains to membership. I quote:

"'ARTICLE II — Membership — Section 1. Eligibility in this

His first two seasons at the Miami helm, Dick Crum's teams lost one and tied one in 22 games. Two of the victories came in the Tangerine Bowl.

Association shall include all persons who have attended Miami University as fully accredited students and are participating or have participated in the coaching profession. It shall also include all persons who did not attend Miami University but who have coached there.

'Section 2. — Active members of this Association shall include only those members who have contributed to the Miami University Fund for the immediate past or present calendar year and earmarked (the gift) for the Cradle of Coaches Association.'

"Dick Crum is an active member who has been contributing to the Cradle of Coaches Association since its inception. He is in the same category as George L. Rider, Woody Hayes, John Brickels and countless other former and current Miami coaches."

Crum himself had another answer . . . an unspoken answer. In the next two years, Miami won 21 games, lost one and tied one. Two of the victories came in the Tangerine Bowl as Miami, champions of the Mid-American Conference, defeated Georgia, 21-10, in 1974, and then South Carolina, 20-3, in 1975.

For years, Miamians who played for John Pont and made coaching their life's work, set aside an evening at the annual gathering of the American Football Coaches Association for dinner and reminiscing. Often, the conversation turned to perpetuating the Cradle of Coaches, to bringing younger coaches along in the Miami tradition.

And for a while, that's as far as it went. Until Bill Narduzzi determined their actions speak louder than words. At the urging of his former coach, Narduzzi, who was on Carm Cozza's staff at Yale, talked with John Dolibois and Doug Wilson in Miami's Office of Alumni Affairs.

Narduzzi's idea, with a little help from his friends like Seb LaSpina, who remains at Yale; Neil Putnam, now on Bill's staff at Youngstown State; John Drew, an assistant at Temple, and Nick Mourouzis, Pont's long-time aide now head coach at DePauw, was simple. All he wanted was some assistance in developing a semi-formal structure that would bring all of the Miami coaches together on a regular basis, thus perpetuating the Cradle of Coaches legend. Dolibois and Wilson were only too glad to cooperate.

When the Miami University Cradle of Coaches Association held its first meeting at Hollywood, Florida, in 1971, those in attendance approved a constitution which stated the purpose of the association: "To foster a spirit of fraternity among Miamians in the coaching profession and to further enhance their unique relationship with Miami University."

By earmarking their annual contributions to the Miami University Fund for the association, coaches remain eligible for active membership, but more importantly, the treasury began to grow. Narduzzi, who had been elected the association's first president, sought the counsel of Miami's current staff as to how monies funneled through the association might best be utilized.

Without fail, year after year, the Miami University Cradle of Coaches Association has voted to aid the current coaching staff by providing funding for at least one assistant — either a graduate student or an undergraduate who has completed playing eligibility — thereby achieving its stated purpose while encouraging continued involvement in the coaching profession by its former players.

Although Narduzzi refuses to take any credit for either the idea or the Association's obvious success, it is perhaps fitting that, since it all started "over a few beers," one of the association's early meetings took place at Buc's, a Canton (Ohio) tavern where Pont once worked.

"We wanted to solidify some things," says Narduzzi, and since all of the Ohio high school coaches had gathered in Canton for the Ohio High School All-Star game, the time and place were right to encourage their involvement.

"I often wondered," said Dick Crum over dinner in Chapel Hill many years later, "what Phil Shriver thought when he came up to Canton and we met in a bar."

Dr. Phillip R. Shriver, Miami's president through many glorious years in athletics — eight consecutive Reese Cups (Mid-American Conference All-Sports Championships) and all those Tangerine Bowl triumphs — had been asked to join Doug Wilson at that Canton meeting.

"I certainly recall it as a good, friendly and positive gathering," Shriver recalled years later. "A lot of enthusiasm. Granted, it might not have been a customary place for a university president to conduct business with alumni, but it would be assumed that the All-Star game would attract a gathering of high school and college coaches. So there they were, and I wanted them to know they had my full support. And they have indeed given us great support all these years."

******

Ara Parseghian was still the Miami coach when Narduzzi arrived on the Miami campus as a freshman in 1955. It's no wonder Ara called him Willie all afternoon during the 1979 telecast of Youngstown State's loss to Delaware in the Division II national championship game. He was Willie to all of us. That 1979 season, when Bill Narduzzi's Penguins finished 11-2, was made all the more memorable for Narduzzi when he was named Division II national Coach of the Year.

Narduzzi has completed eight years at the helm of Youngstown State with an overall record of 54-24-1. Since 1981, however, Youngstown State, along with the Akron Zips, has joined perennial Division I-AA champion Eastern Kentucky in the Ohio Valley Conference.

After three years of high school experience in Ohio, Narduzzi moved to the University of Pittsburgh, where he earned his master's degree working as a graduate assistant, and then earned his way into the Ivy League at Brown.

Yale was his next stop as an assistant, and then it was still more experience at Miami of Florida and the University of Kentucky before his head coaching opportunity came along in 1975.

Just the year before, Narduzzi had been an assistant at Kentucky when Dick Crum was in his first season at the Miami helm. The Redskins had opened that season with a routine victory over Eastern Michigan, but Miami's 13-game winning streak was snapped with a controversial 7-7 tie at Purdue.

"We scored to take what we thought would be a 14-7 lead," explains

Crum, "but over on the extreme right side of the field, they called our wide receiver offside."

That restored the tie, and then Miami had to dodge three bullets in the final minutes to avoid defeat. Purdue had three consecutive field goal attempts and missed all three. But twice Miami was ruled offside. Finally, the flag stayed in the official's pocket, and Miami at least continued unbeaten.

Another romp over Marshall followed the next week, and then came Kentucky. Miami fell behind early, remembers Crum, "then stabilized," as he likes to say, and with the aid of a blocked punt, came back to take a 14-10 lead. Then one of the great Miami players of that era, Linebacker Brad Cousino, made a play Crum calls "a great example of the determined effort which often separates Miami from other teams."

Kentucky had a slippery quarterback who had real quick feet, as the Miami coach remembers, and he made Cousino miss a tackle. He appeared to be off to the races, with Cousino giving chase after the Wildcat player managed to slip away from the rest of the Redskins. Cousino had pretty good speed, but Crum feared he was no match for the quick Kentuckian. Cousino's determined effort saved the touchdown at the three-yard line, and the thus-inspired Redskins rose up and stopped Kentucky on downs. Then, with ten minutes remaining, Miami took over at its own three and marched methodically down the field. When the clock ran down, Miami was on Kentucky's three, and the Redskins had not relinquished possession of the ball.

Crum and Miami then went back to the task of completing a second consecutive Mid-American Conference championship campaign, and after disposing of Cincinnati with relative ease, the Redskins were ready to go back to Orlando and see about wrapping up a second consecutive unbeaten season (Miami teams of George Little and George Rider had gone unbeaten for three years in 1916-17-18, but there were four ties). Another Southeastern Conference team . . . Georgia . . . was Miami's Tangerine Bowl opponent this time. Crum remembers the Redskins rolled to an early lead against the Bulldogs, "then got a little conservative," before finally winning with relative ease, 21-10. I can recall being in Washington, D.C., the following January and visiting with a stunned Georgia assistant, who professed great respect for the way Miami had taken the play completely away from Georgia.

By 1975, Miami was really on a roll. The 1974 Redskins had finished 10th in both wire service polls; and even with a rookie coach, the unbeaten string remained intact. In fact, for three years, 1973 through 1975, Miami never lost its ranking as one of the country's top 20 teams. Mainly because the Redskins continued to march unscathed through the Mid-American Conference, and met every challenge from a so-called "name" opponent. Except one.

Two games into the 1975 season, a 24-game unbeaten string on the line, Miami marched into East Lansing, Michigan. The largest crowd to see a Miami team play up to that time, was in Spartan Stadium to see if Miami could do to Michigan State what it had done earlier to Indiana, Northwestern and Purdue. Miami appeared to control everything but the scoreboard and adapting to the conditions. It was Crum's first loss as Miami head coach.

"We lost 14-13," remembers Crum. "We dropped a couple of kicks, one of our defensive backs slipped and allowed a touchdown, and we missed four field goals."

But that was the only blemish on the 1975 record of the Redskins. A 14-3 victory over Purdue avenged the tie of a year earlier, and Miami again won the MAC. In the Tangerine Bowl Miami "dominated" South Carolina, is the way Crum puts it. Miami's domination of the Tangerine Bowl for three years led the Tangerine Sports Association to name Crum and Rob Carpenter to the Association's Hall of Fame in 1983.

So Miami had a 32-1-1 record for three years, matching Oklahoma's mark. No other team had done better. And the prospects seemed bright for the future. But it wasn't to be, and for the first time since 1942, Miami suffered the embarrassment of a losing season. In fact, after a narrow 14-10 loss at North Carolina, it was all downhill . . . five more losses in succession. But Crum, disappointed as he was, found encouragement in the fact that the team, in spite of early-season injuries that took a toll, didn't quit.

"We had to move Rob Carpenter to fullback, because we didn't have a fullback," says Crum, "and he didn't like it. But he still got his thousand yards. and we came back to win three of the last five."

There was some reason to suspect that the misfortune of 1976 was only temporary; but the way the 1977 season began, the skeptics were ready to get back in business again. Dick Shrider remembers only too well what it was like.

"We started out the year and won a game at the University of Dayton . . . a very close ball game (26-23), and then went down and played probably the poorest game we've played in a long time against a good South Carolina team and got beat very badly (42-19). So there were a lot of people thought 'Oh-oh, here goes another three and eight season.'

"But the next week we went over to Bloomington, Indiana, and we beat a good Indiana team . . . 21-20 in a game that they scored with a minute and fifty six seconds to go and went ahead of us by six. And we got the ball and just methodically went down the field and took it in with 13 seconds to go and kicked the extra point and won 21-20."

Shrider and Crum have different perspectives of the impact of that game. The administrator draws a comparison between the absolute ecstasy in Oxford in 1962 . . . the pandemonium brought on by Miami's victory over Purdue. When the Redskins' caravan pulled into Oxford after the win at Bloomington, "only two people were there to greet us."

Has winning made Miami complacent? There are signs of it. Not among the coaches or players. But elsewhere. It bears watching, but after that Indiana victory, Dick Crum was looking for answers to a different question. Had his team righted itself again?

The record book says yes, because after Miami went over to New Haven and beat Carm Cozza's Yale team, 28-14, the Redskins had the springboard to another Mid-American Conference title, still their most recent. But the league's tie-up with the Tangerine Bowl had gone by the boards, and the California Bowl, where MAC champs have gone since 1981, had yet to surface. So Miami's comeback year wound up at 10-1.

******

As the 1977 season finale at Cincinnati was approaching, Dick Crum somehow had a feeling that game would be his last at Miami.

"Tell you what," explains Crum. "One of the strangest feelings I ever had in my life, and it was almost . . . I don't know why I had it . . . but we always have the senior tackle right out on the 50-yard line at Miami Field. And that last year I was there, we had the senior tackle before the Cincinnati game . . . and all the kids ran off the field, and I was the last guy walkin' off, and I turned around and looked at it . . . and I don't know why, but the thought went through my mind, 'I'm never gonna coach back here again.' I had goose bumps . . . I really felt funny . . . and it was true."

Like others before him, Crum wasn't particularly thinking about

Coach Crum and Randy Walker appeared together on a local television show during Walker's playing days.

leaving Miami, yet he knew his time would come, sooner or later. It came in January of 1978, and it was triggered by the sudden resignation of long-time North Carolina Coach Bill Dooley, who went to Virginia Tech to become head coach and athletic director. Old pal Bo Schembechler wondered if Crum might be interested in the Carolina position. Not much later, Dick heard from Bill Cobey, the North Carolina athletic director, who asked if he'd like to come down for an interview.

"The speed was unbelievable," says Crum as he reflects on the move, "because they called on a Tuesday and asked me if I could come down Wednesday evening and talk with them on Thursday, and bring my wife."

Dick was there on Thursday, and "they really did a job with the interview . . . you saw everything" and on the way back to the airport Cobey wondered how interested Crum was in the job. When Dick acknowledged that he was "very interested," Cobey said he'd be in touch with him the next day.

"He called me at 10 o'clock in the morning," remembers Dick, "and he said, 'If we offer you this job will you take it?'

"I said, 'Yeah, I will,' and he said, 'Well, it looks like we're gonna do that. I'll call you back,' and he called back at 11 o'clock and offered me the job. That was Friday, and I was here that night. It was just 'Wham,' and here we were . . . and it's been a good move."

Before explaining further, Crum wants me to be sure I understand what happens at Miami.

"The thing you've gotta understand about Miami," says Crum, "is that you know when you go there they don't want you comin' there to stay. I mean that's part of the tradition there. You know, 'Come in, do the best you can, and then move on.' And I'd been there nine years . . . a head coach for four years.

"And in lookin' at this job, I thought, 'Ya' know, I'm gonna have to move. There's no question about that.' I liked what I saw here, and academically, I thought they were aimed in the right direction; they wanted student-athletes, it wasn't a football factory, and I just felt real comfortable with the people. That's about how quick it happened; there was no great intrigue involved in it at all."

Like Yale, and Michigan, and so many of the schools where Miami coaches have landed, North Carolina is a comfortable place to be. Obviously, Crum has been more than equal to the competitive challenge. He has added four more successful bowl appearances to his two Tangerine Bowl victories at Miami. His record in post-season games remains perfect.

With beaches to the east, the mountains to the west, and lovely Chapel Hill right in the middle, Dick Crum finds a lot to like about North Carolina. One would suspect that North Carolina has found a lot to like about Dick Crum.

". . . This is a very special year. It's kinda like we are handed a cherished heirloom . . . the Miami football field. We're given this heirloom and told, 'It's yours, you have to do well by it.' We're given this football field with the tradition . . . rich and deep and 'way back . . . it's given to us the very last year. A lot of attention is going to be given to it . . . so therefore . . . we're a special group in that way. Not that we're any better but time, I think, has bestowed this on us. And that's kinda the feeling that we have this year, playing on Miami Field.

"That's the original feeling you have as you approach this season. That feeling, however, is somewhat distant. You know, you have five games . . . that's a lotta football. I think it's taken a new turn now. As I stood out there on the field before the second half of last week's game . . . looked around and saw the largest crowd in the history of that field . . . it started to hit me then. 'My God, we just aren't gonna see it again. It's not gonna be here.'"

Tom Reed, Miami's coach from 1978 through 1982, reflecting on the closing of Miami Field.

XI
AULD LANG SYNE

CENTRAL MICHIGAN never had a chance. The day belonged to Miami. And when students staked out the north goal posts as one of the many souvenirs that would be snatched from the old stadium that day, the game's outcome already had been determined.

The date was November 6, 1982. After 87 years and 333 games, historic Miami Field was seeing its last football game. The second-oldest college-owned football stadium in the United States (Pennsylvania's Franklin Field being the oldest) was giving way to a biological sciences building on its central campus site. Yager Stadium, a 25,000 seat structure at the edge of the campus, would become the new home for Miami football. But before the day would give way to memories and nostalgia and ceremony, the Redskins had some unfinished business.

Early in the first quarter, a good punt return gave the Chippewas excellent field position, inside Miami's 30-yard line. Five running plays later, Central Michigan had a third and two on Miami's ten-yard line. Central went to its main man, Curtis Adams, the Mid-American Conference's leading rusher. He was stopped for no gain. Then Miami's fierce rush caused the field goal kicker, Novo Bojovic, to miss wide on his chip shot attempt. For Central Michigan, that turned out to be the last gasp.

Playing with pride and that fierce determination so characteristic of Miami teams, Miami scored its first points with just a couple of minutes remaining in the first quarter. The big play in an 85-yard touchdown drive was a 46-yard pass from Al Marlow, freshman walk-on quarterback out of Pickerington, Ohio, to senior flanker Mike Haffey, whose dad John had been a Miami classmate of mine.

By halftime, the score had mounted to 16-0, and when a 50-yard run by Miami backup tailback Phil Palcic made it 23-0, the student celebrants took over. That remained the score until the end, but for the final five and a half minutes, the football action was secondary to the action in the north end zone as a coterie of students climbed the goal posts, and by sheer weight, finally brought them down. This in spite of the pleas of the public address announcer to simply lift the posts from the ground.

To set the stage properly for the ceremonies which followed this Miami victory, let's recall my conversation with Coach Tom Reed at mid-point of the week of "The Last Game." He remembers it had been halftime of the previous Saturday's game when the full impact of what was happening hit him, when reality set in.

"You start taking things for granted," he says on Wednesday. "For example, when I go run now . . . I run out in the country . . . I always finish up my last coupla miles at Miami Field, because I'll never get a chance to do that again.

"Then you apply it to this week, in relation to playing the last football game on the field, it has to be a stimulus. I have several letters . . . from Ara . . . Paul Brown . . . Weeb . . . from different people . . . Carm Cozza . . . concerning their feelings about Miami Field. We kinda dedicated this week to Miami Field."

Reed pauses, as if to bring himself back to earth, to focus better on the task at hand. Then he continues.

"This game has to be reality. We've gotta get involved in it. We have to feel the presence of all those who have played before, but we also have to realize that playing football is still blocking, tackling and running. Ara isn't gonna win the game for us, Weeb Ewbank isn't. You have to prepare yourself that way.

"The other thing is that our seniors . . . it's their last home game at Miami . . . This week, as we go out to practice, we all will walk out and go across the field on the way to Cook Field (where Miami practices), and I told 'em to stop and think a little bit about all that has taken place there over the years. Get that feeling, let it get inside you and let it help motivate, stimulate and excite you. But don't think that's gonna win the game for you.

"Another dimension . . . of this football game is the fact that Central Michigan is, without a question, the best football team we will play this year up to this point in time. It's gonna demand our best effort, but I think that's a fitting way to go out on the field, where you are placed in

The author, wearing the light coat, pauses on his way into Miami Field for the last game. The gates will become fixtures at the new stadium this fall.

the situation where you have to have your best effort to win."

Reed went on to point out that Central Michigan had been the last visiting team to win a game on Miami Field . . . that happened in 1980 . . . and the only Mid-American Conference team never to taste defeat on Miami Field (the teams had met twice previously on the historic field). Since entering the Conference, the Chippewas had won three of four overall from Miami.

"Maybe," he concludes before heading for practice, "if we had William & Mary, or somebody like that, it would be easier; but quite honestly, I think this is the way you want it. It's the toughest game we're going to have."

That's essentially what Paul Brown had said to me in his office a day earlier. But Brown also knew it was the type of gut-check Miami teams take, and pass more often than not. The game was over, the closing ceremonies finished, when our paths crossed again. As this great coach put the blankets in the car and said goodby, I remembered what he had said just a few days earlier. Brown had seen Miami play occasionally over the past several seasons and had observed:

"I'll guarantee you they don't measure up in manpower to some others they play. They didn't have the manpower that UC did last year, but they outfought 'em. That's a good sign. They're reflecting something."

As Brown made his way back to Cincinnati and past the crest of the hill where Miami's campus buildings ordinarily come into view, or in this case fade from sight, maybe he even thought about the first time he had seen the "Crimson Towers." It was that kind of day.

******

The closing ceremony. When the hands on the old scoreboard clock finally got as close as possible to "straight-up 12," signalling the end of the game, what happened next was at once moving and memorable. Lest I be accused of losing all objectivity, let me steal a few lines, with permission from the report of Bob Harrod in the November 13 **Indianapolis News.** Wrote Harrod:

> OXFORD, OHIO — The revered, cleat-worn sod of Miami Field shook with a final thunderous cheer last Saturday.
>
> The old field was the arena where thousands of Redskin football players sweat, struggled and bled for 87 autumns.
>
> This was no ordinary 120 yards of grassland, no sleek front lawn, no Astroturf gridiron. Every square inch of this battleground has felt the mark of the men who have contributed to the greatness of the game.
>
> The names of Earl Blaik, Paul Brown, Weeb Ewbank, Ara Parseghian and John Pont are spoken with awe throughout America. They began their journey to reknown at Miami Field.

Harrod's piece didn't end there, but I can still picture the chaos on the field as students and old grads and hundreds of others poured out of the stands and milled around on the field as public address announcer Bernard Phelps tried to get the attention of the nearly 20,000 who had jammed Miami Field for this historic occasion.

"As the Miami Marching Band takes this field for the last time," Phelps intoned above the din," we direct your attention," and here

Phelps had to alter the script, calling for the honored guests to assemble in the south end zone, which by that time was overrun by more souvenir seekers . . . "to the center of the field where M-Men have gathered from throughout the country to commemorate this final game at Miami Field.

"The 57 men leading the M-Men represent 65 teams that have played at Miami Field. Among them are 20 team captains, 23 All-MAC performers, one All-American and 15 members of the Miami Hall of Fame. Nearly three quarters of a century of excellence in intercollegiate athletics is represented by these proud men who symbolize the spirit of this stadium.

"Placed in use in 1896, Miami Field is the second-oldest stadium in the United States. Over these decades, thousands of talented men and women have participated in football and track. And, of course, it is this field that has given Miami the Cradle of Coaches, a unique distinction and a valuable part of the Miami tradition."

As Dr. Phelps, the speech professor, continued to set the stage, from

Tom Jones performing his specialty . . .

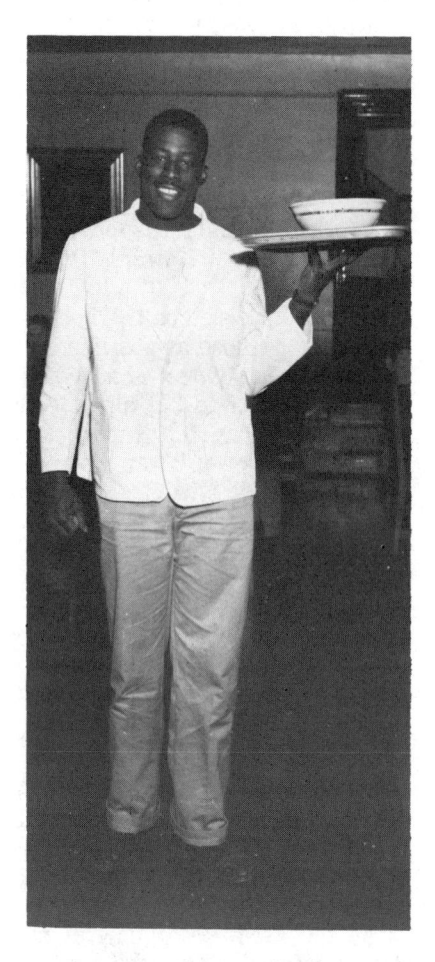

. . . and working his board job.

my press box vantage point I looked directly at Reid Hall. I was reminded of the winter afternoon in 1954 when I was in my room and I was startled by what sounded like an explosion. Investigation uncovered what I learned was one of the "character-building" aspects of Miami. Tom Jones, the NCAA shot put champion, who also was a Miami tackle, was practicing his specialty. The Miami "fieldhouse" in those days was under the stands of the stadium. During the winter and inclement weather, that's where Jones practiced. Occasionally, one of his throws would go too high, and the result was the explosion I heard.

I had another of those "uniquely Miami" experiences early in my freshman year at Miami. As Tom Pagna and others have told us, each of the Miami athletes, stars or substitutes, earned his scholarship with a board job in one of the dormitories. Students learned quickly who the athletes were simply by observing who waited tables or who did dishes. Wayne Embry was a dishwasher in Reid Hall and a classmate. His exploits on the basketball floor are legendary, but it's hard to wipe from one's memory the sight of this 6-foot, 8-inch, 250-pounder with the huge hands reaching in the dish water and "palming" a couple of full-sized dinner plates.

"And now," continued Bernie Phelps, "we direct your attention to the east side of the field (the Reid Hall side) where Former Presidents John D. Millett and Phillip R. Shriver have joined Dr. Paul G. Pearson.

"The 1982 team captains are presenting the game ball to the presidents,

Presidents Millett, Shriver and Pearson, left to right, accept the game ball from Miami's final victory at the old stadium and start it down the line. Paul Drennan waits.

who represent 29 years of Miami leadership. Dr. Pearson is presenting the ball to the 1981 team representative Paul Drennan who starts the ball down the line for one last time."

And as Phelps ticked off the names and years as the ball moved from east to west across the field, the Miami Marching Band played the fight song in the background and the crowd applauded in tribute.

1980 . . . Kent McCormick, son of Sun Bowler Bill, '50, a veteran coach . . . to
1979 . . . Mark Hunter, still holding Miami kickoff return records . . . to
1978 . . . Greg Sullivan . . . to
1977 . . . Jack Glowik, a Reed assistant ... to
1976 . . . Randy Gunlock, whose dad Bill, '51, coached at Bowling Green, Army and Ohio State before turning to business . . . to
1975 . . . Mel Edwards . . . to
1974 . . . Brad Cousino, one of the stars of the 1973-75 era . . . to
1973 . . . Bob Hitchens, Miami's all-time rushing leader, now on the Miami coaching staff . . . to
1972 . . . Bob Williams and John Saccomen . . . to
1971 . . . Rich Dougherty . . . to
1970 . . . Mike Flaig . . . to
1969 . . . Merv Nugent . . . to
1968 . . . Jay Bennett, Oxford attorney . . . to
1967 . . . Ken Root, teammate and close friend of Reed . . . to

Jay Colville passes the ball to Tom Pagna as the ceremony continues.

1965 ... Tom Stillwagon, All-Conference center on the last Miami team I covered ... to
1964 ... Ernie Kellermann, the best quarterback I ever watched ... to
1963 ... Tom Longsworth, a great two-way player and All-MAC fullback, now a corporate jet pilot ... to
1962 ... Gerry Myers, a rugged tight end on the team that upset Purdue ... to
1961 ... Jack Gayheart, a tough, red-headed quarterback ... to
1959 ... Richard Puzzitiello ... to
1958 ... Dave Girbert, an outstanding running back who has turned to the ministry ... to
1957 ... Pat Orloff, an All-Conference guard ... to
1956 ... Dean Porter ... to
1955 ... Jerry Ippoliti, former head coach at Northern Illinois, now the Huskies' associate athletic director ... to

The applause grew louder as Phelps introduced Trainer Emeritus Jay Colville, who was at the middle of the field representing those teams not acknowledged by specific year. And more of Miami's greats stepped forward.

1954 ... Bob Bronston, one in a line of powerful Miami fullbacks whose coaching and administrative work in the Springfield school system are widely heralded ... to
1953 ... Tom Pagna, the marvelous halfback who worked at Ara's right hand for many years ... to
1951 ... Jay Fry, father of a Miami assistant by the same name, himself an assistant at Miami and elsewhere before becoming president of Camp America, a sports camp outside of Oxford ... to
1950 ... Dale Doland, All-Conference guard, a Canadian pro before becoming an industrial executive ... to
1949 ... Ernie Plank, who has gained both a Rose Bowl ring, as an assistant at Indiana, and a Super Bowl ring, as a scout for San Francisco ... to
1948 ... Arch McCartney, businessman ... to
1946-47 ... Bill Hoover, who captained and coached as an Oxford businessman ... to
1944-45 ... Ed (Hooks) Weber ... to
1943 ... Lou Kaczmarek, Franklin, Ohio, high school administrator and longtime coach, whose term on the Cradle of Coaches steering committee expires in 1984 ... to
1941-42 ... Leo Less ... to
1940 ... Dan Schisler ... to
1939 ... Mel Rebholz, long active in the Cincinnati Miami Men's Club ... to
1938 ... Dr. Arthur Evans, Cincinnati urologist and medical school department head ... to
1937 ... Howard Brinker, longtime aide to Paul Brown ... to
1936 ... Ted Rytel ... to
1935 ... Charles Heimsch, eminent Miami botanist and chairman of

	Miami's Athletic Advisory Board . . . to
1934	. . . George Panuska, Cincinnati oil executive . . . to
1933	. . . Stan Lewis, retired Middletown coach . . . to
1932	. . . Glen Isgrig . . . to
1931	. . . Joe Brown . . . to
1930	. . . James A. Gordon, 1932 Olympics 400-meter finalist, who served Miami as acting track coach, assistant in several sports, business manager of athletics and physical education department chairman . . . to
1929	. . . Andy Althauser . . . to
1928	. . . Paul Glick, retired Procter & Gamble executive . . . to
1927	. . . George Vossler, 1982 Miami Hall of Fame inductee . . . to
1926	. . . Bob Whittaker, retired Bowling Green track and football coach . . . to
1924-25	. . . Gordon Wilson, retired Miami English professor and archivist . . . to
1919-21	. . . Elmer (Mike) Essig . . . to
1918-20	. . . Walter McNelly, retired Miami zoology-physiology department chairman, Athletic Advisory Board member and instructional television pioneer.

Next the ball was passed to Russell Baker, age 91, who first saw football on this field as a kid in 1905 and who played on this field on Miami teams from 1909 to 1912 and captained the 1912 team. The oldest living M-Man then passed the ball, as Phelps said over the public address system, "to four members of the famed Cradle of Coaches who represent all Miami coaches everywhere: Weeb Ewbank, '28; Paul Brown, '30; Paul Dietzel, '48; John Pont, '52."

As the crowd roared approval, the ceremony came to an end as Phelps added:

"Head Coach Tom Reed, who also represents the 1966 team, is giving the ball to Jay Peterson and Brian Pillman representing the 1982 Miami Redskins. They are charged to bring that ball back to Yager Stadium on October 1, 1983, where it will be used for the opening kickoff."

Harrod, the **Indianapolis News** writer, described what happened next:
  After that ceremony, the crowd gradually wandered away, many carrying pieces of bleachers, goal posts, turf and bricks — reminders in some future year of the days when Parseghian thrilled with his brilliant runs and Brown passed over the opposition.
  A red-clad Miami marching band stood by while the symbolic ball was being passed from man to man. The strains of the old song went out over Oxford as in days past:
  . . . days of old and days to be.
  Weave a story of thy glory,
  Old Miami, here's to thee.

The tears had already welled in my eyes a couple of times when the band broke into "Auld Lang Syne" as people milled around, many reluctant to leave. From my press box perch, where I'd watched many a game since the two-tiered structure had been added in 1958, I reflected on the events of the day.

It was Yogi Berra, I think, during his managerial days, who uttered the now famous line, "The game's not over until it's over." For Central Michigan, this game had been over even before a local clothier, Jack Samuelson, appeared on the sidelines in the third quarter, dressed like a character out of Miami's past. For years, the legendary Harry Thobe appeared at Miami Field dressed in a white linen suit and sporting a red-banded straw hat, holding aloft a red-and-white parasol. There he would proclaim to the Miami faithful, "I had a dream last night," and of course, the dream was of a Miami victory.

Harry Thobe is only a memory now; but November 6, 1982, was a day for memories. Jack Samuelson, whose Jack's Corner Store was an Oxford landmark for years, took a lot of Miami people on a walk down memory lane in his third-quarter strut.

One more flashback put this day in perspective. I also had been at Miami Field the week before. Recall of that game with Toledo helped affirm once more what I had known for a long time: that the Miami spirit dies hard. On Parents' Day, the largest crowd in Miami Field history was jammed into every available nook and cranny and ringed the field — standing.

With eight minutes remaining, Mike Kiebach's field goal attempt was short and Miami continued to trail by three, 17-14. Things looked grim when just over two minutes remained and Miami finally got the ball on its own 18. The Redskins advanced to the 32. Al Marlow passed 36 yards to Randy Williams, who made a spectacular catch to give Miami new life on the Toledo 32. On fourth and one at the 23, tailback Jay Peterson kept the drive alive by picking up two yards. When Marlow's half-scramble,

A highlight of the 1979 spring practice at Miami was the Varsity-Alumni game. Bo Schembechler coached the offense for the alumni and Weeb Ewbank was in charge of the defense.

half-rollout took Miami down to the ten, the Redskins smelled the end zone. With 45 seconds left, Peterson, behind the awesome blocking of a fired-up Miami line, put Miami in the end zone and in the lead from four yards out. A thrilling finish; and as dusk settled over Miami Field for the last time on the chilly November Saturday, I couldn't help wondering if that comeback a week earlier hadn't been a prelude to the grand finale.

******

Earlier in Miami football history, the rivalry with Ohio Wesleyan University in the old Ohio and Buckeye Conferences was a good one. Ohio Wesleyan is at Delaware, 18 miles or so from Columbus, and Tom Reed can remember riding his bike as a little boy over to the stadium on Saturday afternoons to watch Wesleyan's games.

"There's something about having a university in your town," says Reed. ". . . and I always dreamed at that point in time of playing college football."

It was on that same rainy North Carolina Monday I had talked with Dick Crum down the road in Chapel Hill; and as I talked with the new North Carolina State coach on the campus in Raleigh, I realized the college football he dreamed about in Delaware and college football in the Atlantic Coast Conference are worlds apart. But everybody starts somewhere.

Reed's football start came "in the fourth or fifth grade" with flag football and advanced to the point where he was one of Bo Schembechler's recruits when he came back to Miami to coach in 1963

The old press box at Miami Field. The newer, two-tiered version was under construction during my senior year.

And Reed says Miami wasn't even on his mind when one of Bo's new assistants, Jim Herbstreit, called him.

"I was uncertain between Capital, Toledo and Bowling Green," remembers Reed, "so I went down to Miami on a beautiful May afternoon . . . the sun was shining and everything, and I happened to watch the scrimmage and Bo offered me a scholarship . . . there was no question.

". . . So it was just a matter of fate that, all at once, you receive a phone call and it changes the whole course of your life."

Considering his stature . . . Reed is not big and in his own words was no more than "a plumber" for the Redskins as a running back . . . Reed was in no way intimidated by the "excitable" Schembechler that first

Tom Reed was recruited by Bo Schembechler, and his coaching philosophy is patterned after the Michigan coach.

year. His high school coach had been much the same way, so he felt right at home.

Reed lettered all three of his varsity years for the Redskins and was on the 1965 and '66 teams which shared MAC championships. But from a personal standpoint, his biggest moment may have come during his sophomore year.

"I just worked very hard to try to play. Started a few games my sophomore year, started a few my junior, started a few my senior . . . and just did anything I could to get in, whether it be kickoff return, punt team, kickoff team, whatever else . . . but just being involved in playing, lettering, starting a few games, meant an awful lot to me.

". . . Probably starting as a sophomore against Bowling Green, then in first place in the Conference, was a pretty big moment for me. I'll never forget that one. That was a pretty big one, I guess. The nervousness and the anticipation, the preparation for the game . . . knowing the whole week that as a sophomore you were gonna start against the team that was first in the conference."

Miami and Reed lost that game to Bowling Green, 21-18, yet he still remembers Bo's words of encouragement as he came off the field after game's end.

"'Hey, man,' he said. 'You tried, Keep your head up and we're just gonna keep on goin' from this point on.'"

Reed remembers most the closeness of those teams he played on under Bo. They were few in number, and after a 1-3 start to begin the 1965 season, they grew even closer. The undermanned Redskins had lost to Purdue first, 28-0, in a game that many have said was not as close as the score would seem to indicate. Next there was the "dastardly loss to Xavier, 28-29" and then after a win over Western Michigan, another loss, this one to Kent State, put Miami on the ropes in the Conference.

"Everybody had literally counted us out," says Reed, "and you can imagine some of the turmoil that Bo was goin' through . . . we had I think maybe 38 kids was all we had on that team . . . so we were extremely close. And we started tryin' to mesh and work together and we wound up seven and three and we tied for the Conference championship."

The next year Miami went 9-1, again tying for the MAC title. The team, Reed says, by being extremely close on and off the field and by doing things together had overcome the adversity in the early stages of that 1965 season.

******

Making the transition from player to coach was about as fateful as getting to Miami in the first place. Reed was unsure about what he wanted to do, and a gentle nudge from Bo got him to return to Miami as a graduate assistant and to work with the freshmen. A freshman contest over at Athens where "we got after 'em pretty good . . . and I really enjoyed it" persuaded him to make coaching his life's work, and he's never looked back.

His first full-time coaching job was as an assistant to Gordon Larson at the University of Akron, but much of his coaching apprenticeship has been as a Schembechler disciple. He went from Akron to Arizona, where

Jim Young from Bo's Miami staff was the head coach, and then joined Schembechler at Michigan as the defensive line coach.

Yet even the first job, the one with Gordon Larson at Akron, was Schembechler-influenced. Larson had worked with Bo at Ohio State, and Reed was Bo's recommendation when Larson sought help in filling a vacancy on his staff.

Though he obviously had some influence when Reed was chosen to succeed Dick Crum at Miami, Schembechler felt he wasn't in a position to make a specific recommendation. Reed's assessment of his hiring is uncomplicated. It alludes to his wide range of experience, at an early age, with three different college programs. He fit the Miami mold, too, in that he was young and aggressive, a coach who might require "tightening on the reins," as Reed remembers Dick Shrider telling him.

Any tightening turned out to be self-inflicted, as Miami, after opening the 1982 season with five straight victories, suffered through two consecutive shutouts at the hands of Western Michigan and Ohio University. The students grew restless, no doubt because Miami had failed to win a Conference championship in four years under Reed. And now as 1982 looked lost, homemade signs appeared the next week at the stadium. "Start a new tradition. Fire Reed," said the students who had grown impatient with a five-year record of 34-19-2.

But in the true Miami tradition, another remedy was on the way. North Carolina State made a move, and so did Reed.

******

"Tom Reed had nothing to do with getting this job. It was totally, 100 per cent, the head coach at Miami . . . who it was at that point in time. I know it . . . I mean nobody has told me that, but I know that's exactly how it evolved."

Thus does Reed explain the fact that he is sitting in the head coach's chair in the luxuriant football office complex deep in the woods on the North Carolina State campus in Raleigh rather than back at Millett Hall in Oxford. And lest there be any misunderstanding, Tom was not searching for a job. The job came searching for him.

"In other words," he explains, "I was sitting down one day at my desk and Dick Mochrie, chairman of the selection committee, called me and said, 'Would you be interested in the North Carolina State job?' And I know he was just . . . he didn't know me but he was looking for head coaches: one criterion was an established head coach. And so they went to schools that had produced established head coaches. So I have no qualms about it. I didn't get the job here; Miami University got me this job . . . 100 per cent . . . total."

Reed recalls how Mochrie asked him what his record was. He says he was so surprised by the call that he responded off-handedly that he didn't know. Tom honestly hadn't given any thought to leaving Miami, particularly with the opening of Yager Stadium just around the corner.

After a few days of reflection, he felt he may have overstepped the bounds of courtesy in his earlier conversation with Mochrie, so he called back to apologize. And by that time, after a little further investigation, he felt he would be at least interested in exploring the situation further. A few days later, an interview was arranged.

Before leaving for Raleigh, Reed assured his wife, Cathee, he had every intention of being on hand for the opening of the new stadium, but he also called his old mentor Bo to tell him he was going to Raleigh to look into the North Carolina State job.

"In his normal tone of voice and vernacular," Tom recalls Bo saying, "You're doing what?" And promptly made a couple of telephone calls and quickly assured Tom that it was indeed a new opportunity he should look at thoroughly.

"I had four criteria listed in terms of a job," says Tom. "One, you had to be able to win. The schedule is such that we can. Two, you have to win without cheatin'. And this league probably is the cleanest league in the country. (And why not? It's headed by Robert C. James, previously commissioner of the Mid-American Conference.)

"Not that they are any nicer people, but we are so close together that you are watched by the others in what you do. So I don't think you have to cheat to win.

"Do they want a conservative program? In other words, don't come in and buy your players. Don't look for a championship the cheap way, just build it soundly. Take some time. Graduate your football players. Create some sound individuals. Wear a coat and tie on the road. They want a conservative program. They did want this very badly. I think that's probably one of the biggest things that helped me in obtaining the job.

"The fourth thing was 'Can you get your football players locally?' By six hours in a car can you reach 95 percent of your team. Yes, we can."

So the four criteria that Reed had considered essential to moving into a new coaching situation had been satisfied. But during the course of the interview he discovered two more things about North Carolina State that made the job even more attractive. The first was that unemployment in the state, though at an all-time high, was only 3.9 per cent, a far cry from the depressing facts in Ohio.

And in North Carolina, college football is a part of the culture, the heritage.

"You grow up, you become a Baptist, you become a Methodist or a Presbyterian, and you also become a North Carolina State, Carolina, Wake Forest, Duke fan. It's just one of the things that happens . . . the identifying factor is with the college teams."

The Raleigh-Durham press was summoned to a press conference on December 21 to learn that Tom Reed was following Dick Crum into North Carolina to coach the Wolfpack football team. In the **Durham Morning Herald** the next day, Columnist Ron Morris had this to say about the hiring:

"N.C. State dipped into a well that never seems to run dry when it hired Tom Reed away from Miami of Ohio.

"Reed arrived Tuesday as N.C. State's newest football coach much like Dick Crum arrived at North Carolina five years ago. Crum did not have much of a reputation, nor does Reed. Both, however, carry a tradition. They come from a school that seems to manufacture top-notch coaches."

The headline in the same paper which announced Reed's selection said simply, "State Robs 'Cradle,' Names Reed Coach."

Reed knew that North Carolina State was subject to a slap on the wrist for indiscretions of the previous football administration. The indiscretions involved recruiting; a determining factor in Reed's decision to accept the position at Raleigh was his confidence that the university administration was committed to a football program that did things properly.

******

Football and family are the only two things that matter in Tom Reed's life. He doesn't see any problem with that.

"I have only two things," he says. "My family and football, and I'm totally committed to that, but I don't find a conflict. I think they both enrich each other. The family makes me a better coach, makes me a more understanding person. Football makes me a more understanding person in relation to my family. As long as I'm not out doing a lot of other things, the two go together very, very well . . . very easily.

Building a staff would seem to be a top priority for any coach, but particularly for one just entering his first season. Reed sees his job much differently at North Carolina State than he did at Miami.

"Miami and here are two different situations. At Miami, I liked to take the young men that we had there and bring them on just like Bo did with me. I want 'em around as student assistant, graduate assistant, then hire 'em as a coach.

"Jack Glowik, Dave Hatgas, Jay Fry were three I can think of. Bobby Messaros is back on the campus now coachin' there . . . that was the philosophy there. By having them back through the Cradle of Coaches grant, sometimes as a student assistant, and then having them as a graduate assistant, I had a man for two years.

"Here, it's a little different. Here, I will go out and find a . . . fellow who's an experienced coach. I'll look for a Miami guy obviously, and the reason I would hire one is because I know John Pont well or know Bo well and if they would recommend somebody, then I could take that recommendation. Building a staff here, I'll keep the kids on as graduate assistants, but I probably won't hire them as coaches. I just need more experience.

"The difference is . . . when I bring a coach in here, he has to bring his experience to this place. He doesn't gain his experience while coaching. But that's one of the great things about Miami . . . it does allow you to learn and gain experience while coaching there."

******

Reed, during his Miami coaching years, was outspoken about the recruiting advantages enjoyed by other Mid-American Conference teams because Miami's stadium was so outdated. Without question, when ground was broken on January 30, 1982, for the new sports complex which became a reality with the opening of the 1983 football season, Reed breathed a huge sigh of relief. No question he understood as well as anyone the traditions and history of Miami Field, yet he also understood the need to move on to new horizons.

His personal dream to coach Miami in that opening game at Yager

Stadium after ringing down the curtain at Miami Field was to go unfullfilled. However, as he prepared for "Auld Lang Syne" in the fall of 1982, he still was intensely aware of the history being made, and the history yet to be written.

"As a coach and a player you're saddened by leaving that place out there . . . you just are. Our players now are very saddened . . ." explains Reed the week of the last game. "I mean it just grows on you, you have an affection for it, you love it. You have to realize, though: to grow and develop, you have to change . . . that's all there is to it.

"Young people grow up, and they leave home. They don't want to do it, but it is a necessity. It has to be done, if they're going to grow and develop as they should as strong, mature adults. If we stay at Miami Field, our program is gonna wither. We're not gonna develop, we're gonna wither on the vine. A young man or woman stays at home, they don't develop. It's the same thing.

"You have to go to a new situation, take all that tradition that we have on Miami Field and carry it down to the new field, and it's a new era for us . . . a new beginning for us in some ways, just as it is for the people that leave home.

"We have to instill that in our football program and develop the same feeling for that . . . the same pride we developed in Miami Field. This opens up new horizons for us as a football program . . . we'll enjoy some nice facilities, we'll enjoy some recruiting privileges we've never had before . . .

"So I'm very excited about the future . . . extremely excited about the future."

That future is now in the hands of Tim Rose.

The geographical location of this place and the beauty of it set it apart from all the other universities . . . . Then it got to the place as it developed and grew where everybody wanted to be a part of it. It's been that way for a long, long time.

We got the very finest people . . . a cross section of people . . . to want to come here, and want to be associated. And I think that any success that occurs anywhere is all due to one thing . . . it's due to people.

Dick Shrider, Miami University athletic director since 1965.

XII
A PLACE OF UNMATCHED BEAUTY

THIS IS A book about football at Miami University . . . the people who have played it . . . the people who have coached it. Yet it's more than that. It's a book about an institution, and that institution's people.

And as those people have said over and over, the initial and oft-times lasting impression of Miami University is the beauty of the campus setting. Amidst the beauty, says Dick Shrider, the people of Miami thrive.

"When you have a place like this," says Shrider, " . . . a place where people like to go . . . beautiful trees and a lot of green grass, isolated on a little hill, and a nice little stream that comes down here."

Such a setting, such an environment, maintains Shrider, has led hundreds and hundreds of people . . . good people . . . to Miami, where each has managed to make a special contribution.

"I found out in my short time that I've been here," continues Shrider, "any success that we have had has been due to the fact that we have had more good people . . . That doesn't mean that everybody's perfect, but it does mean this: that there are more quality individuals here than any place I've ever seen.

" . . . So when you start out with that premise . . . that you've got happy people coming to a beautiful situation, and they're quality people . . . it stands to reason that they're going to get things done. Intelligent, happy people working together can do many things that people can't do when they're not happy, they're not surrounded by beauty."

Shrider's vantage point is that of one who once viewed Miami as the opposition, yet has come to see, and be a part of, the Miami tradition. Not surprisingly, says Shrider, Miami people believe in that tradition.

"Miami people helping Miami people. Very strong loyalties . . . almost stronger in many cases than family."

As Shrider sees it, this family concept, producing strong loyalties, has enabled Miami to maintain and continue the tradition of the Cradle of Coaches. And, says Shrider, he has seen the family concept in operation as he has conducted the affairs of the Miami athletic department over the past two decades.

****

Dick Shrider came to Miami in 1957 as head basketball coach. He's never left, and he isn't likely to before he retires a few years down the road.

During his college years at Ohio University, Shrider played basketball against Miami in both his junior and senior seasons. He earned All-Conference honors both years and was an All-Ohio selection as a senior. Athens was Shrider's last stop on a trail of colleges that had included

Ohio State, Michigan and Columbia. A native of Glenford in southeastern Ohio, Shrider began his college years at Ohio State. When he joined the Navy's officer training program, he was transferred to Michigan. And just before leaving for overseas duty, the Navy wanted him to receive some instruction at Columbia.

After a year of professional basketball with the New York Knicks, Shrider embarked on a coaching career which led him from high school assignments in Gallipolis and Fairborn to his first, and only, college job at Miami. He was Ohio's Class A Coach of the Year at Gallia Academy in 1954.

Who would have guessed that when Shrider came to Miami to coach in 1957, one of the Miami players there to greet him would be Jim Thomas, a standout on Shrider's Gallipolis teams? Thomas is an Oxford dentist now, and one of six members of the selection committee for Miami's Athletic Hall of Fame.

In nine years as Miami's head basketball coach, Shrider's teams won two outright Mid-American Conference championships and shared in two others. The last of those championships came in the 1965-66 season, Shrider's last at the helm.

On March 17, 1964, John Brickels died. The man who had been Miami's athletic director through the era of Parseghian, Pont and Schembechler in football and Bill Rohr and Shrider in basketball, was gone, and there was a void. As a temporary measure, Miami President John Millett appointed Shrider acting athletic director.

On making that appointment, Millett had told Shrider that he would

In 1957, Dick Shrider came to Miami as head basketball coach. There to greet him was Shrider's Gallia Academy star, Jim Thomas. Athletic Director John Brickels enjoyed the reunion.

have to relinquish the basketball job. Shrider was reluctant to do that, and when he returned from the basketball coaches meeting at the NCAA tournament, Millett summoned him to the president's office in Roudebush Hall.

"He said," recalls Shrider, 'Do you mean that you feel that strongly?' and I said 'Yeah,' and he said 'What in the hell do you want?'

"I said, 'Well just a couple of things. I would like for Wayne Gibson to be my assistant and I would like to coach basketball for two more years. I've got some young men that I've made some promises and commitments to. I'm not ready to quit coaching then, but I will. That would be the only way I would take it, and I know that's not what you're interested in.'"

Millett was interested. He elevated Shrider to the rank of full professor and Gibson, the assistant football coach who served both Pont and Schembechler, became an associate professor. So Shrider completed his last two years at the Miami basketball helm with back-to-back records of 20-5 and 18-7.

By the time Shrider had spent two years in the dual role as athletic director and basketball coach, he realized the job he was inheriting wasn't the same job he had watched Brickels perform for all those years. Changes in what had been the traditional Miami athletic department already had occurred, and there would be more.

****

"They're not makin' 'em anymore like John Brickels."

Nearly twenty years had passed since John Brickels succumbed to congestive heart failure, and the Dick Shrider who had worked for John was paying fond tribute. Others of us who felt the Brickels influence in our daily lives — any who knew him — could write a similar epitaph.

Back in 1941, Paul Brown found he had to bypass his friend Brickels when building his first staff at Ohio State. They had played against each other in college, they had been in summer school together as Ohio State graduate students, they respected each other as coaches. Brickels had been highly successful at New Philadelphia as Brown was building his reputation at Massillon. Hiring Brickels as an Ohio State assistant was a likely move. So there were feelers from Brown to Brickels — but then Brown had to backtrack. Brown and Ohio State were committed to mending some fences in the Ohio high school community. Brickels had moved recently to Huntington High School, and at just that time selecting a coach from West Virginia over one from Ohio didn't seem right.

"But I won't forget you, John," Brown promised.

Four years later, Brown was beginning to organize his professional Cleveland Browns. By that time Brickels was head basketball coach at West Virginia University and had his team at the National Invitation Tournament. Brown tracked him down in New York and asked him to recruit and organize the club. So far as Brickels was concerned, this illustrated loyalty and promise-keeping. He told the story often in making a point to men of his own staff, later.

Yet this wouldn't be the only indication for Brickels that Paul Brown's memory was as good as his ties to Miami.

In 1949, Miami was looking for a basketball coach to replace W.J. (Blue) Foster. It also was in process of signing a new young football coach, Woody Hayes, who would need a solid, mature assistant. From his own Cleveland Browns staff, Brown recommended Brickels.

Until recently, administration of Miami athletics had been in the hands of Merlin Ditmer, the man who had come in as freshman coach for all sports in the late Twenties. Ditmer had been in failing health for a couple of years; maybe the pressure of making arrangements for Miami's first-ever bowl appearance in 1947 had been the catalyst. James A. Gordon — the same Jim Gordon who had caught Brown's passes and run his way into the 1932 Olympic Games, had been named Manager of Athletics to relieve some of the pressure on Ditmer. It was a stop-gap measure, a potential detour to a promising career in the classroom side of physical and health education.

Dr. Ernest H. Hahne, Miami president, often sought the advice of Paul Brown in matters pertaining to intercollegiate athletics. With obvious need for one person to take command of Miami's athletic ship, much as George Rider had done under Presidents Hughes and Upham, it was time for Hahne to turn to Brown for counsel. Since Brown had steered Brickels to Miami in a coaching capacity, would Brickels be the one to take up the administrative reins?

The answer was forthcoming on June 22, 1950, when Hahne issued a

Assistant Coach-Basketball Coach-Athletic Director Brickels taking notes during a film session with Head Coach Woody Hayes and Ben Ankney.

brief, crisp news statement: Brickels was to become Director of Intercollegiate Athletics, effective immediately. Gordon would become Director of Physical Education for men, and Rider would direct all of his energies to coaching track and field.

Later, through the **Miami Alumnus**, Hahne explained that the new portfolios were part of a new administrative step which he said "ends an extended temporary structure and starts a program which should greatly improve our service in that field to our students."

He explained that Miami's Board of Trustees on June 9 had voted to create a new Division of Physical, Health and Athletic Activities; within that division, a Department of Intercollegiate Athletics with Brickels as Director and a Department of Physical and Health Education under Gordon. The division would be responsible to the President, and Hahne said its administration had been delegated to a three-man executive committee made up of Vice President C.W. Kreger, Gordon and Brickels. This occurred at a time when President Hahne's illness was beginning to require such delegation.

"I know that competition-minded sports fans will be inclined to look only at the intercollegiate side of our picture and consider this a shakeup," Hahne commented. "It's not. It is difficult to explain to outsiders the importance of health and physical education in a university curriculum. We have felt the need of making a number of changes in our scope and our operation.

"I believe we are now coming out of this temporary phase with a well-rounded, well-administered program in both phases. The new division, like our Student Health Division and our Library Division, will be for the service of all schools in our University."

More than thirty years later, the man who followed Brickels as athletic director and who can be considered in many ways beneficiary of the Brickels legacy asserts that "John came on the Miami scene at the right time, when they needed leadership and needed a person to get out and promote things and get the program going a little bit."

According to Dick Shrider, Brickels was a different type of athletic director from those found today.

"He was the tobacco-chewin', cussin', stay-up-all-night, tell-stories type person who knew people all over the world."

We sat in Shrider's office in Millett Hall, a far cry from the second-floor hideaway Brickels occupied in Withrow Court; and as Shrider spoke those words, both of us were reminded of the New Year's morning in Seattle, Washington, when a sleepy-eyed Miami basketball team trudged through the airport before dawn. There was Brickels, who never met a stranger, greeting an old friend, more than 2,000 miles from home, at 4 a.m.

"I don't know of anyone who loved to socialize more than John Brickels," says Shrider. "And John was at his best when he had a drink in his hand, reminiscing about the old days and the places he'd been and the people he'd played with and for.

"His contacts really helped Miami . . . to get the schedule in football and basketball up to where it should be. He had the philosophy . . . he would like to schedule, whenever he could, one big outside game each year in football. He thought that was necessary. And not many other people at that time in the Mid-American Conference or sister institutions our size through the Midwest could get those teams to play 'em."

That's not to say that Miami never had played a "big-name" team before Brickels' arrival. But it was his contacts throughout the Midwest that helped Miami to appear on the schedules of Indiana, Northwestern and Purdue. And there's little doubt the results of those games, both on the scoreboard and at the box office, helped Miami.

If he had done little more . . . and his contributions to Miami did indeed go far beyond that . . . Brickels' impact on Miami's athletic fortunes and her people were enormous. Yet Shrider in retrospect feels Brickels was insecure.

"John Brickels, I felt, was never a secure person. He was always worried about his job. He was worried about little things that he really didn't have to worry about, because he had security."

Maybe that stemmed from his lack of confidence as a public speaker. Speaking engagements go with the territory in the athletic business, but Brickels seemed to dread those occasions when he was called on to address a large gathering.

"This was always a mystery to me," says Shrider, "because he could have a room full of people and entertain those people. At the same time, when he had two or three hundred people it was difficult for him to speak to that group. He shunned that at every opportunity."

Brickels was a tough boss. For years news about Miami reached the outside world through an office called the News Bureau. On completion of Roudebush Hall as a new administration building in 1956, the News Bureau occupied space in the new building. That's where I reported to work when I was hired as sports information director in 1958. Functionally, I was the sports specialist in Bob Howard's News Bureau and reported to him. But I also had to answer to Brickels, at Withrow Court.

He left any commentary on my writing to Howard, but on athletic department matters, there was only one arbiter. You did it John's way. Specifically, that meant he was the official department spokesman. Nobody else, particularly the new kid on the block, need usurp his role.

After we got to know one another better, he used to call me "One-Sport," that sport being football. I don't really think I slighted any of Miami's sports, and I doubt he was serious with his needle; but I never forgot about Miami's determination to have a multi-faceted sports program.

Of the way Brickels ran the athletic department, Shrider says, "I tell our people here, I'd just like to have John Brickels back here for one month . . . for our secretaries to experience working under a man like that . . . for our coaches to realize what this was. I want to tell you one thing: You didn't relax any, because he always challenged you."

It was Brickels' concern about his relationship with Miami Trustees and other influential alumni, particularly in the Cincinnati area, which led eventually to what is now the Miami University Motor Pool. He particularly went out of his way to please C. Vivian Anderson, who chaired Miami's Board of Trustees when Brickels joined the staff in 1949. Anderson would call and ask Brickels to come to Cincinnati to meet with him. Obediently, John would be on his way. But because Brickels' wife Jo needed the family car, John would be forced to take the bus. This inconvenienced both Brickels and Anderson, and eventually the Cincinnatian authorized the Miami athletic director to buy a station wagon for athletic department use. Later, there were two cars, and when Shrider became athletic director, the University in effect repurchased those two cars from the department and the Motor Pool was born.

Like every Miami athletic director, Brickels had to be concerned about finances. Shrider says he constantly was warned that he was "over the budget," but since Brickels maintained authoritarian control over the department's finances, the warning was simply Brickels' way of maintaining discipline in the department. And, as Shrider would learn once he succeeded Brickels, Miami was never overspent.

The athletic department which Brickels was asked to direct was more complex and required more staffing than the four-man department which Rider had started, yet it remained relatively small and stable. Besides football, basketball, baseball and track, Miami also was participating in the Mid-American Conference in cross country, wrestling, tennis and golf. A new swimming facility was under construction, and when Billings Natatorium opened in 1953, swimming was added to the intercollegiate

Changing of the guard: When Ara Parseghian, right, left to go to Northwestern, John Brickels replaced him with John Pont.

roster of sports.

Raymond Ray, a 1938 Miami graduate, was hired as the school's swimming coach and pool director. The tennis coach was Al Moore, and other coaching lined up like this: The baseball coach, Woody Wills, was a football assistant. Brickels, the basketball coach, had no full-time assistant. Parseghian had responsibilities in three sports until named head football coach. Rider, of course, also coached cross country. A football assistant coached wrestling once the football season was over.

Most of these coaches lasted throughout Brickels' tenure. Other than when George Rider retired, the only changes occurred when a football or basketball coach moved on and another moved in. Rare were the days when Brickels needed to roll up his sleeves and wade into the hiring process, but Shrider remembers his thorough approach to the task.

"He would listen pretty much to a lot of people," says Shrider, "and then make up his own mind what he was going to do. He worked very closely with his president. John understood the chain of command and whom he worked for; he would never do anything that Dr. Hahne or Dr. Millett didn't believe in, and he kept them well informed."

The toughest of those hiring decisions Brickels had to make was the last one, the one he made the year before he died. There were several outstanding candidates, all of whom have gone to subsequent coaching successes. Bo Schembechler finally emerged as the choice, and Shrider remembers how Brickels saw it.

"He always thought that Schembechler would be tough to handle, but probably he could get the job done."

If Brickels understood who his boss was, it also was understood clearly by those who worked under him how the chain of command worked in the other direction.

"He thought a lotta people were handed things on a silver platter," explains Shrider. "Assistant coaches he had very little regard for; I mean they had to serve that apprenticeship, and they should know there was a demarcation between an assistant coach and a head coach, and he felt very strongly about that."

From his youth in Newark, Ohio, to an athletic scholarship at Wittenberg, to New Philadelphia High School, to Huntington and then West Virginia University, to the Cleveland Browns and on to Miami, Brickels paid his dues. His message to the Miami staff always was to do likewise.

There were times, not many, when one of us would get a feeling of having done well. Lest we get too complacent, and sensing the self-satisfaction burning within, he would counter, "You may pass me on the way up, but you have to come back down the same way."

Maybe that was the key to John Brickels. There was the gruff, rough-around-the-edges exterior. And the story-telling. Those of us who were touched by John Brickels always will have those memories. That we remember the lessons, too, shows how he ran the ship.

****

Let's go back to the beginning. George Rider was the Miami football coach in 1917 and 1918 when Miami won consecutive Ohio Conference championships and never lost a game. The 1917 team played two scoreless ties, with Kentucky and Wooster, but didn't yield a point in eight games. The 1918 team gave up 13 points, yet won five straight before a scoreless tie with Cincinnati ended the season. Rider was about all there was to the Miami coaching staff in those days, so he coached basketball in the winter and baseball in the spring. (His brilliant career in track at Miami didn't begin until his return in 1924; at this time track was handled by Miami's athletic director and professor of physical education, Alfred "King" Brodbeck.) Miami has had only one undefeated basketball team: George Rider's 1917-18 team which swept a ten-game season. Rider also in the following season coached a basketball team which won seven of 12. And all this as a wartime replacement for George Little.

Native of Michigan, George Rider began his life-long career in athletics at Olivet College. He graduated in 1914; that fall he had been the coach of the football team. The next year found him at the Battle Creek Normal School of Physical Education. That summer, he went to the Illinois Summer School for Coaches. It seems clear it was during that summer at Illinois that the seed may have been planted in young Rider's mind for what eventually became the Miami coaching school.

Through 1915-17 Rider was the Director of Physical Education and Athletics at Hanover College, and then came his two-year stint as Little's Miami replacement. It should be noted that after one year of summer instruction at Illinois, Rider spent the next three summers at Harvard's Summer School of Physical Education as an instructor. He graduated from that program in 1919, and went directly to the University of Maine as Director of Physical Education and Athletics. The next year, he had the same job at Washington University in St. Louis, but was also the football and track coach. He was in St. Louis until 1924, then spent the rest of his life in Oxford.

When Rider, as the newly-named athletic director, immediately set about expanding the staff and persuading President Hughes to establish the new School of Physical Education and Athletic Coaching, few could imagine the impact this man would have in 39 years of service to Miami students.

A look at the record shows that Rider coached five sports at one time or another, and his teams won 317 times, lost 96 times and tied three, a winning percentage of .764. The man clearly was one of the country's great coaches. He is best known for his 36 years as Miami's track and cross country coach, during which time his track teams won nine Buckeye Conference titles and then 10 consecutive Mid-American Conference championships. His cross country teams captured nine Mid-American and 11 All-Ohio crowns.

Rider spent 16 years as Miami's athletic director, and from 1942 to 1950 was director of physical education. In 1957, he was selected to the Helms Foundation Track and Field Coaches Hall of Fame. Two years later, he was honorary president of the International Track and Field Coaches Association. He was president of both the NCAA Track and Cross

Country Coaches Associations.

  In 1969, nine years after his retirement, Rider was elected as a charter member of Miami's Athletic Hall of Fame. One of the men who joined Rider as a charter member, Earl (Red) Blaik, had played football and baseball for him in 1917-18. Rider had hired Jay Colville as Miami's first full-time trainer. And the others, Walter Alston, Paul Brown, Weeb Ewbank, Ara Parseghian and John Pont had learned from him in the

George L. Rider . . . Coach

classroom and on the playing field.

"Coaching and teaching at Miami for thirty-nine years," said Rider at his induction, "has meant some successes, some failures, but most of all, it has meant the privilege of coaching, teaching and working with some of the finest young men in the world. It has been most rewarding to watch average young men grow and develop into better men, and some to become great men, and to feel I may have had some little influence in their becoming champions in their own right.

"Miami has given me the opportunity to establish some wonderful and lasting friendships with some members of the faculty, student body, alumni, and citizens of the grand little village of Oxford. I find in years of retirement that these friends are priceless."

George Rider died in 1979, but his passing never can erase the memories of thousands of athletes and future coaches who sat in his classroom and listened as he taught a course described in the 1926-27 catalog as:

"132. TRACK. Instruction and practice in starting, sprinting, distance running, hurdling, high and broad jumping, pole vaulting, shot putting, discus and javelin throwing, and relay racing. One and one half hours credit. Mr. Rider."

There were more courses, and through the years the course descriptions changed to reflect shifts in emphasis; but for 36 years, Professor Rider commanded the respect of the great and the nearly great.

One personal memory of Coach Rider stands out above all others. It was the spring of 1958, my senior year, and I had just been named officially to the sports information job. Even before I picked up my diploma, I was with the Miami spring sports teams at the Mid-American Conference championships in Kalamazoo, Michigan. Rider's track team was going for its 11th consecutive MAC championship, and it was my baptismal in an official capacity. Phoning the results to the southwestern Ohio newspapers so Sunday morning coverage was assured was my main mission, and I was to return on the bus used by the track team as soon as the team had showered and dressed and I had made my calls.

What neither a rookie publicity man and a veteran coach anticipated was what happened. The host school, Western Michigan, out-pointed Miami for the first time in Conference history, and I must have been on the phone longer than expected. When I stepped outside, there was no bus. In fact, the area was almost deserted. Helpless is but one way to describe my feeling as I contemplated the next move. Less than five dollars in my pocket, and aware only that I was a long way from home.

When the only Western Michigan staff member still around volunteered to take me in the direction of Marshall, Michigan, to see if I could catch up with the bus there, I gladly accepted, unable to think of a better alternative. My heart skipped a beat when we approached the famous Win Schuler's restaurant and there was no bus in sight. And my new-found friend wouldn't be able to take me any further. In desperation, I went inside to use the phone. There, just preparing to leave after having finished dinner, were John Brickels, Dick Shrider and Dr. Fred Cottrell, Miami's faculty representative. Persistent needling for what seemed like an eternity and no dinner were a small price to pay for a ride back to Oxford.

As this manuscript reached its final stages, Editor Howard received a handwritten note, postmarked Greeley, Colorado, from George Rider's widow Una. Wrote Mrs. Rider:

"Dear Bob

I noticed you serve as Robert Kurz' ... editor. After thinking about the Book etc. etc. I wondered if he knew how much my husband, George, figured in the building up of the Athletic Dept. at Miami after George was first hired to rebuild it (and to 'build character'). There are not many around who were there then."

Mrs. Rider makes a good point. And her letter goes on to point out several of her husband's contributions, all of them well-documented by the record book. But then, in the unmistakable hand of a lady who lovingly stood by her husband, Mrs. Rider says it all:

"A more important thing that he did was his hard work and putting his all-out effort and influence on the 'Powers that Be' as long as it took, to get the Training School for Coaches started. This wasn't easy. This School of Training was responsible to a big degree for Miami putting out coaches well-trained."

Rider's love for his boyhood home in Michigan never diminished, and Shrider, who came on the Miami scene late in Rider's career, remembers how he would always vacation in Michigan, where he could fish and enjoy the outdoors to his heart's content.

"I remember George," says Shrider, "as the straightest of straight arrows. If somebody was bad, they were 'a double jackass,' and if they were really, really bad, and he had a few of those, they were 'a triple jackass.'"

As anyone who has ever been there can attest, springtime in Oxford is one of the grandest times of the year. For decades, one of the grandest weekends of spring was the one when hundreds of high school athletes converged on the Miami campus for George Rider's meet — The Miami University Track and Field Meet for High Schools. (Now officially the George L. Rider-Miami Relays, it's more conveniently called the Rider Relays.) For some, this was their introduction to Miami. Not surprisingly, many returned as Miami student-athletes.

"Basically," says Shrider, "he was a track coach . . . first, last and always, and felt that was the most important program in the intercollegiate athletic department, and he should, rightly so. Every coach should feel that way . . .

"A nationally known figure, a pleasant person to be around, a no-nonsense guy, he really believed in what he thought was right. Basically, the thing about George Rider . . . he was a guy that stood for integrity and honesty and discipline and there was really only one way . . . his way. He was a little bit set in his ways."

For nearly four decades, his ways bore fruit, and as Shrider says, "he was Mister Miami for a long, long time."

****

When I was riding the buses to Athens and Bowling Green and other garden spots of Ohio, John Brickels sat in the first seat on the left, right behind the driver. In the first seat on the right sat Jay Colville. Other positions and people changed places, but those two remained. Until the day John Brickels died.

"I'm a person who believes," explains Shrider, "if something isn't broke, don't try to fix it. Whether you want to, or whether you don't, if you work for a man as long as I did for John . . . I worked for him for seven years . . . you are going to do quite a few things the way he did it. And we were going along pretty well at that time."

Shrider still rides those buses, to more places now since the Mid-American Conference has expanded. And due to the faltering economy, Conference travel is strictly limited to over the road.

"I travel all the time with the basketball team and the football team. I'm sure I inherited that from him," says Shrider. "I'm with that football team and that basketball team every place they go. As I look around the Mid-American Conference, no one else does that.

"Now that was a Brickels thing. He believed you should be right on top of the situation and know what's going on. That's not all bad. Because you're right on top of it. You know how much money is being spent. You plan the trip. You plan the meals. You do all those things . . . I think one thing that does do; that creates a closer relationship between the players and the athletic director, the players and the coaching staff, because they know you care about 'em."

Not everything has stayed the same, though. Shrider has outlived some of Brickels' old haunts like the Phoenix Hotel in Findlay on the trip to Bowling Green. Never again will he have to conduct a man-hunt like he did for Carm Cozza when the freshman basketball coach went up to take a nap when the team arrived in Findlay one afternoon. It was time for the pre-game meal, and Cozza wasn't responding to a knock on the door of the room to which he was assigned, and had been issued a key. Cozza made two mistakes. He left the elevator on the wrong floor, and he didn't realize that, in the Phoenix, a room key was a room key. If it fit the door, use it. Cozza finally was located, sleeping peacefully in the room beneath the one where he was supposed to be.

Travel and accommodations are merely the nuts and bolts of running the Miami athletic department today, however. As Shrider, who has run the department longer than anyone else, is quick to acknowledge.

"The job's changed dramatically, though, because we expanded to the broad-based program where we had to go to 12 men's sports, plus the fact that I inherited a new program, the women's program.

"Now, don't get me wrong. I'm not griping about the situation I've got, because I don't know of a better place in the world to work than Miami University, and that's the reason I've stayed here. But I'll tell you, with all your women's programs, and all your men's programs, and all the problems we've had nationally as far as Division I-A classification is concerned . . . it's really a busy time."

Made even more busy by Shrider's membership on the National Collegiate Athletic Association Council as vice president of District 4. And he also serves on the NCAA Division I Basketball Committee.

The Mid-American Conference began in 1946. In all the years, only Ed Saxer of Toledo and Fred Picard of Ohio University, both faculty representatives, and now Shrider, have served on the powerful NCAA Council. And Shrider is the first MAC representative on the basketball committee.

"I feel good about it," explains Shrider, "because Miami and the Mid-American Conference were treated very shabbily as far as the Division I Basketball Committee was concerned. In all those years . . . that wasn't right. There are nine members, and you shouldn't have somebody on there all the time, I realize that, but we should have had someone on there. We didn't have much of a voice . . . it was very important to Miami and the Mid-American Conference that whoever won our MAC championship could go on to compete in the NCAA tournament, and we almost lost that."

As far as Miami's and the Mid-American Conference's recent problems with reclassification were concerned, Shrider says of the NCAA Council, "It wasn't so important that I was there, but it was important someone in the Conference was there."

Since Shrider's Conference longevity outstrips every other athletic director, president or faculty representative, maybe he underestimates the role he played in the NCAA decision in January 1983 which restored all the MAC schools to Division I-A status in football. Certainly he doesn't underestimate the importance of that decision as far as Miami and the Conference are concerned. When the announcement was made at the NCAA convention in San Diego, Shrider proclaimed:

"The reclassification of the Mid-American Conference from I-AA to I-A is the greatest milestone in Conference history. It is also the greatest Conference victory that has ever been achieved. With adversity came strength and unity. I have never seen the members of the MAC so unified. The MAC is back in its rightful position in NCAA football, and that is Division I-A."

The athletic department born under George Rider in the Twenties and brought to full maturity in the Fifties under John Brickels bears little resemblance to the Miami athletic program today, however.

"We've had a few things come our way. This building you're in right now," says Shrider as we sit in his office in Millett Hall, "was a great thing to happen to Miami University. Our ice program was a good thing to happen to us. And now, the thing that's about ready to unfold this year is a dream come true.

"Having that stadium down there, and all the great facilities, because our stadium facilities and our track were so shabby we were almost at the place that we were ashamed of them. People constantly making cracks about our inadequate facilities, and it hurt us in recruiting.

"When I first came to Miami, Withrow Court was an acceptable place to play basketball. The stadium was a pretty good stadium. And the track . . . everybody else had a cinder track . . . it was OK. But we got so far behind. Now we've got Millett Hall, and with the stadium we've got going in and the track we've got going in, our facilities will be second to none. And Miami again will be on top of the Mid-American Conference facility-wise."

Withrow Court had been the basketball home of the Redskins through the Thirties and Forties and Fifties and until 1968. There were occasions when the building, accommodating a maximum of 3,500, even with people sitting on the floor under each basket, got a little snug, but it was the scene of many memorable games and source of much lore.

Consider the night in 1957 when students started lining up outside Withrow Court before 5 o'clock to see the fabulous Oscar Robertson of Cincinnati play in a freshman game that would start at 6. Or the night crafty Cam Henderson, the wiley old Marshall College coach, needled Brickels with a proposal that they drive his team bus into the building so its headlights could improve the lighting. (A couple of years later he tested a newer Miami coach, William D. Rohr: "Billy, in West V'ginyuh we got barns lit bettuh'n this!"

And Withrow Court was the four-year home of Miami's own NBA great, Wayne Embry. Second-leading scorer in Miami history, Embry twice had 40 points or more in Withrow Court. He scored 42 in an 87-74 victory over Kent State in 1957, and he had 40 in his final home game, an 89-79 win over Xavier in 1958.

On December 2, 1968, the Miami basketball scene shifted to the new Millett Assembly Hall, a multi-purpose building named for the 16th president of Miami. A crowd of 9,135 was there to see Miami bow to Kentucky, 86-77.

Ice hockey got a home at Miami in 1976 as a new two-sheet ice arena opened on land where the football Redskins had practiced for many years. An unofficial, coachless Miami hockey club had been roaming to Cincinnati, Troy and Indianapolis at unbelievable hours to find ice time for practice and games. Now it had its own ice, and a coach. Hockey acquired varsity status in 1978. By 1983, Miami advanced to the Central Collegiate Hockey Association playoffs.

At Miami tradition, or maybe it's just sentiment, sometimes impedes progress. Strange though it may seem, there were those who opposed closing Miami Field. And Shrider concedes that if only sentiment were involved, he'd line up on the side of the traditionalists.

"I would have been for that," Shrider says of the cry to keep the old stadium where it stood, "if there would have been enough room to do it, and you could have adequate parking and you could have taken all the other things that were so desperately needed, like locker rooms and facilities for our women's program, an adequate place to play field hockey and softball, and a new track and everything, and you see now, we'll be able to comply . . . not only comply but justifiably have locker rooms and equipment and everything that's equal for men and women . . . and that's the way it should be.

"And this athletic complex that's going down over the hill is going to be the greatest thing that's ever happened to our athletic program since I've been here, because now we can have a really great place to play football and put a lot of people in. It got so discouraging to see Parents' Weekend and Homecoming over there and our people . . . four or five thousand people . . . have to stand up. That's not what it's all about."

With all that has happened in the last two decades to change, and enhance, the face of Miami athletics, there is one thing that may never change. Miami coaches come for the opportunity, not for the money.

"As you overlook our salaries for the Miami University football staff year in and year out, it would be about average," says Shrider. "It wouldn't be as high as the entire Mid-American Conference, simply because we have a turnover every four or five years. Our coaches are younger than most coaches in the Conference."

At Miami, what the new, young coach has is an opportunity to win. And in most cases, the overwhelming support of the community . . . faculty, students, alumni . . . in making it easier. Of course, there is the reputation. Like the Randy Walkers and the other young men who come to Miami to play and learn and later coach, young coaches come to Miami in hopes of moving on.

"Now we don't look for a coach who's looking for an opportunity to come in and coach and then move on . . . use this for a stepping stone," says Shrider. "We want him to come in and do a job, and if that happens, that's fine, and that's what does happen."

To a man, the football coaches Shrider has hired . . . Bill Mallory, Dick Crum, Tom Reed . . . have all rolled up their sleeves, gone to work, and said they were happy; they wanted to stay. But none stayed.

"My job is a little more difficult from this standpoint," explains Shrider. "I don't always feel I can hire the best man . . . I don't always feel that way. In most cases I can, but sometimes we've let some really great candidates slip through our hands who have no Miami connection.

"But on the other hand, you have enough good, successful Miami people out there, that you can go ahead and get them."

And when that time has come, every four or five years, Shrider has had only one thought.

"When I've got that list of people in front of me that are coming in for interviews, I want to get the best possible coach for Miami University at that particular time in history that I can humanly pick. And if I don't pick him, it's because I made an honest mistake. I haven't made one out of fear, or I haven't made one out of leaning toward another candidate."

In 1983, Shrider went to the well again, following those guidelines. He selected Tim Rose.

"In my own mind right now, as I sit here, I don't think there's a better candidate anywhere else, or a better coach anywhere else, than Tim Rose to do the job for Miami . . . I really feel that way."

Miami has meant many good things to me, but generally speaking it is like the thrust of the second stage of a space rocket. The college education provides the extra boost that enables one to be propelled toward a better life orbit.

In my case it has been a big factor in helping me in the teaching aspect of sports. Also by participation in the Miami athletic program it was possible for me to get a start in professional baseball.

Most important, however, has been my association and friendship with the coaches, trainers, teachers, students and others connected with the University. I am proud of Miami's tradition, growth and continued success. My sincere thanks for inviting me to be a part of Miami.

Walter (Smokey) Alston,
Los Angeles Dodgers manager,
upon his election to Miami's
Athletic Hall of Fame
as one of eight charter members.

XIII
HALL OF FAME

ON MAY 19, 1960, Miami University paid singular honor to three of its alumni coaches whose accomplishments had brought singular honor to Alma Mater. A special, one-time honorary degree Doctor of Athletic Arts was conferred simultaneously, as climax to the annual Student Recognition Convocation, upon Walter Emmons Alston, Paul Eugene Brown and Wilbur Charles Ewbank.

Ewbank at the time was coach of the World Champion Baltimore Colts. Alston at the time was manager of the World Champion Los Angeles Dodgers. And Brown's Cleveland Browns had been World Champions three times. In citing the three as extraordinary teachers, organizers and administrators in professional sports, Miami President John D. Millett noted that these were traits which Miami had recognized many times through honorary degrees for achievements in business, the arts, and various professions. Once previously, he noted, a brilliant former college coach had been so honored: Earl Blaik, by then a vice president of Avco Manufacturing Corporation, had been among representative Miami alumni in six separate fields awarded honorary degrees at Sesquicentennial Commencement the previous year.

When Millett sought the blessing of University Senate for the three doctorates in Athletic Arts, he encountered opposition from a few faculty conservatives. An impasse was avoided when Dr. Clarke Crannell, a senior psychology professor, rose, surveyed the roomful of academic doctors, and suggested:

"It would seem to be appropriate to remind ourselves that in today's culture, our colleges and universities have become accustomed to conferring the doctorate upon quite a wide variety of persons, including dentists and physicians."

In a collective chuckle, Senate approved.

There was scarcely a second thought eighteen years later when such recognition was conferred by President Phillip R. Shriver on Ara Parseghian. The former Miami-Northwestern-Notre Dame coach by this time was head of Ara Parseghian Enterprises, a radio-television personality, a new member of the University's Board of Trustees. The degree was Doctor of Humanities, and with scant mention of sports prowess he was cited for unselfish service in promotion of humanitarian causes, especially the fight against multiple sclerosis, and for leadership in Miami's Goals for Enrichment campaign.

In 1969, these five shared yet a different recognition, being among the eight charter members of Miami's Athletic Hall of Fame. Members are enshrined in a special place of honor in Millett Assembly Hall and are recognized for the manner in which their careers in athletics have honored Miami.

To be eligible for the Hall of Fame, one must meet the following qualifications:

(1) An athlete must have earned two letters in one sport or one letter in two or more sports.

(2) A coach or athletic administrator must have lettered at Miami University or served on the Miami University staff for at least five years.

(3) An athlete must have graduated at least five years prior to selection.

(4) The record of the individual must be so outstanding that there is no question as to his qualifying for the Hall of Fame. Thus, each candidate must be passed by all members of the Selection Committee.

That first year, Jay Colville, John Pont and George Rider accompanied Alston, Blaik, Brown, Ewbank and Parseghian into the Hall of Fame. They were chosen from among 200 placed in nomination by members of Tribe Miami, the lettermen's organization.

****

Just east of Oxford sits Darrtown, the boyhood home of Walter Alston. Darrtown is still Alston's home, and he'd just as soon be there, enjoying a game of pool, as anywhere.

The sports world remembers Alston as the little-known figure in the Dodger organization who was tapped by Branch Rickey in 1953 to manage the Brooklyn Dodgers, and did so for 23 years, first in Brooklyn and later in Los Angeles. When he retired after the 1976 season, he left behind a legacy of seven National League championships and four World Series titles. It is a record that has catapulted him into baseball's Hall of Fame at Cooperstown.

Every fall, the baseball season behind him, he returned to Darrtown, where he could run over to Oxford and watch an occasional basketball game (he had been a two-sport star for Miami), or help out an old friend by agreeing to be interviewed by a journalism class.

It was in such a setting that I first met Alston, the soft-spoken man whose familiar #24 was known by millions of baseball fans. Gilson Wright, who preceded Bob Howard as director of the Miami News Bureau, taught what few journalism courses Miami offered when I was an undergraduate. Every year, we could count on Alston stopping by for an hour so we could gain a little more experience for a feature-writing or news-writing class.

Always, one of the first things you noticed about Alston was his huge hands. That, and his command of the situation. To any question posed by an aspiring journalist, there was a thoughtful answer. And straightforward. The only things gray about Alston in his managing days were his road uniform and a touch of gray hair around the temples. Everything else was black or white.

Alston remembers when the Miami basketball team beat Ohio University during the 1933-34 season. Ohio was heavily favored, but as he held Ohio's leading scorer to just four points, Miami won, 30-26. Another memorable moment was the day he hit three home runs and a double in a Miami baseball game against Youngstown.

Frank Rickey, a brother of Branch, had watched Alston play shortstop at Miami. The day after graduation he signed Alston to a contract for $125 a month.

"According to the Cardinals," says Alston, "that was $25 above the average."

Alston went to the Cardinals' main office in St. Louis while awaiting assignment to a minor league club.

"I stayed at the YMCA in St. Louis for about a week," says Alston. "Each day I would report to the Cardinal office to see Branch Rickey. They finally decided to send me to Greenwood."

Greenwood was Greenwood, Mississippi, and as Alston recalls it, he drove all the way to Greenwood from St. Louis with Eddie Dyer in a two-seated roadster. Dyer was a scout for the Cardinals and later would manage the St. Louis team.

"We got to Greenwood around noon," recalls Alston, "and I jumped into a uniform and found myself at shortstop that day. The first time up I hit the ball back to the pitcher, but I think I got a hit later in the game."

But, says Walt, "they saw enough of me at shortstop to move me to third base the next game." He spent the rest of that 1935 season as Greenwood's third baseman, batting .326 in 82 games and playing well enough to gain honorable mention on the East Dixie League All-Star team. Most of his early career was as a player and coach in the minor leagues. Four times in his minor league career he hit 25 or more home runs. But in his only major league plate appearance, with the Cardinals in 1936, he struck out.

Alston remained with the Cardinal organization until July 1944, when he was released by Rochester of the International League. Upon release from the Cardinals, he received a telephone call from Branch Rickey, who had moved to the Dodger organization. Rickey offered Alston the position of player-manager of the Trenton team in the Interstate League. The rest is history. He managed in the Dodger organization until retirement.

****

In September 1914, a young red-head from Dayton enrolled at Miami. Earl (Red) Blaik played on a couple of Miami's great football teams: George Little's 1916 bunch and the 1917 squad coached by George Rider — both undefeated. He also had been a sophomore on the 1915 team captained by his Dayton neighbor and Beta Theta Pi fraternity brother, Marvin (Monk) Pierce.

Immediately on graduation from Miami in 1918, Blaik sought and won an appointment to West Point. This somehow provided further eligibility, and he lettered on a fine 1920 Army team. Graduated from the academy after that season, he completed his military commitment before giving much thought to what he intended doing with his life. We have noted in an earlier chapter that he made frequent trips from Dayton to Oxford to help with the coaching, while seemingly firmly established in real estate and construction with his father in Dayton. Then he spent the 1925 and 1926 seasons at Wisconsin helping his former Miami coach, Little, who had gone there from Michigan. The lure of a temporary coaching assignment at West Point was strong, and what began as an avocation became a vocation. By 1934, this West Point assistant had become head coach at Dartmouth. He would stay for seven years and compile a record of 45 wins, 15 losses and four ties.

Blaik moved back to West Point in 1941 and coached Army's football teams for 18 years. He had six undefeated teams, coached 26 All-American players, compiled a record of 121-33-10 and was voted Coach of the Year in 1946. He also was athletic director at West Point for 11 years, from 1948 to 1959. When inducted into Miami's Athletic Hall of Fame in 1969, Blaik had this to say about his Miami experience:

"Miami taught me my philosophy of life — 'You Have To Pay The Price.' This has been a priceless heritage that stood the rugged test of college days as well as the challenge of the years in the professions of coaching and business.

"Since this is a gathering to honor former athletes, perhaps the lessons of Miami may be appropriately stated in terms of the gridiron. Through the years as a coach the lessons became fixed opinions and simply stated are: (1) Football is secondary to the purpose for which the player is in college; (2) Championship football and good scholarship are entirely compatible; (3) The purpose of the game of football is to win and to dilute the will to win is to destroy the purpose of the game.

"Thus, in this football creed is the essence of my philosophy 'You Have To Pay The Price.' And whether it is business, sports, politics, or the professions, there is small satisfaction and less self respect if one has not paid the price to achieve the potential of which one is capable.

"Indeed the experience of my Miami days laid the foundation for any achievement which has come my way and I shall remain forever indebted to 'Old Miami.'"

No more than eight individuals in a single calendar year may be enshrined in Miami's Athletic Hall of Fame. From 1969 through 1983, the 75 Miamians selected for the Hall symbolize Miami athletics. We have seen how the first eight inductees wrote much of the history of Miami athletics. Let's take a closer look at some of the others.

1970

The second class of inductees included Carm Cozza, Yale's great coach; Wayne Embry, the huge basketball player who rewrote the Miami record book and attained legendary status in the NBA because of his physical stature; Jim Gordon, the man who caught Paul Brown's passes and ran in the Olympics; Chet Pittser, the football coach who was Paul Brown's, Weeb Ewbank's and Gordon's mentor, and the captains of the 1921 and 1925 football teams, Virgil Perry and Tom Sharkey.

*****

Only Embry of the six was not a multiple-sport standout. Even Pittser, best known as a football coach, coached the Miami baseball team in the spring. But Embry, who was a big, awkward kid when Coach Bill Rohr found him at Tecumseh High School near Springfield, Ohio, was a basketball player, one who developed a measure of finesse to go along with his awesome physical attributes.

Twice Embry led Miami to the Mid-American Conference championship and into the NCAA tournament, and both times he was the All-MAC center. He played professional basketball for 11 years, with the Cincinnati Royals, Milwaukee Bucks and Boston Celtics. While with Cincinnati, he was an Eastern Division NBA All-Star five times. Despite giving away several inches in height to some of the league's premier centers, like Wilt Chamberlain and Bill Russell, Embry's strength enabled him to hold his own in the land of the giants. A successful Milwaukee businessman, Embry today maintains contact with the Bucks and serves as a special consultant to the Milwaukee franchise.

Embry used the occasion of his induction to point out an ongoing concern of Miami's black athletes and suggest that Miami pave the way for greater opportunities for blacks at the school.

"As Miami continues to grow, I hope she will overcome some of the attitudes that existed and will become a pacesetter in developing attitudes of brotherhood and equality for all mankind. I have confidence in this becoming a reality, just as Miami has achieved the reputation of being a pacesetter in producing fine coaches, athletes and leaders in our country."

****

"Athletics were an important part of my education," said Jim Gordon on being inducted. "They taught me the meaning of dedication, hard work, sacrifice and respect. I think these values have great meaning. I think they are what athletics are all about. I think they are very much a part of what Miami stands for. I am proud to have them as a part of my Miami heritage."

Few men in Miami's sports history excelled in two sports as Gordon did. He led Miami to three consecutive Buckeye Conference track championships from 1929 to 1931. He ran all the sprints up through the

Jim Gordon . . .1932 Olympian

440, ran on the mile relay team and also ran the low hurdles. But his specialty was the 440, and he recorded his best time for that distance, :47.8, in the 1932 Olympic 400-meter trials.

Dick Shrider, who worked with Gordon when he chaired the physical education department, says his quiet demeanor masked his competitive spirit. "He was a tremendous competitor. He loved that stuff . . . he loved to get in the blocks with people and get out there and lay it on the line. But after it was all over, he was a quiet person . . . you wouldn't even know what a great athlete he was."

****

Virgil Perry starred as a sophomore on Miami's undefeated 1921 team that won the Ohio Conference championship and was one of those rare athletes in that day who played football without a headgear. Captain of the 1923 team, Perry also excelled in track and held the Ohio Intercollegiate Athletic Association broad jump record. He finished third in the NCAA meet in Chicago in 1923 with a leap of 23 feet, 4 inches.

****

Captain of Chet Pittser's 1925 Miami football team was Tom Sharkey, who also happened to share the world record for the 100-yard dash at :09.6. Before graduation in 1926, Sharkey had also participated in basketball and boxing. Obviously deeply involved both on and off the field, Sharkey earned his M.D. degree from the University of Cincinnati and was in the practice of internal medicine in Dayton. He became president of both the Miami University Alumni Association and the American Diabetes Association. He died in 1979.

1971

John Brickels, Paul Dietzel, Bill Mulliken and Mel Olix were the four inductees in 1971. The reader remembers Brickels as the feisty Miami athletic director who passed away in 1964, and Dietzel as the center on Miami's Sun Bowl team who went on to Coach of the Year honors at LSU.

Quarterback on that Sun Bowl team was Mel Olix. That year, his sophomore season, Olix completed 71 of 133 passes for 1,081 yards and eight touchdowns. In 1948, Olix helped lead Miami to its first Mid-American Conference football championship. He threw a dozen touchdown passes. Today, he is a highly-regarded orthopedic surgeon.

****

It was a late summer evening in 1960 when Miamians watching the Olympics from Rome, Italy, saw a tall, blond Miami junior spin out of the last turn in the 200 meter breaststroke finals and launch his famous finishing kick. Even though the televised version came to us on a delayed basis, it would confirm what we already knew. It was still a thrill to see Bill Mulliken's powerful stroke overtake the Japanese swimmer and win the Gold Medal for the United States.

Mulliken's Gold Medal victory may have been viewed as a surprise in some quarters, but it certainly was no fluke. He had been NCAA champion, Pan-American Games champion and holder of a whole host of Mid-American Conference records. And as far as Mulliken was concerned, he felt Miami was the perfect place for him to attain some of his personal goals. He had a three-workouts-a-day schedule: distance work in the morning before breakfast and class, work on his stroke around noon, and practice with the team in the afternoon. And Billings Natatorium was a facility ideal for Mulliken's regimen.

Mulliken began his response to his selection to the Hall of Fame with this tribute to Miami: "Miami is opportunity. Miami was the opportunity for me to stretch and reach in many directions; to develop as a rounded person. It was the opportunity for me to find, approach and test my limits. It was an exceptional, well rounded, total educational opportunity."

And he concluded: "Miami was the first place I ever saw or heard in person, then-Senator John F. Kennedy, Eugene Ormandy and the Philadelphia Philharmonic, Roberta Peters, John Kenneth Galbraith, Paul Dietzel and Louie Armstrong; just to name a few. Miami caused me to reach and stretch in many ways. No school can do more."

Bill Mulliken . . . 1960 Olympic swimming champion

1972

They marched into the Hall of Fame together, these two southpaws: Bo Schembechler, the left-handed pitcher, offensive tackle and coach, and his star player, left-handed quarterback Ernie Kellermann. They were joined by another basketball player, Earl Blaik's Dayton neighbor and Miami's first great distance runner.

****

Bob Brown's Miami basketball career was interrupted by the war, like many athletes in his day, yet he ranks among the top all-time career scorers. His 1277 points puts him behind only Archie Aldridge, Wayne Embry and Jeff Gehring. On February 2, 1947, in a game against Evansville in Withrow Court, Brown scored 39 points, a Miami record until Dick Walls came along five years later. He earned All-Ohio honors at center in both 1946-47 and 1947-48. A successful business and civic leader in Houston, Texas, he has served Miami in recent years on the Executive Council of its Alumni Association.

****

The 1913 Miami football team upset Denison, 19-0. A sophomore from Dayton named Marvin Pierce, Blaik's neighbor, accounted for all the points with a touchdown, four field goals and an extra-point placement. Nicknamed Monk, he was not only an outstanding football player, a quarterback and halfback, but starred in three other sports at Miami . . basketball, baseball and tennis. His baseball career was highlighted by a series of games on successive days against Wittenberg, Wooster and Oberlin. As an outfielder, Pierce got a single and double in three at bats against Wittenberg. The next day he pitched the full game against Wooster, and on the third day against Oberlin he returned to the mound in relief to strike out eight in the remaining five innings.

****

Charles Shugert, a 1932 Miami graduate, captured three consecutive Buckeye Conference cross country titles and won the two-mile run in both the Ohio AAU and the NCAA in 1932. His NCAA championship in Chicago came in the then record time of 9:16.7. He had been second in the same event a year earlier.

1973

Fifty years of Miami's football history and another Olympic champion were represented by the inductees into the Hall of Fame in 1973.

One of only two men to serve as a Miami football team captain for two consecutive years, George Booth was elected to that honor in both 1907 and 1908. He was a "roving center" on defense and is given much credit for Miami's having an undefeated 7-0 record in 1908 while allowing only Oberlin among the seven opponents even to score. Some "oldtimers" claim that Booth played football for seven years at Miami, but Booth said that was not so. "I played every minute of every game for Miami for five years," he recalled. "When I wasn't on defense, I kicked off, punted and did just about everything except pass."

Booth recalled that often on road trips the pre-game meal consisted of a "bushel of ham sandwiches and lots of hot coffee."

****

In 1982, when Miami Field was retired, Russell Baker, the oldest living Miami football player to have played on the historic field, was there. As captain of the 1912 team, he was representing his era in the ceremonial passing of the game ball through the years. Baker was a "triple-threat" who is believed to be one of the first collegiate football players in the Midwest to throw a long pass. And, said a Miami publication of that era, "Baker could throw a football into a tomato can, kick it into a coffin corner and, playing behind an average line, was rarely stopped by the opposition."

****

There is no denying the passing combination of Paul Brown to Jim Gordon was one of Chet Pittser's primary offensive weapons during his coaching regime; but when Brown graduated in 1930, a running back named Wilbur Cartwright really came into his own. Known by a variety of nicknames, such as "Catchproof Cartwright," "The Chief," "The Buckeye Bullet" and "The Redskin Rambler," Cartwright was regarded by many in that period as one of the most exciting running backs in Miami football history. Few who were there will forget the Homecoming game in 1930 when Cartwright scored three touchdowns on runs of 78, 90 and 92 yards and gained a total of 344 yards, even though Miami lost to Ohio Wesleyan, 23-20. George Gauthier, the legendary Ohio Wesleyan coach, stated: "Cartwright was a master at making the fullest possible use of his interference. He always maneuvered himself so that he kept a blocker or two between himself and the opposing tacklers."

In a game against Ashland the week before, Cartwright had scored five touchdowns and kicked an extra point. The five touchdowns, the 31 points and the 344 rushing yards remain Miami single game records. Over the season, he gained 1,168 yards, which was more than all nine opponents gained that year. He was selected All-Ohio in 1930 and All-Buckeye in 1930 and 1931.

****

Cartwright's senior season was Warren (Chisel) Ott's sophomore year. Unlike Cartwright, Ott was a multi-sport standout. Playing offensive and defensive end, Ott gained All-Ohio honors twice and All-Buckeye honors three times. He was a leading player on the 1932 and 1933 Miami teams which won successive Buckeye Conference championships.

When Miami dedicated Withrow Court in 1932, Ott was one of the starting guards, along with a baseball player named Walter Alston. After graduation, Ott opted for a coaching career. He spent more than 30 years in the Ohio high school ranks, three years at Oberlin and 34 years at Bowling Green, where at one time or another he was head coach in football, basketball, cross country and track.

****

It was August of 1949 when Woody Hayes, wrapping up some last-minute recruiting, finally got around to Quarterback Jim Root. In three varsity years, one under Hayes and two under Ara Parseghian, Root's career totals showed 161 completed passes out of 289 attempts for 2,485 yards and 24 touchdowns.

"It's great going to school here," Root was saying at the reunion of the

Miami welcomed Bob Schul home in 1964 after his Gold-Medal-winning effort in Tokyo. Participating in the ceremonies were Bob Epskamp, who succeeded George Rider as track coach, Acting President Charles Ray Wilson, Dick Shrider, Schul, Rider and Student Body President Mike Oxley, now a Congressman.

Salad Bowl team a few years ago, "but to be here, go to school, be married and play football all at the same time . . . those were super years and years that we'll never forget."

Root went on to describe what being a Miami graduate meant to him. "Unquestionably, Miami gave me a super education. You know, education is a lot of things. Education is really getting to know people . . . knowing how to deal with people . . . knowing how to handle a stress situation . . . knowing how to get along in the world . . . and I didn't burn up the books here, but I did graduate. And as for being in coaching, what else could help you more than Miami has helped all of us in coaching?"

****

Four years after Bill Mulliken's Gold Medal victory in Rome, the scene shifted halfway around the world to Tokyo, Japan. It was 1964 and the sport wasn't swimming, it was track and field. And the man breaking the tape, a wide smile lighting up his face, was unmistakably a Miamian. Bob Schul, a Miami senior from West Milton, Ohio, had won the 5,000 meters, the first American to capture that event.

In a sense, these two Olympic champions had similar dedication, although that dedication was manifested in different ways. Schul first had enrolled at Miami in 1956, but he quit school in 1958 to join the Air Force. Most of his Air Force career was spent in California, where he trained under Mihaly Igloi, famed Hungarian trainer of distance runners. It was while he was in the Air Force that Schul began to run in international competition.

He re-enrolled at Miami in September of 1963, and ran on Miami's track team during the spring of 1964. From April to June, he set five Miami varsity or Miami Field records, three American records and two National Collegiate records at distances ranging from a mile to 5,000 meters. After school closed for the summer, he returned to California to train for the Olympics.

On June 27, Schul won the 76th National AAU championship 5,000-meter run with a clocking of 13:56.2. On September 11, he qualified for the Olympics in 13:55.6, and on October 19 he won the Gold Medal in 13:48.8.

Ten years after he first enrolled, Schul finally earned his degree from Miami. Today, Schul operates Bob Schul's Pro Shop, a sporting goods store in Troy, Ohio, and coaches track at Wright State University.

1974

In each class of inductees, it seems, there is an underlying symbol of a strength, or indeed the different strengths, of Miami. The 1974 class was a case in point. Three of the inductees, Tirrel Burton, Tom Pagna and Richard (Doc) Urich had spent most of their post-graduate days as assistant coaches working at the right hand of Miami head coaches. Each of their careers is chronicled, in some measure, earlier in these pages. One of the three, Burton, grew up in Oxford, and as he looked back at what Miami had meant to him, he perhaps saw it in unique perspective.

"I grew up in Oxford. Attending Miami, running track, playing football and later returning to coach football with Bill Mallory's staff, have all been special chapters in my life.

"As a youngster I recall the excitement of a football Saturday, a jam-packed Withrow Court, a track meet at Miami Field. Afterwards, at home in bed, I fantasized and dreamt of myself duplicating the athletic feats of the Miami greats of that era.

"The traditional 'landmarks' of Miami such as Benton Hall, Fisher Hall, Slant Walk, and Cook Field were only extensions of my back yard.

"After returning from a three-year tour of duty in the Army, I had different goals, not only to play football, but to get a degree from one of the most prestigious universities in the country. I wanted to teach and to coach and the foundation and the philosophy for everything I have done since was influenced by some of the most respected men in the field — John Brickels, Ara Parseghian, George Rider, Jim Gordon, Tom Van Voorhis, Dick Mackey, Walt Gregg, Bo Schembechler, and many others. "To be selected as a member of the Miami Athletic Hall of Fame is an honor that surpasses any dream and is particularly meaningful to one who grew up in 'Redskin Country.'"

****

My good friend Bill Whitmore, the sports information director at Rice University in Houston for many years and president elect of the College Sports Information Directors of America, calls him the "Silent K." When Don Knodel was first introduced as the new basketball coach at Rice University, Whitmore thought it would be especially difficult to teach a bunch of folks who had talked Texan all their lives to say Knodel (the "K" is silent); so he immediately helped them out by giving Knodel the nickname.

Knodel came to Miami and played first under John Brickels and later for Bill Rohr. A 5-9 guard, he scored 828 points during his three-year career and three times was named to the All-Conference team while helping lead Miami to two Conference championships. He also was a competent baseball player.

A coaching career followed for Knodel, and it started in high school at Marion Harding and later Oxford's Talawanda High School. His first college experience was as a Miami assistant in 1955-56, and from there he moved on to assist at Vanderbilt before landing the Rice job in 1966. He guided the Owls to the Southwest Conference title in 1969-70 and was named the SWC's Coach of the Year.

Upon being named to Miami's Athletic Hall of Fame, Knodel had this to say: "Miami gives every young person the opportunity to meet his destiny and regardless of his failures or successes, he is never really forgotten. Assistance is always extended from the vast reservoir of successful people in the Miami Fraternity of Coaches. I myself have had several instances to fill my cup from it."

****

George Munns also was an Oxford native, but Burton wasn't dreaming of his exploits in his youth. Munns was an outstanding athlete in five sports at Miami from 1916-1919. He participated three years each in football, basketball and baseball, two in track and captured the Tobey Tennis Trophy.

He is best remembered as a three-year All-Ohio halfback who never lost a game in football. Playing under George Little in 1916 and George

Rider the next two years, he helped Miami to win three consecutive Ohio Conference titles and compile a record of 18 wins, no defeats and four ties. In those three years, Miami outscored the opposition 636-25.

Munns was also a member of Miami's 1917-18 basketball team that went undefeated in 10 games and captured the Ohio Conference crown.

1975

Bo Schembechler mentioned that one of his failings early in his Miami coaching career was his inattention to defense. He corrected that oversight when, in his second year at the helm, he recruited Bob Babich to play linebacker. From 1966 through 1968, this Youngstown product was the anchor of Miami's defense. At times, he seemed to be on a one-man search and destroy mission.

The youngest man to be selected for induction into the Hall of Fame, Babich twice earned the Most Valuable Player accolade of his teammates. He was selected as Miami's Athlete of the Year for the 1968-69 season. A two-time unanimous All-MAC linebacker, he was voted Defensive Player of the Year in the Conference as he captained the 1968 team. Indicative of the value of his presence is this little-known fact: of 30 games at Miami when he was in the lineup, the Redskins allowed one touchdown or less on 19 occasions. There were six shutouts. Babich was chosen a first team All-American by the American Football Coaches Association and was a first round draft pick of the San Diego Chargers. He was a regular with the Chargers before being traded to the Cleveland Browns.

****

I walked into John Brickels' office one January day in 1957. I had just returned from Christmas vacation, and as Sports Editor of **The Miami Student,** I felt a need to catch up on the latest developments. There was one. Bill Rohr, the basketball coach at the time, was in the office, and he and Brickels were talking about Rohr being under consideration for the vacant coaching position at Northwestern. There had been some speculation in the Chicago papers about that, but nothing definite. Rohr was explaining to Brickels that if Northwestern offered him the job, he thought he would take it. That offer might come at any time.

The Student didn't publish until Friday, and as a summertime employee of **The Chicago Tribune,** I thought they might be interested. I called **The Tribune** and suggested they check it out. If Northwestern was interested in Rohr, I said, Rohr seemed interested in Northwestern. And I gave the **Tribune** some background on the Miami basketball coach. That night, a telegram from Chicago told me everything had been verified, and a check was on the way. The next morning, readers of **The Chicago Tribune** learned that Bill Rohr was expected to follow Ara Parseghian from Miami to Northwestern and would be named the head basketball coach later that day.

Rohr, of course, was the protege of Paul Brown. He attended Ohio Wesleyan and made his entry into coaching as a Brown assistant at Massillon. After his discharge from service in 1946, he became head basketball coach at Portsmouth High School. With Brickels having been steered to Miami by Brown, it's not surprising that, when Brickels gave up basketball coaching to concentrate on his administrative duties, he turned to Rohr as his successor.

Miami teams under Rohr won 91 of 138 games, never had a losing season, captured four Mid-American Conference championships and appeared in three NCAA tournaments.

Ohio University summoned Rohr to take command of its athletic program in 1963, so after leading Northwestern to some of its better years in the Big Ten basketball wars, Rohr took on the challenge of athletic administration. In 1976, he was the president of the National Association of Collegiate Directors of Athletics. In July 1978, he resigned from Ohio University to return to Oxford and enter the insurance business.

****

A basketball player who served as honorary co-captain with Bob Brown during the 1947-48 season, the captain and Most Valuable Player on George Blackburn's 1948 team and the fullback on some of Chet Pittser's earliest teams round out the 1975 class of honorees.

Paul Schnackenberg was an All-Ohio guard for three years under Blue Foster and was an All-Mid-American Conference choice in the first two years Miami competed in the league. To this day many consider him Miami's finest ball-handler.

****

Paul Shoults won All-Conference and All-Ohio honors twice in his four-year football career and led Miami to its first MAC championship in 1948. He was a three-year letterman in baseball as well. His coaching career began at Fairview High School in Dayton after a year of professional football. He joined Ara Parseghian's staff at Miami in 1952 and stayed with Parseghian as an assistant at Northwestern and Notre Dame. He is now the athletic director at Eastern Michigan University, a recent addition to the Mid-American Conference.

****

Harry Stryker was an All-Ohio and All-Buckeye Conference fullback from 1925 through 1927. An outstanding runner, pass receiver and punter, he helped Miami hand Oberlin its first defeat in four years in the 1926 season as he turned a fake punt into an 85-yard touchdown run.

1976

Few assistant coaches receive the attention reserved for Bill Arnsparger. He played on Miami's 1948 and '49 football teams, and began his coaching career as an assistant to Woody Hayes in 1950. When Hayes went to Ohio State the next year, Arnsparger went along.

In 1954, Arnsparger rejoined his former high school coach, Blanton Collier, at the University of Kentucky, where he was associated with Don Shula. Arnsparger spent two years as an assistant at Tulane, but in 1964, became an assistant to Shula at Baltimore. With the exception of two and a half years as head coach of the New York Giants, Arnsparger has been a Shula aide ever since, first at Baltimore and then with the Miami Dolphins. His title, Assistant Head Coach — Defense, speaks volumes about why he is held in such esteem.

****

Jeff Gehring and his twin brother, John, a high jumper, came out of Toledo's Ottawa Hills High School, and it was apparent from the beginning that Jeff's basketball skills would have an impact on the Redskins' fortunes. In his sophomore season, he became the first Miami player to score more than 400 points. His three-year total of 1,295 points places him third on Miami's all-time career scoring list, behind Wayne Embry and Archie Aldridge, who came along later.

Twice an All-Conference performer, Gehring helped lead Miami to a 49-24 record over three seasons, including a 20-5 mark in 1964-65, when the Redskins tied for the Conference championship and became the first Miami team in history to win 20 games. Gehring averaged 18 points a game over three years, with a field goal percentage of .478 and a free throw percentage of .789. His best single-game scoring output was 38 points against Ball State in 1963.

****

Dick Klitch followed Bill Rohr from Portsmouth to Miami and immediately became a basketball and tennis standout for the Redskins. He played on three Mid-American Conference championship teams in basketball and one in tennis. He teamed with Fred Haring to win the MAC #1 doubles title in 1953 as the Redskins captured the team title. Klitch captured the #1 singles title in 1955. He was co-captain of the 1954-55 basketball team which won the MAC title, and had career totals of 821 points and 589 rebounds.

****

Another Portsmouth entry was Arthur (Red) Thatcher, who lettered three times each for Chet Pittser's football team's and George Rider's track teams. A center, he was selected second team All-Buckeye as a senior, then helped Miami win the Buckeye and Big Six track titles.

1977

Coaching and teaching have been the lifetime work of each of the 1977 inductees.

Bob Bronston was one of the great fullbacks in Miami history as he helped Ara Parseghian's teams to a 30-6-1 record during his four-year career from 1951 to 1954. Bronston gained 1,161 yards and scored 80 points during his Miami career, which was climaxed when he was named team captain his senior year. He returned to his hometown, Springfield, to coach. He now is the Dean of Students at Springfield North High School.

****

Donald Weaver (Red) Emery finished fourth in the NCAA two-mile run in 1926 and eighth in the mile in 1927. He taught and coached at Cleveland Lincoln High School prior to his retirement.

****

Alfred Gansberg was a football and baseball player under Coach Chet Pittser, played basketball under Roy Tillotson, and was the president of the Miami University Foundation before he passed away in 1976.

****

Bob Jencks, the pass-catching and place-kicking star of Miami's 10-7 upset victory over Purdue in 1962, played on the Chicago Bears' world championship team in 1963, before moving to Indiana State University as a part-time assistant while working on his doctorate in economic geography. Today, he is professor of geography at the University of New Hampshire.

****

John McVay, team captain and center for the 1952 football Redskins, has had a distinguished coaching and administrative career in football, beginning with a nine-year mark of 41-7-2 at Canton Central Catholic High School and highlighted by his role as administrative vice-president during the San Francisco '49ers Super Bowl year. In between, he coached in college as a Michigan State assistant and as head coach at Dayton, and in the professional ranks with Memphis of the World Football League and as head coach of the New York Giants.

In 1932, Vernon Cheadle graduated from Miami and headed for Harvard, where he would pursue his master's and doctoral degrees. He left behind a string of athletic successes which were highlighted by a record discus throw of 132 ft., 8⅞ in. in the Buckeye Conference championships his senior year. He also tossed the shot and played basketball and football. A noted botanist, Dr. Cheadle was chancellor of the University of California, Santa Barbara, from 1962 until his retirement in 1977.

****

Darrell Hedric, the winningest basketball coach in Miami history, sits in his office in Millett Hall, and recalls how he found his way to Miami from nearby Franklin, Ohio.

"I played for a guy by the name of Mickey McDade," says Hedric of his high school days. "He was from Massillon, Ohio, a Miami graduate, and played on the Miami basketball team here . . in the era of Ray Mears, Ara Parseghian, Schnackenberg, Brown . . that era, and of course was a personal friend of Bill Rohr. And Bill Rohr had just taken the head basketball job over from John Brickels in 1951, and so it was kind of a setup that I was gonna come to Miami University."

Hedric came to Miami with a coaching career in mind. Graduated in 1955, Hedric played industrial basketball in Akron with Goodyear Tire and Rubber and had an Air Force commitment which he completed in the fall of 1957. He had come back to Oxford to see his girl, who was to become his wife, when he ran into Brickels and Shrider. It was Shrider's first season, and Brickels asked Hedric if he would be a graduate assistant.

That sparked a coaching career. After a junior high school job at Chillicothe, he coached at Taft High School, Hamilton, Ohio. He was back at Miami as a full-time assistant to both Shrider and his successor, Tates Locke, then ascended to the head coaching position in 1970.

Under Hedric, Miami has won four Mid-American Conference championships and qualified for the NCAA tournament three times. One of those times was in 1978, when Miami's first round opponent was defending NCAA champion Marquette. The Redskins trailed by 11 when an elbowing incident involving John Shoemaker apparently lit a fire among the rest of the players, and brought the crowd, now pro-Miami, into the game. The Redskins tied it in regulation, then won in overtime, 84-81. Perhaps an even bigger Miami basketball victory was the 102-92 Miami upset of the North Carolina Tar Heels in Chapel Hill in the 1972-73 season. A headline in the campus newspaper which the Redskins noticed just before the pre-game meal was the catalyst for a 102-92 Miami upset. What so riled the team? The headline said, "Miami Who?"

****

Ray Mears lettered two years on Coach Blue Foster's Miami teams that featured Bob Brown and Paul Schnackenberg, but he made his reputation as coach. Mears went first to Wittenberg, where in six years his team won 121 games and lost only 23. He became known as a defensive genius as his teams posted the best defensive average in the country for four straight years. His 1961 team captured the NCAA college division national title, and in 1962 he moved on to Tennessee. At the time of his induction into the Hall of Fame, his Volunteer teams had won three Southeastern Conference championships, and he had posted a record of 278-112. Health problems forced his retirement from coaching, but he is now the athletic director at the University of Tennessee-Martin.

Mention of Mears raises one of those sidebars that show how involved the Cradle story can be. One of his assistants at Tennessee was the late Cliff Wettig, a Wilmington graduate but a Miami letterman, veteran of two and a half Miami basketball seasons under Blue Foster. Wettig had coached basketball, tennis and soccer at Grove City and Slippery Rock before Mears beckoned. After Tennessee, he was athletic director and basketball coach at Samford University in Birmingham.

Now Cliff Wettig's daughter Pam is starting her ninth year as Miami women's basketball coach. And seeking her third consecutive MAC crown. She has been MAC women's basketball Coach of the Year the past two seasons. And you guessed it: her proteges are infiltrating the coaching ranks as assistants at several colleges.

Just this year the University of Cincinnati elevated Sandy Smith, Miami '71, to head women's basketball coach.

****

Raymond Ray was a pioneer of sorts. Graduated from Miami in 1938, he became the first swimming coach at Fenn College (now Cleveland State). When Miami opened Billings Natatorium in 1952, Ray became Miami's first swimming coach. He performed the job with distinction for 22 years. He had a Miami record of 148-89-2 and three Mid-American Conference championsips. Besides Olympic champion Bill Mulliken, Ray coached five All-Americans and 88 MAC champions. And one of his proudest accomplishments may have been bringing the 1955 NCAA Swimming and Diving Championships to Billings Natatorium.

****

Edward Sauer played tackle alongside Earl Blaik on the 1917 Miami team, and in the two years he had him on the team, Coach George Rider called Sauer the "best tackle I ever had." Sauer played on teams that posted an 18-1-3 record in three years, and he was selected All-Ohio all three years.

After graduation in 1920, Sauer played professional football with the Dayton Triangles. He became a football referee in high school and later in the National Football League.

1979

One has a sense of history when examining the careers of the four Miami student-athletes who entered the Hall of Fame in 1979.

Bob Whittaker began his college career at Bowling Green, which was near his home of Norwalk. But he transferred to Miami in 1925 and made his Miami mark as a halfback on the 1925-26-27 teams and with a record-setting javelin throw of 171 ft., 3 in. in 1928. He returned to Bowling Green for his master's degree, then went on to establish one of the state's outstanding high school football coaching records at Sandusky High School from 1930-40. His teams had five undefeated seasons. In one stretch they won 38 straight games.

Whittaker returned to Bowling Green State University as head football coach, 1941 through 1954, and had two terms as head track coach, 1942-48 and 1953-60. He was succeeded as the Falcons' track and cross country coach by another Miami graduate, Mel Brodt, '49, who in 1972 coached the irrepressible Dave Wottle to an Olympic gold medal at 800 meters. The Robert H. Whittaker all-weather track adjacent to Doyt Perry Stadium at BG is named for this Miami Hall of Famer.

****

Pat Roudebush was a son of an Oxford and Miami legend. His untimely death while attending Harvard Law School after 1934 graduation from Miami cut short a career which showed uncommon promise.

Wallace Pattison Roudebush, Jr., literally grew up on campus. His father was Miami's long-time business officer, an early member of the Athletic Advisory Board, the man for whom Miami's administration building is named. The family home was the brick house which William Holmes McGuffey built in the 1830's when he was preparing the series of readers which were such an important educational tool of the early West. The University has converted it into a McGuffey Museum. Its location for a century was at the south edge of the campus; now it is virtually at the heart of a greatly expanded university.

Pat was a brilliant student, recipient of the Hinckley Award to an Outstanding Junior Man, senior class president, Phi Beta Kappa and Miami nominee for a Rhodes Scholarship. At the end of his first year in law school, he had been named to the editorial board of the **Harvard Law Review.**

George Rider insisted Roudebush was one of Miami's finest all-round athletes. He lettered in football on Pittser's 1931 team and was letterman and spark as quarterback on Frank Wilton's first two Miami teams, both Buckeye Conference champions. He was co-captain of the 1933 baseball team and captain of the '34 squad.

Pat Roudebush had been accustomed to working with younger boys as a camp counselor each summer — and just before he was to begin his second year of law school, he was brought home seriously ill from an infection incurred in a fall over a tennis court roller at summer camp. It was an infection which today's antibiotics almost certainly would have curbed easily; yet he died within a few days on September 7, 1935.

****

As we have learned in previous chapters, Bill Hoover came to Miami from Louisville, Ohio, one of the early recruits of Stu Holcomb and Sid Gillman. He had to take a few years out for the service, but he returned to complete his education, and Oxford has remained his home ever since, as an assistant coach for three years and then as a successful businessman.

In the three post-war seasons after Hoover returned from Navy duty, he helped Miami compile a three-year record of 23-5-1. He is joined in the Hall of Fame by five teammates from those teams who climaxed their careers with the Sun Bowl victory over Texas Tech: Paul Dietzel, Mel Olix, Ara Parseghian, Paul Shoults and Richard (Doc) Urich.

****

A little school at New Carlisle, near Springfield . . Tecumseh High School . . had a lot to do with Miami's basketball success in the mid-Fifties and early Sixties. First there was Wayne Embry, and then came Dave Zeller out of Tecumseh High School. As a sophomore, Zeller led Miami to a Conference co-championship, averaging 13 points a game. His scoring average was about the same the next year, but he made the All-MAC first team as a senior when he led the league in scoring with a 22.9-point average for MAC games. His all-games average was 22.3. He also led the league in free throw shooting that year with 91 of 103 for a percentage of .883.

He played one season of professional basketball with the Cincinnati Royals, as a teammate of Embry, but returned to Miami the next year as a graduate assistant to Dick Shrider. The year after that, 1963, he launched a high school coaching career which has included six years as the head coach at Northeastern High School near Springfield. Since 1969, he has been the head coach at Piqua.

1980

A teammate of Pat Roudebush, two highly successful coaches in football and tennis and Miami's all-time leading ground gainer make up the Hall of Famers that launched the decade of the Eighties.

Len Fertig lettered three years each in football and baseball from 1931 through '34. He was selected first team All-Buckeye Conference in his senior season as a fullback. Like Roudebush, he shared Miami's back-to-back Buckeye Conference championships in 1932 and 1933.

Fertig earned All-American recognition that senior season by accounting for at least two touchdowns in each of three separate games. Against Wittenberg, he scored on a 72-yard run and a one-yard plunge and threw a 20-yard scoring pass. In his final game against Cincinnati, he was a defensive standout as well, being in on half of the tackles in a 6-2 Miami victory. A catcher and outfielder in baseball, he signed a professional contract with the Philadelphia Athletics after graduation.

****

Bob Hitchens' number 40 is displayed in Miami's trophy case alongside John Pont's number 42. For three consecutive years, Hitchens received All-Conference honors as a tailback for Bill Mallory's teams. His junior season was a banner year: he established five Miami records; was selected Miami Most Valuable Player; MAC Offensive Player of the Year and Miami Athlete of the Year, and gained All-American honors from the Associated Press.

He holds the single game record for most rushes with 45 in a 21-8 Miami victory over South Carolina in 1972. Hitchens' season marks include 326 carries for 1,370 yards and 15 touchdowns, good for 90 points. He also holds four career records with 773 carries for 1,370 yards and 34 touchdowns . . . 204 points.

As a co-captain his senior year, 'Hitchens' helped lead Miami to the 11-0 season that was climaxed by the Mid-American Conference title and the Redskins' victory over Florida in the Tangerine Bowl.

Following graduation, Hitchens played professional football for two years with the New England Patriots, Kansas City Chiefs and Pittsburgh Steelers. The next three years he was an assistant football coach at Carnegie-Mellon University, which captured three President's Athletic Conference championships and two semi-final berths in the NCAA District III playoffs. Since 1980, Hitchens has been a member of the Miami coaching staff, first under Tom Reed and now under Tim Rose. It is perhaps no coincidence that Bill Mallory, Hitchens' coach, joined Bob in the Hall of Fame in 1980. Mallory thus became the most recent of the Miami coaches to be enshrined in the Hall.

****

Steve Strome came to Miami as a basketball and tennis player, returned as an assistant basketball coach under Tates Locke for three years, then in 1969 switched to tennis and started a ten-year reign of terror in Mid-American Conference tennis as Miami's head coach.

He guided the Redskins to seven MAC championships in 10 years. He had an overall record of 167-64 and a winning percentage of .723. At one time, the Redskins had a 46-match winning streak against Conference foes. During Strome's tenure, Miami had 27 singles and 14 doubles champions in the MAC. Five times he was voted Mid-American Conference Coach of the Year. Strome left Miami in 1979 to accept the head coaching position at Louisiana State University. In 1983, he became the head tennis coach at Duke University.

1981

The Hall of Fame class of 1981 paints a portrait of the depth and breadth of Miami athletics. Included among the inductees are the winningest coach in Miami baseball history, Miami's only two-time Olympian, a former football star who has served on Miami's athletic staff for more than 25 years, one of Ohio's most successful high school football coaches and another teammate of Pat Roudebush on the championship teams of 1932 and '33.

****

Jack Bacheler is a 1966 graduate of Miami who earned All-America honors in 1964 when he finished seventh in the NCAA cross country championship. He did it again in 1966 when he placed second in the steeplechase in the NCAA Track and Field championships. Bacheler also captured the three-mile run in the Mid-American Conference Track and Field championships in 1965 and '66 and helped lead the Redskins to the All-Ohio and MAC cross country championships in 1965.

He is the only Miamian to participate in two Olympics as an athlete. At Mexico City in 1968 Bacheler was a finalist in the 5,000 meters, the same event Miamian Bob Schul had won in 1964. Bacheler finished ninth in the marathon at Munich in 1972. Between Olympic performances, running for the Florida Track Club, Bacheler captured National AAU championships in cross country and the 10,000 meters in 1969 and the six-mile run in 1970.

"After two lackluster academic years," said Bacheler when he was inducted, "whose purpose must have been to illustrate what I was not cut out to do or be, a Miami zoology professor, Marion Boesel, explained to me that my life-long hobby of insect collecting could be shaped into an interesting career. That conversation, his recommended course in entomology, and a subsequent degree in zoology provided a clear path toward graduate school and an exciting livelihood."

Now an associate professor at North Carolina State with a Ph.D. in entomology, Bacheler has continued his association with running by working with distance runners. In 1979 and '80 he coached the North Carolina State women's cross country team to the AIAW national championships.

Reflecting further on his Miami career Bacheler said, "Those difficult workouts, the job required of a grant-in-aid athlete, and the budgeted lifestyles were somehow satisfying, and the friendships made at Miami established a respect and love for athletics in general and distance running in particular that I hold to this day. To Miami University I owe a debt of gratitude which can never be repaid."

****

Since 1956, when he returned to Miami as an assistant football coach, Wayne Gibson has worked in the athletic department in various capacities. Nobody, since Jay Colville retired from full-time duty, has had longer continuous service. When Gibby was enshrined in the Athletic Hall of Fame, he saw Miami from a different perspective.

"Studying history at Miami," he said, "has no doubt influenced my feeling about the values I have received at this unique institution. I have observed the campus at times when it was alive with students, staff and events, and during vacation periods when the only beauty was the design of the buildings and their surroundings. This gives a person two great spectrums of its character. It makes you realize that from a physical standpoint Miami has few equals. Even more important, it drives home the point that a beautiful and well-kept campus is necessary, but the true value is in the people and attitudes that make up the University."

****

When Paul Brown was pointing certain of his Massillon athletes in Miami's direction, one of those who accepted the challenge was Mel Knowlton. Knowlton earned three letters each in baseball and basketball and was named All-Buckeye Conference in both sports. He participated in football for two years as a player and was a student assistant with the freshman football team for two years. He was also a member of the Athletic Board of Control (recently renamed Athletic Policy Committee).

After graduation he returned to Massillon where he coached under Brown. From 1946 to 1969 Knowlton was the head football coach at Alliance High School, where his teams compiled a 24-year record of 150-85-8, capturing the state championship in 1958. He was named Ohio Coach of the Year in 1954. Knowlton was president of the Ohio High School Football Coaches' Association in 1957 and was named to that group's Hall of Fame in 1972. After retiring from coaching he remained as athletic director at Alliance until 1978.

****

"I feel very fortunate, not only having been a student at Miami, but also having the opportunity to come back as a member of the coaching staff and faculty," responded Bud Middaugh when informed of his selection to the Hall of Fame.

"My association with Miami University has been very rewarding. Not only did I receive a fine education, but most important the staff, alumni and friends of the University that I came in contact with had so much influence on my life. Of those the most influential person was Woody Wills. Woody was my coach and had a great influence in my pursuing the coaching profession.

"While playing under Coach Wills, and the association with the other Miami coaches, I received a sense of values which include self discipline, personal pride, sacrifice, and desire to compete and excel."

Bud Middaugh guided 12 Miami baseball teams to a record of 359-173 for a winning percentage of .673. His teams captured three MAC championships and appeared in the NCAA playoffs four times. Middaugh's 1977 team set an all-time Miami record for most wins in a season with 45. Four players gained All-America recognition, nine were selected All-District, 17 made first team All-MAC and 20 signed professional baseball contracts.

A four-year letterman at shortstop under Wills, Middaugh was selected All-Conference his senior year. After graduation he coached three years at Lorain Admiral King High School and compiled a record of 52-14. He returned to Miami in 1977 as an assistant baseball coach and the following year accepted the head coaching assignment following Wills' retirement. He quickly moved Miami to baseball prominence as the Redskins captured their first-ever MAC titles in 1973 and '74. Since 1980, Middaugh has been the head coach at the University of Michigan and has taken the Wolverines to the College World Series at Omaha for three of four years.

****

For the third year in a row, a member of the 1931-33 Miami football teams who played one year under Chet Pittser and two under Frank Wilton was selected for the Hall of Fame. This time, it was Bill Stewart, an outstanding tackle on offense and defense. He was chosen All-Buckeye Conference three years and All-Ohio in 1932. Stewart also earned All-America honorable mention and participated in track.

Following graduation from Miami, Stewart went to Springfield High

School as an assistant coach in football, basketball and track and head of the intramural program. He later became business manager of the Springfield city schools and taught industrial arts.

1982

When Paul Brown persuaded that group of high school athletes from Massillon to visit the campus, and Ray Brown gave Howard Brinker the job on his farm which helped him pay for his college education, Brinker probably didn't realize that he would one day return to Miami as a Hall of Famer.

From 1935 through 1937, Brinker played center on Coach Frank Wilton's teams, and in his junior year, the Redskins shared the Buckeye Conference title with a 7-1-1 record. Brinker graduated in 1939, and began a coaching career which has spanned three decades. He started under 1981 inductee Mel Knowlton at Edmund Jones Junior High School in Massillon, then moved with Knowlton to Steubenville High School. He took over as head coach in 1941, and though his Steubenville coaching assignment was interrupted by three years of military service, he returned and remained through the 1948 season. In 1949, he became line coach at Ohio University, and stayed for three years before rejoining Paul Brown on the Cleveland Browns. He remained with the Browns until Brown asked him to come to Cincinnati in 1974. Brinker was defensive coordinator under Brown, Bill Johnson and Homer Rice until 1979.

****

Ted Downing, who came to Miami from Evanston Township High School in Illinois is the best high jumper in Miami history. The first man in Ohio to clear 7 feet in the high jump, Downing did it 15 times, the first time when he won the NCAA Indoor championship in 1967 with a jump of 7 feet, ¼ inches. That jump earned Downing All-America honors that year, and he repeated the next year when he placed third. Downing won the Mid-American Conference title in both 1967 and 1968, and also won the Penn Relays title and the International Meet of Champions in Winnipeg, Canada. He was selected Miami's Athlete of the Year for 1967-68. Upon his induction into the Hall of Fame, Downing had this to say about his Miami experience:

"To be elected to the Miami University Athletic Hall of Fame is more than a tremendous honor, it is a culmination and a recognition of all the associations and experiences made possible by the university. The extent of my gratitude seems impossible to measure. I remain very much indebted to Miami for providing me the opportunities and experiences to grow as a person."

****

Miami's Athlete of the Year for 1960-61 was a football player-wrestler named Joe Galat. From Painesville, Ohio, Galat had an even greater impact when he turned to coaching and in six years as Miami's wrestling coach he guided the Redskins to a dual meet record of 53-18-1, and four Mid-American Conference championships. Eighteen of his wrestlers won individual MAC championships, and Galat himself was MAC Coach of the Year twice. In 1963-64, he was runner-up in the balloting for National Rookie Coach of the Year honors.

Galat was also an assistant football coach under Bo Schembechler for four years, and after leaving Miami he continued in football, assisting Carm Cozza at Yale, John McVay with the New York Giants and the Memphis Southmen, Bill Narduzzi at Youngstown State and Eddie Biles in Houston with the Oilers. He also had a stint as an assistant coach at Kentucky. He was appointed head coach of the Montreal Concordes in the Canadian League not long after his induction into the Hall of Fame.

Said Galat at his induction: "The person that had the most influence on my athletic philosophy is Jay Colville, who always kept every contest in perspective. He is the Will Rogers and Ernest Hemingway of the training room. My life-long goal has always been to reach the coveted position on the training room wall that Jay has reserved for the great and near great."

Galat retains fond memories of the wrestlers he coached at Miami, and says of those years that "the highlight would have to be the MAC championships in 1967 that Miami hosted and won before a full house in Withrow Court."

******

Sherman Smith was the quarterback who helped Miami compile a four-year record of 39-4-1 from 1972-75, including the three straight Tangerine Bowl victories. Now with the Seattle Seahawks in the National Football League, Smith ranks third on Miami's all-time total offense list with 3,200 yards. Included in that total were 2,187 yards in 503 carries and 95 of 224 passes for 1,013 yards. He scored 12 touchdowns and passed for nine more. He was named to the All-MAC first team his senior year. Smith displayed the depth of his feeling for Miami when he was inducted as he said:

"My fondest memories of Miami are the many life-long friendships that developed with my teammates and classmates. Even though we were of different races, cultures and backgrounds, we demonstrated what it takes to make a great team besides ability and good coaching. We demonstrated togetherness, that was our secret weapon, that was our 12th man. It is because of this togetherness and, our special friendships that could not be developed in the classroom, that makes me proud to say that I played on three of the greatest football teams in Miami's history.

"I am deeply grateful to the outstanding people of Miami for making my four years a very positive total experience. Finally, I would like to say that I am very grateful for this wonderful honor. Being inducted into the Miami University Athletic Hall of Fame is my finest hour, because I will be named with many great men, and I can truly become a permanent part of Miami."

****

Ernie Vossler was an All-Ohio fullback and a champion in the shot put, an outstanding athlete for Miami from 1927-30. A 205-pound fullback from Franklin, Ohio, he was a triple-threat performer. One of his outstanding performances came against Denison in 1929 when he rushed for more than 200 yards as Miami won 31-0.

Vossler captured three Buckeye Conference shot put titles, his best effort of 47 feet, 6 inches coming in his senior year. He qualified for the

NCAA championships in 1929, and also threw the discus and the javelin for Miami.

1983

The latest additions to Miami's Athletic Hall of Fame each made significant contributions on the field of play to recent moments of glory in tennis, basketball, wrestling and baseball. They underscore emphatically the expansion and development of Miami athletics into a broad-based program. They illustrate why Miami has been such a dominant force in the annual battle for the Reese Cup, indicating all-around supremacy in Mid-American Conference athletics.

****

Dave Brown, a 1975 graduate, won seven Mid-American Conference championships in tennis, beginning in 1972. He was a four-time champion at #2 singles and teamed with Ken Daniels to win three titles at #1 doubles. Brown became the second of only four players to win seven MAC titles. During Brown's career, Miami won the MAC championship in 1972, '74 and '75. Those championships were the first of nine Miami won in 11 years.

Brown came to Miami from Wilmette, Illinois, and currently is a

Miami won its first Reese Cup, emblematic of overall accomplishment in the Mid-American Conference, in 1955. Athletic Director John Brickels smiled over MAC championships in football under Ara Parseghian, in track and cross country under George Rider, in basketball under Bill Rohr and in swimming under Raymond Ray.

partner in a sporting goods store in Colorado.

****

Phil Lumpkin, a high-scoring guard from Dayton, was a key factor during the 1972-73 basketball season when Miami went into Chapel Hill and upset North Carolina, then won the Mid-American Conference title and advanced to the NCAA tournament. That year, Lumpkin was named Miami's Athlete of the Year. Over his four-year career, he scored 1243 points, which places him sixth on Miami's all-time scoring list.

Lumpkin was drafted by the Portland Trailblazers and played three years in the NBA with Portland and the Phoenix Suns. He returned to Miami to complete work toward his undergraduate degree, which he received in 1981.

****

Under Coach Joe Galat, Miami won back-to-back Mid-American Conference wrestling championships in 1964 and '65, and 147-pounder John Schael was a big factor as he won titles both years in his weight class. After graduation in 1966, Schael was the head wrestling coach at the University of Chicago for ten years, before he turned to athletic administration and became the athletic director at Washington University in St. Louis.

****

Gary Wright's 25-8 record makes him the winningest pitcher in Miami baseball history, and there is little doubt that his career 1.64 earned-run average combined with his won-lost record were key ingredients in 1973 and '74 when Miami won Mid-American Conference championships. Wright, on top of his pitching prowess, was a two-time academic All-America with a 3.77 grade point average in accounting. He was awarded an NCAA post-graduate scholarship, and now is a lawyer in Fairborn, Ohio, his hometown.

****

Seventy-five people in 15 years have been inducted into Miami's Hall of Fame. In no way are those 75 more than a path to follow as this story has unfolded. Because those 75 can tell stories of 75 more. And on and on it goes. It's a people story with a beginning, and an ending that's yet to be written. The final chapter is a new beginning.

"Let's face it. The excellence over thirty-forty years has been tremendous. Any coach in this particular seat is charged with the duty and responsibility to maintain it . . . and that'll be difficult. But it's something I feel up to, and I think we have the people, and the manpower and the tradition to definitely get it done.

"The schedule is very tough. I think we're playing teams that are not only so-called major powers, but successful major powers . . . teams that have a tremendous tradition in their own league in their own part of the country. The league is balanced like it's never been before. There isn't a more balanced league in the country.

"But I'm not pessimistic. I'm optimistic. I mean we're at Miami. We're at the Cradle of Coaches. We've got great people to line up and wear the white helmets with the red 'M' on 'em, so I'm not pessimistic, I'm optimistic, but I think you have to look at things in realistic terms."

Tim Rose, Miami's newest football coach, looking to the future shortly after his appointment was announced.

XIV
YAGER STADIUM ... AND A GUY NAMED ROSE

THEY SAW HIM coming, and when he entered the room with Dick Shrider, they were standing, applauding. They had gathered . . . the press and many in the Miami family . . . to learn the identity of the newest Miami head football coach. And when Tim Rose walked into that room in Millett Assembly Hall on January 5, 1983, the response was spontaneous.

Miami President Paul G. Pearson, who had delayed his departure for an extended alumni speaking tour as the announcement became imminent, looked out over the crowd and smiled.

"I think the first thing I want to do," he said, "is to put into proper perspective one point: In the press conference announcing my own appointment as president two years ago, the audience was about half the size of the audience that is here today. I think that puts into perspective the two appointments."

Turning serious, Pearson further acknowledged the unusual media turnout and incidental gathering of friends from campus and community, thanking each for "the support that each of you gives to the University." Then he began talking of Miami's approach to intercollegiate athletics, football in particular. Citing the leadership qualities that Rose had demonstrated in his five years as defensive coordinator and his ability to relate to the many Miami constituencies, the Miami president told how the new coach impressed him.

"Most of all, Tim fits well the Miami image, because of his high standard of ethics, because of his determination to see that our athletes receive solid academic experience and graduate, and because of his quest for excellence on the field of competition."

Seldom is an assistant coach distinguishable; but it was the Tim Rose sideline personality, his obvious rapport with the people around him as he led the Miami defense, which prompted the audience reaction as he strode into the room.

A 1963 graduate of Xavier University, Rose was an outstanding high school coach before he joined Tom Reed's Miami staff in 1978. He began his coaching career as an assistant in Cincinnati, first at Elder High School and later at Moeller, which has become a dominant force in Ohio high school football in recent years.

At St. Mary High School in Lorain, Ohio, Rose got his first head coaching experience. His eight-year record, from 1967 through '74, was 56-16-7. He was Ohio's Class A Coach of the Year his first year as a head coach and eventually conference Coach of the Year five straight times.

From Lorain, he moved to Boulder, Colorado, as head coach for three years. There he compiled a 19-10-1 record.

Responding to a question about the adjustment required in making the transition from assistant to head coach, Rose was characteristically candid.

"I think it's much easier the second time around in both capacities," he said. "I thought I was a better assistant here at Miami after having been a head coach for eleven years, and I think I'll be a better head coach after having been an assistant.

"There are going to be adjustments. Don't get me wrong. But I think I'm better qualified now than five years ago because of seeing it as assistant coach. So I think the transition will be relatively smooth."

Rose's response to his introduction as Miami's 29th head football coach reflected a depth of feeling for the position, and for those who had preceded him.

"There are an awful lot of feelings that come to one at a time like this in his life," Rose began, "and obviously I'm no exception. Certainly a tremendous source of personal pride at this time, and really a sense of

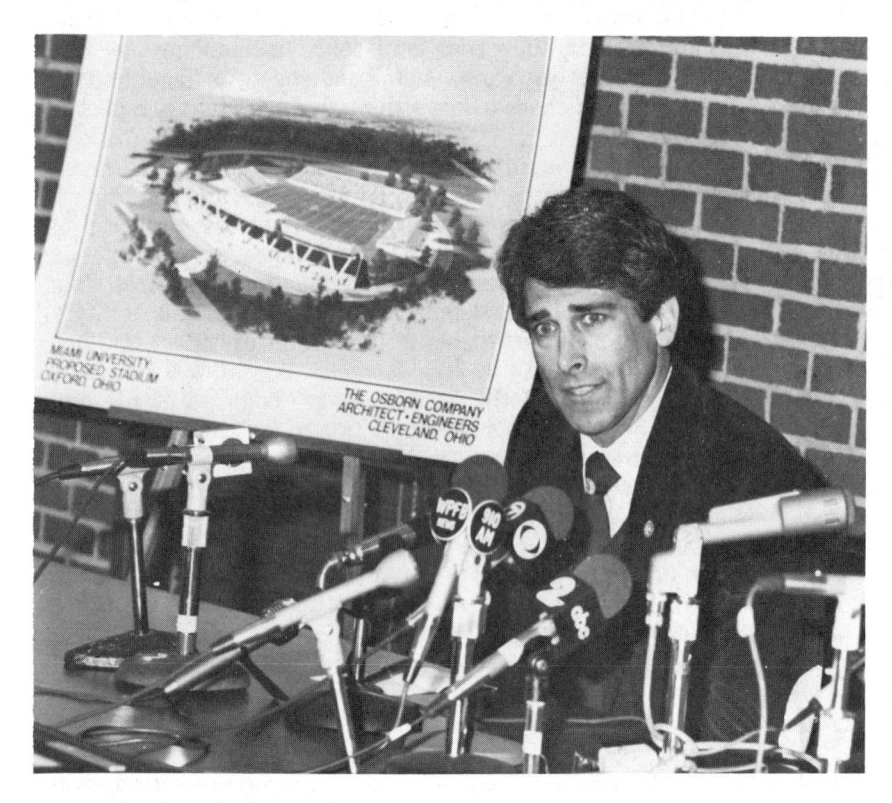

Tim Rose responding to a reporter's question at the press conference announcing his appointment. The architect's rendering of the new Yager Stadium provides the backdrop.

awe. Because since I've been coaching, I've heard people like Weeb Ewbank, Parseghian, Hayes, Pont, Schembechler, Reed, Mallory, Crum, all speak at clinics, and now to be a part of that heritage simply puts me in a state of awe.

"At the same time, the thing that stands out most in the feelings I have today and the way I feel at this moment is simply a very strong feeling of duty and responsibility, above all else. A duty and responsibility to the Miami community, for the past heritage and traditions ... to the alumni, to the students, to the players, to the administration. And by golly, I'll do everything I can, within the power of my abilities ... mental and physical, to get it done, because that is the overwhelming feeling today ... duty and responsibility."

****

There is the tradition at Miami. More than half a century has flashed by since the days of Red Blaik, and George Rider, and Jay Colville. But Tim Rose can't dwell on the past, he can only see the past as a key to unlock the future. He knows the challenge and he accepts it. A coach can do no less.

"I think as a young coach," he says when asked why he chose coaching, "you got into it because, number one, you love sports, and number two, you love to compete. Those are the main reasons. You aren't good enough to be a pro athlete. It's totally intriguing . . . the tactical part of it, the organizational part of it, the motivational part of it . . . that's why you get into it.

"And I think as you get older, you kind of evolve into more of a thing person . . . the competitive 'X' and 'O' thing . . . into being in it for people reasons. The relationships you have with your players, with your coaches. The camaraderie before combat. The camaraderie after combat, win or lose. Seeing kids come through your program, and then seeing them years later and seeing them be solid citizens.

"I think there is a metamorphosis. I think when you start off, you're a young, competitive, wild buck that wants to compete and coach. And I think the older you get, the longer you stay, you realize you're in it, yes, for that, but you're in it primarily for the relationships. The feelings that I don't think insurance salesmen get, I don't think Bendix washer salesmen get, I don't think many people get 'em. I think it's a unique feeling that you just don't want to trade that camaraderie that is unbelievable . . . a warm feeling among men . . . among competitors."

At age 41 the oldest first-year Miami football coach since the days of George Little and George Rider, and maybe ever, Tim Rose has had time to experience his evolution as a coach. And as he sees it, it all goes back to basics. Does he consider himself a teacher?

"Above all else," he responds without hesitation, "coaching is teaching. Not only a mental skill, but a physical skill. You're a teacher first. Those who teach, coach. If you don't think of yourself as a teacher, your chances of being successful are slim. You have to be a teacher. By all means, I'm a teacher, hopefully a good one."

Football, maintains Rose, is a basic game . . . blocking, tackling, running, passing and catching. As a teacher of football at Miami, that's what is taught.

"That would be a basic tenet" of the Cradle of Coaches, says Rose.

"Anybody who coached here or came from Miami . . . I think that's one thing they would mention very strongly . . . you must teach the basics before you go on to other things.

"Sometimes there is a tendency to want to stray from that, because you can get enchanted by the tactical part of it . . by the planning and that sort of thing. The big thing in terms of fundamentals is to be sure you ask your kids to do what they can do. Don't ask 'em to do something that they can't physically do."

Rose refers to Woody Hayes and Bo Schembechler to help explain the evolution taking place in football today, an evolution he is necessarily a part of, though not as a strong proponent.

"Everything is cyclical," he says. "This period right now just kinda hearkens back to the mid-Sixties, when Alabama had Steve Sloan and Kenny Stabler and those people, it was predominantly a passing era.

"Then in the late Sixties when Royal brought the wishbone in . . . and Bill Yeoman with the triple option . . option football became the thrust of college offense until the late Seventies when we've seen the passing game come back. And I think the passing game has come back because of the need to fill up the stadiums . . . because the have-nots in college football could not catch the haves by playing their game.

"If you were gonna play Woody or Bo in the Big Ten and believe their philosophy, which is super-sound, and beat them at their game, you weren't gonna get it done, and I think the record proves that. The people who came in with the idea no mistakes, pitch sweep, play great defense and win . . . they weren't gonna beat Woody or Bo.

"I think they then saw a way to beat those people . . . the great haves . . . by being diversified, by doing something that they didn't do, and I think you've seen that change.

"So the evolution has taken place out of necessity, and the realization you couldn't beat those super-powers or the real good teams in the conference by doing exactly what they were doing."

The job Rose inherited — perhaps **earned** is more accurate — is not without its pressures.

Of course he's aware that any non-alumnus skipper at the Cradle of Coaches, of all places, will be under scrutiny.

And a new stadium brings new demands: You want to fill it, to live up to it, to justify it. For the opening of the new 25,676-seat Yager Stadium on October 1, 1983, Miami built hopes of playing before more people than ever had watched a single football game in Oxford. To be sure, those standing-room-only crowds that ringed old Miami Field had become commonplace in recent years, yet there had been times in the not-too-distant past when it would have taken three Saturdays to draw that many.

And there is the schedule. Even before that October 1 dedication of Yager Stadium, the Redskins would have opened the 1983 season with two visits to the Carolinas: South Carolina first at Columbia, then North Carolina at Chapel Hill. Miami had beaten each before, yet the odds lessen considerably these days with the manpower difference. Mid-American Conference schools now limit football grants-in-aid to 75 over a four-year period. Most NCAA Division I schools utilize the maximum 95. Through 1988, Miami schedules list Houston, Washington, Oklahoma State, LSU, Syracuse and Minnesota.

While Miami's success against "major" opposition has brought media attention to the Redskins ever since 1954, its has been Miami's 12 Mid-American Conference championships that have caught the attention of the rest of its league. Miami's last title came in 1977, and every Miami coach from Gillman to Rose has known that Miami is the target.

Thus tradition becomes a weapon in the hands and minds of the rest of the Mid-American; a tool for Rose as he looks to the future.

"The Cradle of Coaches means to me, or anybody who is a part of it . . and I may be classified as an orphan," says Rose . . "it means, number one, tremendous success; people that have understood the work ethic. I think the Cradle of Coaches and the people who maybe coined that phrase and became a part of the Cradle of Coaches are guys that have set the coaching work ethic for the last twenty, thirty years, at least since I've been involved in coaching.

"Whether you want to start with Woody, who was a non-Miami guy, or Ara, or John Pont, or Bo, or anybody that coached . . . those people set the work ethic . . . certainly in the Midwest, because of their influence, and I think around the country. Not only at the college level, but the pro level. These people have set a tremendous success standard and work ethic standard.

"Number two, I would suppose it means that it's very much a close fraternity of people who have gone to Miami . . and I'd like to think in some small way those of us who have coached at Miami. It's a very select group of people who kinda believe the same things.

"Certainly the offenses and defenses weren't exactly the same, but the philosophy of coaching, of dealing with people, I think by and large has been the same."

Rose acknowledges his playing career at Xavier was unspectacular, and he remembers Miami as "an ugly rival." And though the games were fiercely competitive, there was mutual respect for each team's rugged, dogged character.

"There was always tremendous respect for Miami," remembers Rose. "I don't think you could come to the campus and play a game or be here and not have a tremendous respect, and even in some ways, maybe awe, because it seemed to epitomize and be the type of campus that college was supposed to be, in terms of the physical structure and the physical beauty. Not just from Tim Rose, but I think from anybody that's set foot in Oxford, Ohio."

Ah, the physical beauty of Miami and Oxford. If you're keeping score, it's Miami 1809 (the year the University was founded) and the opponents zero. Rose doesn't think that's about to change, and it still plays a significant role in recruiting, although there is an occasional dissenter.

"Sure it does," answers Rose to a question on the continuing role of Miami's picturesque campus setting in recruitment of student-athletes.

"But it depends on your perspective. Beauty is in the eye of the beholder. We had a young man a couple of years ago who came here and didn't like it because it was old. He didn't understand tradition, I suppose."

Rose isn't sure, either, if today's young man holds the physical features, the aesthetics, as high as mom and dad and the old grads. It's still a part of the recruiting sales pitch, but Tim wonders if the athletes visiting the campus aren't somehow "a little bit more nearsighted."

Even as Tom Reed's defensive coordinator, Tim's sideline mannerisms . . . his enthusiasm . . . caught the attention of fans.

"But I think the thing that makes a place a place or gives it its uniqueness is the people. This town, the campus, the academics, the whole Miami picture, just inspires people to have those types of feelings. It's not just the physical beauty. It's the people . . . they make Miami what it is."

****

As Tim Rose begins his third decade as a football coach, a person meeting him for the first time realizes that he has had ample time to formulate a philosophy or two about coaching. And to see how, given the complexities and travails in the world of college athletics today, his age and experience are to his, and Miami's, benefit.

"Coaching is such a multi-faceted job today," says Rose. "The idea of sitting in an office and working on 'Xs and Os' and brainstorming and coming up with great plays and great defenses and doing nothing else is . . . there's no way you can exist in a college program doing that.

"You have to attempt to be a lot of different things, realizing you aren't going to please everybody. But you have to be, among other things, a public relations person, an organizer, you have to attempt to be a motivator, a tactician, a father-confessor on occasion, you have to be able to counsel athletes, you have to be able to deal with problems, you have to be a job-finder, you have to be a liaison between different interest groups.

"It's a multi-faceted job that I don't think a young coach can handle. I don't think I could have handled this job at twenty-five, or thirty or thirty-one. I don't even think, five years ago, coming from high school, I could have handled the job. I think you have to be experienced, not only in college coaching, but experienced in terms of leadership. It helps to have been a head coach in some capacity and understand the obligation."

So looking at his appointment in that light, Rose realizes there is no place in the college game today for the strict 'Xs and Os' coach. There is a need, on the other hand, to deal with every facet of the job as effectively as possible without," says Rose, "sacrificing the essentials of coaching, which is being with your players . . . being a force in terms of their lives."

Recalling how Ara Parseghian felt his early ascendency to a head coaching position had been a factor in his decision to step aside after 25 years as a head coach and comparing that to Rose's 20-year wait for his first collegiate head coaching position, there was the inevitable comparison. Rose thinks he understands Parseghian's position in light of his own, and it is no surprise that his thoughts are at once clear and insightful.

"I think timing is important in terms of what you spend your life doing. In my case, I'm very lucky right now," says Rose, explaining that he has a goal to coach until he's 70. "Now, whether I make it or not, I don't know. The good Lord willing, and if the enthusiasm and the intensity remain, and if I can handle it and get it done, that would be my goal right now."

But Rose also understands that if he is to come within hailing distance of attaining his goal, he needs to have a plan to avoid the "burn-out" difficulties which have caused some coaches to cash in their chips prematurely.

"Burn-out is something that's very real," thinks Rose. "It's true in the business world, it's true in teaching, it's true in coaching. If you love your job, if you love doing what you're doing, you have to try to guard against that. And the only way I see trying to guard against that is balance in your life.

"I don't see how you can be like a Vermiel (Dick, the Philadelphia Eagles' coach who resigned last year) and stay in the office until two o'clock and sleep on the couch and get up and go to work at six.

"Losing is difficult enough, and I think you have to have balance in your life, whatever that balance is, whatever allows you to handle pressure. It may be a chance to run, it may be a very strong family tie. Hopefully, it'll be something that's sound and good for you. But you need balance; without it, I see burn-out as being an inevitability.

"And I don't think it has to be that way. I'm not saying you don't have to work hard, but I know too many coaches who waste time, who equate time and work. I don't buy it. I think you've gotta work hard. You've gotta put in an inordinate amount of time, but you also have to find time for your family. You have to find time for things that are important."

Even at that, says Rose, burn-out is a possibility, because coaching is a profession that demands a winner. He doesn't pretend "to have all the answers," but he has a plan, and he strives to achieve the balance he thinks he needs.

"I'm not talkin' about a tremendous diversity, because the job doesn't allow that. But you have to have some balance. Psychologists will tell you that. People who have only one interest in their lives, generally don't survive emotionally."

And it appears Rose has plans to survive.

****

John Millett was president and John Brickels athletic director when Miami University began to make serious plans for a new stadium almost 30 years ago. One of the early options was to build east of the campus, on valley land now occupied by Miami's riding stables. Phillip Shriver succeeded Millett, and Dick Shrider succeeded Brickels, and Vice President Lloyd Goggin worked with all of them — and with yet a third president, Paul Pearson, before that groundbreaking which all of them except the deceased Brickels shared on January 30, 1982. Long before that, the site had been moved up the valley, and the stadium dream had grown to include an entire sports complex.

"Osborn Engineering and I have been working on this project for 20 years," sighed Shrider a few weeks before the actual opening and dedication set for the first home game of the 1983 season, October 1.

Fulfillment of the dream was made possible through a bequest of Fred C. Yager, Miami '14; through the Goals for Enrichment campaign to which many Miami coaches lent support, and through a capital improvements appropriations bill passed by the Ohio legislature.

Besides the Yager Stadium, the new outdoor athletic complex includes three football practice fields, one of them with lights and Superturf artificial surface; a 10-lane, all-weather Chevron track with its own bleachers; softball and field hockey fields for women; two soccer fields, and locker and training-room facilities for all sports involved in the complex. The "near" side of the stadium is literally a building including classrooms and a Cradle of Coaches Room displaying memorabilia of the many coaches whose careers had been influenced by their Miami associations.

"I think you'll see the greatest turn-around in program in football that you ever have seen at Miami, this fall," Shrider continued as he displayed the blueprints and mockup to a visitor for the umpteenth time. "I think you'll see things that you never dreamed were possible here, as for dreams that we've had and things that we can do now that we've got the space and the seating capacity to do it."

That aspect of the dream, Shrider explained, would include treating fans to a potpourri of activities "in a carnival-like atmosphere." Near Millett Hall, a band playing by a mammoth red and white tent set up as pre-game headquarters for metts and brats and liquid refreshment. Down at the stadium, an expanded public address system broadcasting the fight songs of colleges all over the country as tailgaters would start arriving nearly three hours before game time. You might even find a supply of ice, he said.

"We're going to cater to the people now that we're in a position to, and really put on a show for 'em when they come in here," Shrider added. "We're gonna try to really make this an experience that they have enjoyed from the time they got here until they left."

Shrider's 20-year dream was almost a reality as he talked, yet he still was fantasizing as he described his pilgrimages to the construction site.

"You know, I walk up in that stadium every once in a while, and I walk up there . . we don't have the 15 rows of seats finished down toward the field yet . . so when I get up to about row 25 I think, 'Boy, this is a beautiful sight,' and then when I get up to about row 40 and I say, 'Gosh, I've never seen anything this high in Oxford before, I just can't believe this,' and then I go up in the seats around fifty and look down there and think 'Boy, this is gettin' high, there's gonna be some people that are gonna think this is too high,' and then when I get up to row sixty-four, it's awesome. It really is an awesome sight to look down over that valley and see how beautiful that's going to be, and you just close your eyes and see it."

Tim Rose approaches recruiting during the Yager Stadium era with his eyes wide open. He realizes the door has been opened, and no longer will a Miami coach have to show architect's drawings to a prospective Miami football player. This year's recruits will be playing in the new stadium on the freshly-sodded turf.

The new stadium, says Rose, "will make a tremendous difference in terms of recruiting, as far as keeping some very outstanding recruits very interested in Miami. It'll make a big difference.

"Because in the past, we would drive very slowly around this beautiful, majestic, traditional campus, point out all the great academic buildings, and by the time we got to the corner of High and Patterson (where Miami Field sat), we'd kick that car into about fifty miles an hour and say, 'Oh, yeah, we play over there.'"

And then Rose, like Shrider, paints a word picture of the impact of Yager Stadium on the 1983 recruit.

"I don't think you can sit up on this hill in your car and look out over that valley and not picture that thing on a fully-bloomed autumn afternoon as being anything but majestic and college football at its best."

The knock on the door was an unwanted interruption at that point, but the player who appeared in the doorway represented the player-coach relationship which Rose values so highly. This one was seeking reinstatement to the team. These are the conditions, said Rose matter-of-factly as the player stood and listened intently, nodding in agreement. Rose stood.

"Welcome back," he said.

Rose describes the new era at Miami as "a glorious time to be coming in," as he ticks off the new stadium, the schedule and the Mid-American Conference tie-up with the California Bowl as additional benefits to "everything else that's true about Miami."

****

By the late Forties and early Fifties, the coaching school at Miami officially had become part of the Department of Health and Physical Education. The idea was still the same. Ara Parseghian taught a class in football. Bill Rohr taught basketball. George Rider taught track. And Woody Wills taught baseball.

Jobs for teachers aren't plentiful right now, and without jobs for teachers, there aren't any jobs for coaches. Projections show that might change by the late Eighties, or into the Nineties, and the demand for teachers will be on the rise again. The ever-present cycles, you know.

Meanwhile, they still come to Miami wanting to teach and coach. Not in great numbers, like Pont and Cozza and Schembechler, and Pagna and Burton and Mourouzis, and all the rest. But they come. And Tim Rose, the orphan, has a message for them.

"I always tell 'em, if you're thinking of coaching, and you don't go to Miami, you're nuts, because we aren't called the Cradle of Engineers. This is the Cradle of Coaches. If you don't go to Miami, you gotta be crazy."

EPILOGUE

Not long after Miami launched its coaching school in 1925, products of that school were scattered at high schools throughout Ohio. In 1930, you will recall, Weeb Ewbank had counted over 180 Miami graduates in coaching and teaching positions over the state.

In 1983, Miami is known as the Cradle of Coaches far beyond the Buckeye state, and Miami graduates in coaching and related athletic fields number well over 700. In keeping with Miami tradition, more than 500 of those are involved in coaching or athletic administration at the high school level.

Once the Cradle of Coaches Association was launched in 1971, Miami's Office of Alumni Affairs and the Sports Information Office were confronted with the dual task of fund-raising and record-keeping. As the amount pledged to support the graduate assistants has grown, so have the numbers of Miamians who have directed their annual gifts to the Miami Loyalty Fund to the Cradle.

Stan Lewis, '35, a long-time coach and athletic administrator in the Middletown area, has retired to Florida, and remains a member of the Cradle of Coaches Association. So does Larry Lyons, '57, swimming coach at Sycamore High School near Cincinnati. And Roberta Anne Flath, '72, on the staff at Culver Military Academy in Indiana. These three are representative of hundreds of Miami graduates who, since as far back as 1925, when Miami President Upham announced the School of Physical Education and Athletic Coaching, have helped guide young people who sought enjoyment and satisfaction in athletics.

The high school coach, a Miamian, is the catalyst. Miami spawns another coach, and so it goes, a cycle without end. And from the hundreds of high school coaches scattered throughout the country, there emerge those who, in 1983, are the focal point of the legend of the Cradle of Coaches.

Professional Sports
Jerry Angelo, '71, scout, Dallas Cowboys
Bill Arnsparger, '50, assistant coach, Miami Dolphins
Earl Biederman, '57, scout, Cincinnati Bengals
Ed Biles, '53, head coach, Houston Oilers
Paul Brown, '30, general manager, Cincinnati Bengals
Wayne Embry, '58, special consultant, Milwaukee Bucks
Joe Galat, '62, head coach, Montreal Concordes
John Mackovic, '66, head coach, Kansas City Chiefs
John McVay, '53, general manager, San Francisco '49ers
Ernie Plank, '50, scout, San Francisco '49ers
John Shoemaker, '78, assistant coach, Los Angeles Dodgers
Doc Urich, '51, assistant coach, Green Bay Packers
Jerry Wampfler, '54, assistant coach, Philadelphia Eagles

Mack Yoho, '58, assistant coach, Hartford Knights
College Administration
Bob Bockrath, '64, associate athletic director, University of Arizona
Tom Bryant, '55, athletic director, Centre College
Jon Falk, '71, equipment manager, University of Michigan
Wayne Gibson, '48, associate athletic director, Miami University
Bud Haidet, '57, tickets/promotion, Miami University
Hugh Hindman, '50, athletic director, Ohio State University
Jerry Ippoliti, '58, assistant athletic director
    Northern Illinois University
Harley Knosher, '57, athletic director, Knox College
Ruth Long, '74, assistant athletic director, Walsh College
Ray Mears, '49, athletic director, University of Tennessee-Martin
Don Miller, '70, equipment manager, Miami University
Mike Palmisano, '66, assistant athletic director, University of Michigan
Mary Parker, '60, women's athletic director, Ohio Wesleyan University
Bob Purcell, '50, equipment coordinator, Miami University
John Schael, '66, athletic director, Washington University (St. Louis)
Paul Shoults, '49, athletic director, Eastern Michigan University
Robert Wayne Starcher, '67, athletic director and baseball coach,
    Malone College
Elizabeth Vanhorn, '46, women's athletic director, Denison University
Nobby Wirkowski, '51, athletic director, York University (Canada)
Athletic Trainers
Tom L. Agne, '75, Ohio Wesleyan University
Tom Healion, '52, New England Patriots
Patricia Jayson, '72, University of Dayton
Lisa L. Kelleher, '79, assistant, Oregon State University
Brandt McFarlin, '76, Chicago White Sox
John McNeeley, '67, Cleveland State University
Marv Pollins, '61, Cincinnati Bengals
Ron Ribaric, '71, Central Florida University
College Football
Dick Adams, '71, University of Hawaii-Maui
Jim Bengala, '71, East Carolina University, assistant
Tirrel Burton, '56, University of Michigan, assistant
Ron Corradini, '61, Indiana University, assistant
Carmen Cozza, '52, Yale University
Tom Dimitroff, '58, Guelph University (Canada)
John Drew, '59, Temple University, assistant
Gary Durchik, '67, Northern Illinois University, assistant
Jay Fry, '76, Miami University, assistant
Mark Gentile, '75, Gardner-Webb University, assistant
Jack Glowik, '78, North Carolina State University, assistant
Jerry Hanlon, '56, University of Michigan, assistant
Dave Hatgas, '79, Miami University, assistant
Jack Himebauch, '65, University of North Carolina, assistant
Bob Hitchens, '74, Miami University, assistant
Bob Kappes, '50, Ohio University, assistant

Paul Krasula, '68, West Virginia University, assistant
Sebastian LaSpina, '58, Yale University, assistant
Bill Mallory, '57, Northern Illinois University
Denny Marcin, '64, University of North Carolina, assistant
John Matsko, '76, University of North Carolina, assistant
Bob Messaros, '77, Miami University, assistant
Nick Mourouzis, '59, DePauw University
Bill Narduzzi, '59, Youngstown State University
Joe Novak, '67, Northern Illinois University, assistant
Gus Pachis, '64, Illinois State University, assistant
Chris Pagliaro, '58, Santa Barbara City College
Don Peddie, '66, Central Michigan University, assistant
Peter Peterson, '77, Kenyon College
Mike Poff, '73, Central Michigan University, assistant
James Purtill, '78, University of Toledo, assistant
Tom Reed, '67, North Carolina State University
Bo Schembechler, '51, University of Michigan
Paul Schudel, '66, University of Michigan, assistant
Dave Smith, '72, Findlay College, assistant
Rick Spisak, '73, Miami University, assistant
Gary Troll, '71, Southwestern College, assistant
Dick Tomey, '64, University of Hawaii
Randy Walker, '76, University of North Carolina, assistant
Bill Wiggins, '76, Ashland College, assistant
Ron Zook, '76, University of Kansas, assistant

College Men's Basketball

Randy Ayers, '78, West Point, assistant
Tom Bryant, '55, Centre College
Charles Coles, '65, University of Detroit, assistant
Donald Ehler, '50, University of Dayton, assistant
James Hallihan, '67, Iowa State University, assistant
Darrell Hedric, '55, Miami University
Herb Hilgeman, '72, Southwestern at Memphis
Richard Hopkins, '50, Shawnee State
Mark Huffman, '79, Mt. Union College
Harley Knosher, '57, Knox College — also golf
Jerry Pierson, '66, Miami University, assistant
Gerald Sears, '71, Ashland College
John Michael Street, '79, University of Akron

Additional Collegiate Sports

Ron Bush, '68, Bluffton College, track and cross country
Mel Brodt, '49, Bowling Green State University, track and cross country
John Cahill, '69, Nevada-Las Vegas, swimming
Robert Coons, '67, Cal State-Bakersfield, track and cross country
Linda Donkelaar, '73, Mesa Community College, track and cross country
Judith George, '62, DePauw University, field hockey
Danny Hall, '77, University of Michigan, assistant baseball
Debra Ann Hockemeyer, '78, Manchester College, softball
Connie Inman, '58, Tennessee Tech, tennis

Julie Ann Illner, '63, Southern Illinois University, field hockey
Janiece Kelley, '66, Baldwin-Wallace College
Barbara Lawson, '67, Austin College, basketball and tennis
Martha Litherland, '71, Defiance College, basketball and softball
Mary Ruth Maurer, '79, Mt. Union College, basketball and softball
John McMichen, '82, Miami University, baseball assistant
Bud Middaugh, '61, University of Michigan, baseball
Wally Morton, '70, Cleveland State University, swimming
Mary Ann Myers, '82, Miami University, basketball assistant
Mark Osgood, '79, Ashland College, wrestling
Ray Riordan, '56, Towson State, swimming
Sue Ramsey, '78, Miami University, basketball assistant
Joe Rogers, '66, Hillsdale College, track and cross country
Mike Salupi, '74, Coe College, wrestling
Bob Schul, '66, Wright State University, track and cross country
Bob Shaw, '69, Miami University, swimming
Sandy Smith, '71, University of Cincinnati, basketball
Steve Strome, '64, Duke University, tennis
Jack Suydam, '61, Central Connecticut State, swimming
David Thomas, '59, University of Arizona, wrestling